The Super-Easy Tower Air Fryer Cookbook for Beginners

Crispy, Healthy, Quick, Delicious and Affordable Recipes for Beginners

Gerald Seale

Table of Contents

Chapter 5: Beef, pork & Lamb Recipes 34

Chapter 6: Fish And Seafood Recipes 47

Chapter 1: Introduction

In the ever-evolving landscape of kitchen appliances, one innovation has truly stood out as a game-changer for health-conscious individuals and culinary enthusiasts alike - the Tower Air Fryer. This revolutionary kitchen gadget has gained immense popularity for its ability to transform the way we cook, allowing us to enjoy our favorite fried foods with a fraction of the guilt and calories. In this comprehensive guide, we will delve into the world of the Tower Air Fryer, exploring its history, benefits, features, tips for use, and essential cleaning and maintenance guidelines. By the end of this journey, you'll have a thorough understanding of how this appliance can elevate your culinary adventures and contribute to a healthier lifestyle.

History of the Tower Air Fryer

To truly appreciate the Tower Air Fryer and its impact on modern cooking, it's essential to understand its historical context and the development of air frying technology.

The Birth of Air Frying

The concept of air frying dates back to the early 20th century, with various iterations and experiments involving hot air circulation to cook food. However, it wasn't until the 21st century that air frying technology saw a significant breakthrough. Philips, a renowned Dutch electronics company, is credited with introducing the world's first commercial air fryer in 2010. This appliance marked the beginning of a culinary revolution, offering a healthier alternative to traditional deep frying.

The Emergence of the Tower Air Fryer

The Tower Air Fryer emerged as a notable player in the air frying arena, making its mark in the kitchen appliance industry. With a history steeped in British engineering excellence, the Tower brand has been synonymous with quality and innovation since its inception in 1912. Over the decades, Tower has continuously evolved to meet the changing needs of consumers, and the introduction of the Tower Air Fryer was a testament to their commitment to modernizing cooking methods.

Benefits of the Tower Air Fryer

The Tower Air Fryer offers a myriad of advantages that have made it a must-have appliance in kitchens around the world. Let's explore these benefits in detail.

1. Healthier Cooking

One of the most compelling reasons to invest in a Tower Air Fryer is its ability to prepare crispy, delicious foods with significantly less oil compared to traditional deep frying methods. The appliance uses hot air to circulate around the food, crisping it up to perfection. This means you can enjoy your favorite fried dishes with up to 80% less fat, making it an excellent choice for those striving for a healthier diet.

2. Versatility

The Tower Air Fryer is a versatile kitchen companion that can handle a wide range of cooking tasks beyond just frying. It can bake, grill, roast, and even reheat food effectively. This versatility allows you to experiment with various recipes and cooking techniques, from crispy chicken wings to tender roasted vegetables.

3. Time Efficiency

With its rapid heating and cooking capabilities, the Tower Air Fryer significantly reduces cooking time. It preheats quickly and cooks food faster than traditional ovens, making it ideal for busy individuals and families who want to prepare meals in a hurry without sacrificing quality.

4. Energy Efficiency

Compared to conventional ovens and deep fryers, the Tower Air Fryer is remarkably energy-efficient. Its compact design and efficient heating elements ensure that it uses less electricity, saving both energy and money in the long run.

5. Easy Cleanup

Cleaning up after cooking can be a chore, but the Tower Air Fryer makes this task a breeze. Most models feature non-stick cooking baskets and trays that are dishwasher-safe, reducing the time and effort required for maintenance.

6. Reduced Odor

Traditional frying methods often leave your kitchen smelling of oil and fried food for hours. With the Tower Air Fryer, you'll experience minimal odor thanks to its enclosed cooking chamber and efficient air circulation.

7. Preserves Nutrients

Air frying helps retain more of the nutrients in your food compared to deep frying, which can deplete vitamins and minerals due to high temperatures and excessive oil absorption.

8. Customizable Cooking

Most Tower Air Fryer models come equipped with adjustable temperature and timer settings, allowing you to customize your cooking experience. Whether you prefer a golden-brown crust or a crispy texture, you have full control over the outcome.

Features of the Tower Air Fryer

The Tower Air Fryer boasts an array of features designed to make your cooking experience enjoyable and hassle-free. Let's take a closer look at these innovative characteristics.

1. Rapid Air Circulation

The heart of the Tower Air Fryer's cooking prowess lies in its powerful fan and heating element. These components work together to circulate hot air evenly around the food, ensuring consistent cooking and crispy results without the need for excessive oil.

2. Temperature Control

Most Tower Air Fryer models offer adjustable temperature settings that typically range from 180°C (360°F) to 200°C (392°F). This versatility allows you to fine-tune the cooking temperature to suit your specific recipes.

3. Timer Function

A built-in timer is a crucial feature that lets you set precise cooking durations. Once the timer reaches zero, the appliance will automatically switch off, preventing overcooking or burning your food.

4. Capacity Options

Tower offers a variety of Air Fryer models with different capacities to cater to various household sizes. Whether you're cooking for one or a large family, you can find a Tower Air Fryer that suits your needs.

5. Preheat Function

Many Tower Air Fryers come with a preheat function, which quickly brings the appliance to the desired cooking temperature, reducing overall cooking time.

6. Digital Display

Some Tower Air Fryers feature a digital display that provides easy-to-read information about temperature, time, and cooking settings. This user-friendly interface simplifies operation.

7. Safety Features

Safety is a top priority for Tower, and their Air Fryers are equipped with features like automatic shut-off and cool-touch handles to prevent accidents and ensure peace of mind during use.

8. Recipe Booklet

To help users make the most of their Tower Air Fryer, many models include a recipe booklet filled with inspiration and step-by-step instructions for delicious dishes.

9. Non-Stick Coating

The cooking baskets and trays in Tower Air Fryers often come with a non-stick coating, making food release and cleanup a breeze.

10. Compact Design

The Tower Air Fryer's compact and sleek design takes up minimal counter space, making it an excellent addition to kitchens of all sizes.

Tips for Using the Tower Air Fryer

Now that we've explored the history, benefits, and features of the Tower Air Fryer, let's delve into some essential tips and tricks for making the most of this remarkable kitchen appliance.

1. Preheat for Optimal Results

Before placing your food in the air fryer, preheat it for a few minutes to ensure even cooking and achieve that coveted crispy texture.

2. Use the Right Amount of Oil

While the Tower Air Fryer is designed to use less oil, some recipes may benefit from a light spritz of cooking spray or a small amount of oil. Use an oil sprayer to apply a thin, even layer for enhanced flavor and texture.

3. Avoid Overcrowding

For the best results, avoid overcrowding the cooking basket. Leaving enough space between food items allows the hot air to circulate freely and ensures everything cooks evenly.

4. Shake or Flip Midway

To ensure uniform cooking, shake the basket or flip the food halfway through the cooking process. This step is especially important for items like fries or chicken wings.

5. Experiment with Seasonings

Get creative with seasonings, herbs, and spices to enhance the flavor of your dishes. Experimentation is encouraged, and you'll discover exciting flavor combinations along the way.

6. Use Parchment Paper or Foil

When cooking foods that might stick to the basket, consider using parchment paper or aluminum foil with small holes punched through it to allow air circulation. This prevents sticking and simplifies cleanup.

7. Keep an Eye on Cooking Times

The Tower Air Fryer cooks faster than traditional methods, so keep a close eye on your food to prevent overcooking. Use the timer and adjust it according to your preferences.

8. Pre-Packaged Foods
Many pre-packaged frozen foods are designed for air fryers. Be sure to check the packaging for air fryer-specific instructions, as they may require different cooking times and temperatures compared to conventional ovens.

9. Clean Regularly
To maintain the Tower Air Fryer's performance and longevity, clean it after each use. Remove the cooking basket and tray, wash them with warm, soapy water, or place them in the dishwasher if they are dishwasher-safe. Wipe down the interior and exterior of the appliance as needed.

10. Explore New Recipes
Don't limit yourself to the basics. The Tower Air Fryer can handle a wide range of recipes, from appetizers to desserts. Explore online recipe communities, cookbooks, and Tower's own recipe resources to expand your culinary repertoire.

Cleaning and Maintenance of the Tower Air Fryer

Proper cleaning and maintenance are essential to ensure the longevity and efficiency of your Tower Air Fryer. Here's a step-by-step guide to keeping your appliance in top condition.

1. Unplug and Cool Down
Always unplug the Tower Air Fryer and allow it to cool down before attempting to clean or perform maintenance tasks. This ensures your safety and prevents accidental burns.

2. Remove and Clean Removable Parts
Remove the cooking basket, tray, and any other removable parts from the air fryer. Check your appliance's manual to confirm which parts are dishwasher-safe. Wash them with warm, soapy water or place them in the dishwasher accordingly.

3. Wipe Down the Interior
Use a damp cloth or sponge to wipe down the interior of the air fryer, including the heating element. Be gentle to avoid damaging the non-stick coating or any sensitive components.

4. Clean the Exterior
Wipe the exterior of the appliance with a damp cloth or sponge to remove any grease or food residue. Pay special attention to the control panel and digital display, if applicable.

5. Check the Heating Element
Inspect the heating element for any food particles or debris. If necessary, use a soft brush or a damp cloth to

clean it carefully. Do not immerse the air fryer in water or submerge the heating element.

6. Empty the Crumb Tray
Some Tower Air Fryer models have a crumb tray located at the bottom. Remove and empty this tray regularly to prevent buildup and potential fire hazards.

7. Reassemble and Store
Once all the components are clean and dry, reassemble the Tower Air Fryer. Store it in a dry, cool place with proper ventilation. Avoid placing heavy objects on top of the appliance.

8. Perform Regular Maintenance
To ensure the long-term functionality of your Tower Air Fryer, refer to the user manual for any specific maintenance recommendations. This may include periodic inspections or component replacements.

9. Address Odors
If your air fryer develops persistent odors, try placing a bowl of water with a few slices of lemon in the cooking basket and running the appliance at a low temperature for a short time. This can help eliminate unwanted smells.

Conclusion

The Tower Air Fryer is a culinary marvel that has transformed the way we cook, allowing us to enjoy our favorite fried foods without compromising on health or flavor. With its rich history, numerous benefits, innovative features, and handy tips for use and maintenance, this kitchen appliance has earned its place as an indispensable tool for home cooks and food enthusiasts alike. Whether you're aiming to lead a healthier lifestyle, save time in the kitchen, or explore new culinary horizons, the Tower Air Fryer is a versatile and reliable companion that can help you achieve your goals. So, embark on a flavorful journey, experiment with exciting recipes, and savor the delicious, guilt-free results that only the Tower Air Fryer can deliver.

Chapter 2: Measurement Conversions

BASIC KITCHEN CONVERSIONS & EQUIVALENTS

DRY MEASUREMENTS CONVERSION CHART
3 TEASPOONS = 1 TABLESPOON = 1/16 CUP
6 TEASPOONS = 2 TABLESPOONS = 1/8 CUP
12 TEASPOONS = 4 TABLESPOONS = 1/4 CUP
24 TEASPOONS = 8 TABLESPOONS = 1/2 CUP
36 TEASPOONS = 12 TABLESPOONS = 3/4 CUP
48 TEASPOONS = 16 TABLESPOONS = 1 CUP

METRIC TO US COOKING CONVER SIONS
OVEN TEMPERATURES
120 °C = 250 °F
160 °C = 320 °F
180° C = 360 °F
205 °C = 400 °F
220 °C = 425 °F

LIQUID MEASUREMENTS CONVERSION CHART
8 FLUID OUNCES = 1 CUP = 1/2 PINT = 1/4 QUART
16 FLUID OUNCES = 2 CUPS = 1 PINT = 1/2 QUART
32 FLUID OUNCES = 4 CUPS = 2 PINTS = 1 QUART = 1/4 GALLON
128 FLUID OUNCES = 16 CUPS = 8 PINTS = 4 QUARTS = 1 GALLON

BAKING IN GRAMS
1 CUP FLOUR = 140 GRAMS
1 CUP SUGAR = 150 GRAMS
1 CUP POWDERED SUGAR = 160 GRAMS
1 CUP HEAVY CREAM = 235 GRAMS

VOLUME
1 MILLILITER = 1/5 TEASPOON
5 ML = 1 TEASPOON
15 ML = 1 TABLESPOON
240 ML = 1 CUP OR 8 FLUID OUNCES
1 LITER = 34 FL. OUNCES

WEIGHT
1 GRAM = .035 OUNCES

100 GRAMS = 3.5 OUNCES
500 GRAMS = 1.1 POUNDS
1 KILOGRAM = 35 OUNCES

US TO METRIC COOKING CONVERSIONS
1/5 TSP = 1 ML
1 TSP = 5 ML
1 TBSP = 15 ML
1 FL OUNCE = 30 ML
1 CUP = 237 ML
1 PINT (2 CUPS) = 473 ML
1 QUART (4 CUPS) = .95 LITER
1 GALLON (16 CUPS) = 3.8 LITERS
1 OZ = 28 GRAMS
1 POUND = 454 GRAMS

BUTTER
1 CUP BUTTER = 2 STICKS = 8 OUNCES = 230 GRAMS = 8 TABLESPOONS

WHAT DOES 1 CUP EQUAL
1 CUP = 8 FLUID OUNCES
1 CUP = 16 TABLESPOONS
1 CUP = 48 TEASPOONS
1 CUP = 1/2 PINT
1 CUP = 1/4 QUART
1 CUP = 1/16 GALLON
1 CUP = 240 ML

BAKING PAN CONVERSIONS
1 CUP ALL-PURPOSE FLOUR = 4.5 OZ
1 CUP ROLLED OATS = 3 OZ 1 LARGE EGG = 1.7 OZ
1 CUP BUTTER = 8 OZ 1 CUP MILK = 8 OZ
1 CUP HEAVY CREAM = 8.4 OZ
1 CUP GRANULATED SUGAR = 7.1 OZ
1 CUP PACKED BROWN SUGAR = 7.75 OZ
1 CUP VEGETABLE OIL = 7.7 OZ
1 CUP UNSIFTED POWDERED SUGAR = 4.4 OZ

BAKING PAN CONVERSIONS
9-INCH ROUND CAKE PAN = 12 CUPS
10-INCH TUBE PAN =16 CUPS
11-INCH BUNDT PAN = 12 CUPS
9-INCH SPRINGFORM PAN = 10 CUPS
9 X 5 INCH LOAF PAN = 8 CUPS
9-INCH SQUARE PAN = 8 CUPS

Chapter 3: Appetizers And Snacks Recipes

Tortilla Chips

Servings: 4
Cooking Time: 5 Minutes
Ingredients:
- 8 white corn tortillas
- ¼ cup olive oil
- 2 tablespoons lime juice
- ½ teaspoon salt

Directions:
1. Preheat the air fryer to 350°F.
2. Cut each tortilla into fourths and brush lightly with oil.
3. Place chips in a single layer in the air fryer basket, working in batches as necessary. Cook 5 minutes, shaking the basket halfway through cooking time.
4. Sprinkle with lime juice and salt. Serve warm.

Bagel Chips

Servings: 2
Cooking Time: 4 Minutes
Ingredients:
- Sweet
- 1 large plain bagel
- 2 teaspoons sugar
- 1 teaspoon ground cinnamon
- butter-flavored cooking spray
- Savory
- 1 large plain bagel
- 1 teaspoon Italian seasoning
- ½ teaspoon garlic powder
- oil for misting or cooking spray

Directions:
1. Preheat air fryer to 390°F.
2. Cut bagel into ¼-inch slices or thinner.
3. Mix the seasonings together.
4. Spread out the slices, mist with oil or cooking spray, and sprinkle with half of the seasonings.
5. Turn over and repeat to coat the other side with oil or cooking spray and seasonings.
6. Place in air fryer basket and cook for 2minutes. Shake basket or stir a little and continue cooking for 2 minutes or until toasty brown and crispy.

"fried" Pickles With Homemade Ranch

Servings: 8
Cooking Time: 8 Minutes
Ingredients:
- 1 cup all-purpose flour
- 2 teaspoons dried dill
- ½ teaspoon paprika
- ¾ cup buttermilk
- 1 egg
- 4 large kosher dill pickles, sliced ¼-inch thick
- 2 cups panko breadcrumbs

Directions:
1. Preheat the air fryer to 380°F.

2. In a medium bowl, whisk together the flour, dill, paprika, buttermilk, and egg.
3. Dip and coat thick slices of dill pickles into the batter. Next, dredge into the panko breadcrumbs.
4. Place a single layer of breaded pickles into the air fryer basket. Spray the pickles with cooking spray. Cook for 4 minutes, turn over, and cook another 4 minutes. Repeat until all the pickle chips have been cooked.

Fast And Easy Tortilla Chips

Servings:2
Cooking Time: 3 Minutes
Ingredients:
- 8 corn tortillas
- 1 tablespoon olive oil
- Salt, to taste

Directions:
1. Preheat the air fryer to 390ºF (199ºC).
2. Slice the corn tortillas into triangles. Coat with a light brushing of olive oil.
3. Put the tortilla pieces in the air fryer basket and air fry for 3 minutes. You may need to do this in batches.
4. Season with salt before serving.

Roasted Chickpeas

Servings: 1
Cooking Time: 15 Minutes
Ingredients:
- 1 15-ounce can chickpeas, drained
- 2 teaspoons curry powder
- ¼ teaspoon salt
- 1 tablespoon olive oil

Directions:
1. Drain chickpeas thoroughly and spread in a single layer on paper towels. Cover with another paper towel and press gently to remove extra moisture. Don't press too hard or you'll crush the chickpeas.
2. Mix curry powder and salt together.
3. Place chickpeas in a medium bowl and sprinkle with seasonings. Stir well to coat.
4. Add olive oil and stir again to distribute oil.
5. Cook at 390°F for 15 minutes, stopping to shake basket about halfway through cooking time.
6. Cool completely and store in airtight container.

Apple Rollups

Servings: 8
Cooking Time: 5 Minutes
Ingredients:
- 8 slices whole wheat sandwich bread
- 4 ounces Colby Jack cheese, grated
- ½ small apple, chopped
- 2 tablespoons butter, melted

Directions:
1. Remove crusts from bread and flatten the slices with rolling pin. Don't be gentle. Press hard so that bread will be very thin.
2. Top bread slices with cheese and chopped apple, dividing the ingredients evenly.

3. Roll up each slice tightly and secure each with one or two toothpicks.
4. Brush outside of rolls with melted butter.
5. Place in air fryer basket and cook at 390°F for 5minutes, until outside is crisp and nicely browned.

Crab-stuffed Mushrooms

Servings: 4
Cooking Time: 20 Minutes
Ingredients:
- ½ cup shredded mozzarella cheese
- 8 portobello mushrooms
- 1 tbsp olive oil
- ¼ tsp salt
- 3 oz lump crabmeat
- 3 tsp grated Parmesan cheese
- ¼ cup panko bread crumbs
- 1 tbsp ground walnuts
- 3 tsp mayonnaise
- 2 tbsp chopped chives
- 1 egg, beaten
- 1 garlic clove, minced
- ¼ tsp seafood seasoning
- 1 tbsp chopped cilantro

Directions:
1. Clean the mushrooms with a damp paper towel. Remove stems and chop them finely. Set aside. Take the mushroom caps and brush with oil before sprinkling with salt. Combine the remaining ingredients, excluding mozzarella, in a bowl. Spoon crab filling mixture into each mushroom cap. Top each cap with mozzarella and press down so that it may stick to the filling.
2. Preheat air fryer to 360°F. Place the stuffed mushrooms in the greased frying basket. Bake 8-10 minutes until the mushrooms are soft and the mozzarella is golden. Serve.

Bacon Butter

Servings:5
Cooking Time: 2 Minutes
Ingredients:
- ½ cup butter
- 3 oz bacon, chopped

Directions:
1. Preheat the air fryer to 400°F and put the bacon inside. Cook it for 8 minutes. Stir the bacon every 2 minutes. Meanwhile, soften the butter in the oven and put it in the butter mold. Add cooked bacon and churn the butter. Refrigerate the butter for 30 minutes.

Bacon-wrapped Cabbage Bites

Servings:6
Cooking Time: 12 Minutes
Ingredients:
- 3 tablespoons sriracha hot chili sauce, divided
- 1 medium head cabbage, cored and cut into 12 bite-sized pieces
- 2 tablespoons coconut oil, melted

- ½ teaspoon salt
- 12 slices sugar-free bacon
- ½ cup mayonnaise
- ¼ teaspoon garlic powder

Directions:
1. Evenly brush 2 tablespoons sriracha onto cabbage pieces. Drizzle evenly with coconut oil, then sprinkle with salt.
2. Wrap each cabbage piece with bacon and secure with a toothpick. Place into ungreased air fryer basket. Adjust the temperature to 375°F and set the timer for 12 minutes, turning cabbage halfway through cooking. Bacon will be cooked and crispy when done.
3. In a small bowl, whisk together mayonnaise, garlic powder, and remaining sriracha. Use as a dipping sauce for cabbage bites.

Wrapped Shrimp Bites

Servings: 4
Cooking Time: 15 Minutes
Ingredients:
- 2 jumbo shrimp, peeled
- 2 bacon strips, sliced
- 2 tbsp lemon juice
- ½ tsp chipotle powder
- ½ tsp garlic salt

Directions:
1. Preheat air fryer to 350°F. Wrap the bacon around the shrimp and place the shrimp in the foil-lined frying basket, seam side down. Drizzle with lemon juice, chipotle powder and garlic salt. Air Fry for 10 minutes, turning the shrimp once until cooked through and bacon is crispy. Serve hot.

Spicy Chickpeas With Paprika

Servings: 4
Cooking Time: 10 Minutes
Ingredients:
- 1 15-ounces can chickpeas, rinsed and drained
- 1 tablespoon olive oil
- ½ teaspoon ground cumin
- ½ teaspoon cayenne pepper
- ½ teaspoon smoked paprika
- Salt, to taste

Directions:
1. At 390 degrees F/ 200 degrees C, preheat your air fryer.
2. In a suitable bowl, add all the recipe ingredients and toss to coat well.
3. Add the chickpeas in an air fryer basket in 2 batches.
4. Air fry for about 8-10 minutes.
5. Serve.

Parmesan Crackers

Servings: 6
Cooking Time: 6 Minutes
Ingredients:
- 2 cups finely grated Parmesan cheese

- ¼ teaspoon paprika
- ¼ teaspoon garlic powder
- ½ teaspoon dried thyme
- 1 tablespoon all-purpose flour

Directions:
1. Preheat the air fryer to 380°F.
2. In a medium bowl, stir together the Parmesan, paprika, garlic powder, thyme, and flour.
3. Line the air fryer basket with parchment paper.
4. Using a tablespoon measuring tool, create 1-tablespoon mounds of seasoned cheese on the parchment paper, leaving 2 inches between the mounds to allow for spreading.
5. Cook the crackers for 6 minutes. Allow the cheese to harden and cool before handling. Repeat in batches with the remaining cheese.

Enchilada Chicken Dip

Servings:6
Cooking Time: 20 Minutes
Ingredients:
- 1 cup chopped cooked chicken breasts
- 1 can diced green chiles, including juice
- 8 oz cream cheese, softened
- ¼ cup mayonnaise
- ¼ cup sour cream
- 2 tbsp chopped onion
- 1 jalapeño pepper, minced
- 1 cup shredded mozzarella
- ¼ cup diced tomatoes
- 1 tsp chili powder

Directions:
1. Preheat air fryer to 400ºF. Beat the cream cheese, mayonnaise, and sour cream in a bowl until smooth. Stir in the cooked chicken, onion, green chiles, jalapeño, and ½ cup of mozzarella cheese. Spoon the mixture into a baking dish. Sprinkle the remaining cheese on top, and place the dish in the fryer. Bake for 10 minutes. Garnish the dip with diced tomatoes and chili powder. Serve.

Crispy Old Bay Chicken Wings

Servings:4
Cooking Time: 15 Minutes
Ingredients:
- Olive oil
- 2 tablespoons Old Bay seasoning
- 2 teaspoons baking powder
- 2 teaspoons salt
- 2 pounds chicken wings

Directions:
1. Spray a fryer basket lightly with olive oil.
2. In a large zip-top plastic bag, mix together the Old Bay seasoning, baking powder, and salt.
3. Pat the wings dry with paper towels.
4. Place the wings in the zip-top bag, seal, and toss with the seasoning mixture until evenly coated.

5. Place the seasoned wings in the fryer basket in a single layer. Lightly spray with olive oil. You may need to cook them in batches.
6. Air fry for 7 minutes. Turn the wings over, lightly spray them with olive oil, and air fry until the wings are crispy and lightly browned, 5 to 8 more minutes. Using a meat thermometer, check to make sure the internal temperature is 165°F or higher.

Ham And Cheese Sliders

Servings:3
Cooking Time: 10 Minutes
Ingredients:
- 6 Hawaiian sweet rolls
- 12 slices thinly sliced Black Forest ham
- 6 slices sharp Cheddar cheese
- ⅓ cup salted butter, melted
- 1 ½ teaspoons minced garlic

Directions:
1. Preheat the air fryer to 350°F.
2. For each slider, slice horizontally through the center of a roll without fully separating the two halves. Place 2 slices ham and 2 slices cheese inside roll and close. Repeat with remaining rolls, ham, and cheese.
3. In a small bowl, mix butter and garlic and brush over all sides of rolls.
4. Place in the air fryer and cook 10 minutes until rolls are golden on top and cheese is melted. Serve warm.

Cheesy Green Wonton Triangles

Servings: 20 Wontons
Cooking Time: 55 Minutes
Ingredients:
- 6 oz marinated artichoke hearts
- 6 oz cream cheese
- ¼ cup sour cream
- ¼ cup grated Parmesan
- ¼ cup grated cheddar
- 5 oz chopped kale
- 2 garlic cloves, chopped
- Salt and pepper to taste
- 20 wonton wrappers

Directions:
1. Microwave cream cheese in a bowl for 20 seconds. Combine with sour cream, Parmesan, cheddar, kale, artichoke hearts, garlic, salt, and pepper. Lay out the wrappers on a cutting board. Scoop 1 ½ tsp of cream cheese mixture on top of the wrapper. Fold up diagonally to form a triangle. Bring together the two bottom corners. Squeeze out any air and press together to seal the edges.
2. Preheat air fryer to 375°F. Place a batch of wonton in the greased frying basket and Bake for 10 minutes. Flip them and cook for 5-8 minutes until crisp and golden. Serve.

Buffalo Breaded Cauliflower Bites

Servings: 4
Cooking Time: 25 Minutes
Ingredients:
- 1 cup all-purpose flour
- 1 cup water
- 1 teaspoon garlic powder
- 1 large head cauliflower, cut into florets (4 cups)
- Cooking oil
- ⅓ cup Frank's RedHot Buffalo Wings sauce

Directions:
1. In a large bowl, combine the flour, water, and garlic powder. Mix well. The mixture should resemble pancake batter.
2. Add the cauliflower to the batter and stir to coat. Transfer the cauliflower to another large bowl to drain the excess batter.
3. Spray the air fryer with cooking oil.
4. Transfer the cauliflower to the air fryer. Do not stack. Cook in batches. Spray the cauliflower with cooking oil. Cook for 6 minutes.
5. Open the air fryer and transfer the cauliflower to a large bowl. Drizzle with the Buffalo sauce. Mix well.
6. Return the cauliflower to the air fryer. Cook for an additional 6 minutes, or until crisp.
7. Remove the cooked cauliflower from the air fryer, then repeat steps 4 through 6 for the remaining cauliflower batches.
8. Cool before serving.

Onion Puffs

Servings: 14
Cooking Time: 8 Minutes
Ingredients:
- Vegetable oil spray
- ¾ cup Chopped yellow or white onion
- ½ cup Seasoned Italian-style panko bread crumbs
- 4½ tablespoons All-purpose flour
- 4½ tablespoons Whole, low-fat, or fat-free milk
- 1½ tablespoons Yellow cornmeal
- 1¼ teaspoons Granulated white sugar
- ½ teaspoon Baking powder
- ¼ teaspoon Table salt

Directions:
1. Cut or tear a piece of aluminum foil so that it lines the air fryer's basket with a ½-inch space on each of its four sides. Lightly coat the foil with vegetable oil spray, then set the foil sprayed side up inside the basket.
2. Preheat the air fryer to 400°F.
3. Stir the onion, bread crumbs, flour, milk, cornmeal, sugar, baking powder, and salt in a bowl to form a thick batter.
4. Remove the basket from the machine. Drop the onion batter by 2-tablespoon measures onto the foil, spacing the mounds evenly across its surface. Return the basket to the machine and air-fry undisturbed for 4 minutes.

5. Remove the basket from the machine. Lightly coat the puffs with vegetable oil spray. Use kitchen tongs to pick up a corner of the foil, then gently pull it out of the basket, letting the puffs slip onto the basket directly. Return the basket to the machine and continue air-frying undisturbed for 8 minutes, or until brown and crunchy.
6. Use kitchen tongs to transfer the puffs to a wire rack or a serving platter. Cool for 5 minutes before serving.

Potato Pastries

Servings: 8
Cooking Time: 37 Minutes
Ingredients:
- 2 large potatoes, peeled
- 1 tablespoon olive oil
- ½ cup carrot, peeled and chopped
- ½ cup onion, chopped
- 2 garlic cloves, minced
- 1 tablespoon fresh ginger, minced
- ½ cup green peas, shelled
- Salt and ground black pepper, as needed
- 3 puff pastry sheets

Directions:
1. Boil water in a suitable pan, then put the potatoes and cook for about 15-20 minutes
2. Drain the potatoes well and then mash the potatoes.
3. Heat the oil over medium heat in a skillet, then add the carrot, onion, ginger, garlic and sauté for about 4-5 minutes.
4. Then drain all the fat from the skillet.
5. Stir in the mashed potatoes, peas, salt and black pepper. Continue to cook for about 1-2 minutes.
6. Remove the potato mixture from heat and set aside to cool completely.
7. After placing the puff pastry onto a smooth surface, cut each puff pastry sheet into four pieces and cut each piece into a round shape.
8. Add about 2 tablespoons of veggie filling over each pastry round.
9. Use your wet finger to moisten the edges.
10. To seal the filling, fold each pastry round in half.
11. Firmly press the edges with a fork.
12. Set the temperature setting to 390 degrees F/ 200 degrees C.
13. Arrange the pastries in the basket of your air fryer and air fry for about 5 minutes at 390 minutes.
14. Work in 2 batches.
15. Serve.

Zucchini Slices With Parsley

Servings: 4
Cooking Time: 15 Minutes
Ingredients:
- 2 zucchinis, sliced
- 1 tablespoon olive oil
- 4 tablespoon parmesan cheese, grated
- 2 tablespoons almond flour
- 1 tablespoon parsley, chopped

- Black pepper
- Salt

Directions:
1. At 350 degrees F/ 175 degrees C, preheat your air fryer.
2. In a suitable bowl, mix together cheese, parsley, oil, almond flour, black pepper, and salt.
3. Top zucchini pieces with cheese mixture and place in the air fryer basket.
4. Cook zucchini for almost 15 minutes at 350 degrees F/ 175 degrees C.
5. Serve and enjoy.

Olive Oil Sweet Potato Chips

Servings: 5
Cooking Time: 20 Minutes
Ingredients:
- 3 sweet potatoes
- 2 teaspoons extra-virgin olive oil
- 1 teaspoon cinnamon (optional)
- Salt
- Pepper

Directions:
1. Peel the sweet potatoes using a vegetable peeler. Cut the potatoes crosswise into thin slices. You can also use a mandoline to slice the potatoes into chips.
2. Place the sweet potatoes in a large bowl of cold water for 30 minutes. This helps remove the starch from the sweet potatoes, which promotes crisping.
3. Drain the sweet potatoes. Dry the slices thoroughly with paper towels or napkins.
4. Place the sweet potatoes in another large bowl. Drizzle with the olive oil and sprinkle with the cinnamon, if using, and salt and pepper to taste. Toss to fully coat.
5. Place the sweet potato slices in the air fryer. It is okay to stack them, but do not overcrowd. You may need to cook the chips in two batches. Cook the potatoes for 10 minutes.
6. Open the air fryer and shake the basket. Cook the chips for an additional 10 minutes.
7. Cool before serving.

Spiced Roasted Pepitas

Servings:4
Cooking Time: 25 Minutes
Ingredients:
- 2 cups pumpkin seeds
- 1 tbsp butter, melted
- Salt and pepper to taste
- ½ tsp shallot powder
- ½ tsp smoked paprika
- ½ tsp dried parsley
- ½ tsp garlic powder
- ¼ tsp dried chives
- ¼ tsp dry mustard
- ¼ tsp celery seed

Directions:

1. Preheat air fryer to 325ºF. Combine the pumpkin seeds, butter, and salt in a bowl. Place the seed mixture in the frying basket and Roast for 13 minutes, turning once. Transfer to a medium serving bowl. Stir in shallot powder, paprika, parsley, garlic powder, chives, dry mustard, celery seed, and black pepper. Serve right away.

Cheesy Jalapeño Poppers

Servings:4
Cooking Time: 10 Minutes
Ingredients:
- 8 jalapeño peppers
- ½ cup whipped cream cheese
- ¼ cup shredded Cheddar cheese

Directions:
1. Preheat the air fryer to 360ºF (182ºC).
2. Use a paring knife to carefully cut off the jalapeño tops, then scoop out the ribs and seeds. Set aside.
3. In a medium bowl, combine the whipped cream cheese and shredded Cheddar cheese. Place the mixture in a sealable plastic bag, and using a pair of scissors, cut off one corner from the bag. Gently squeeze some cream cheese mixture into each pepper until almost full.
4. Place a piece of parchment paper on the bottom of the air fryer basket and place the poppers on top, distributing evenly. Air fry for 10 minutes.
5. Allow the poppers to cool for 5 to 10 minutes before serving.

Crab Toasts

Servings: 15
Cooking Time: 5 Minutes
Ingredients:
- 1 6-ounce can flaked crabmeat, well drained
- 3 tablespoons light mayonnaise
- ½ teaspoon lemon juice
- 1 teaspoon Worcestershire sauce
- ¼ cup shredded sharp Cheddar cheese
- ¼ cup shredded Parmesan cheese
- 1 loaf artisan bread, French bread, or baguette, cut into slices ⅜-inch thick

Directions:
1. Mix together all ingredients except the bread slices.
2. Spread each slice of bread with a thin layer of crabmeat mixture. (For a bread slice measuring 2 x 1½ inches you will need about ½ tablespoon of crab mixture.)
3. Place in air fryer basket in single layer and cook at 360°F for 5minutes or until tops brown and toast is crispy.
4. Repeat step 3 to cook remaining crab toasts.

Spiced Nuts

Servings: 3
Cooking Time: 25 Minutes
Ingredients:
- 1 egg white, lightly beaten
- ¼ cup sugar
- 1 teaspoon salt
- ½ teaspoon ground cinnamon

- ¼ teaspoon ground cloves
- ¼ teaspoon ground allspice
- pinch ground cayenne pepper
- 1 cup pecan halves
- 1 cup cashews
- 1 cup almonds

Directions:

1. Combine the egg white with the sugar and spices in a bowl.
2. Preheat the air fryer to 300°F.
3. Spray or brush the air fryer basket with vegetable oil. Toss the nuts together in the spiced egg white and transfer the nuts to the air fryer basket.
4. Air-fry for 25 minutes, stirring the nuts in the basket a few times during the cooking process. Taste the nuts to see if they are crunchy and nicely toasted. Air-fry for a few more minutes if necessary.
5. Serve warm or cool to room temperature and store in an airtight container for up to two weeks.

Eggplant Fries

Servings: 4
Cooking Time: 8 Minutes
Ingredients:

- 1 medium eggplant
- 1 teaspoon ground coriander
- 1 teaspoon cumin
- 1 teaspoon garlic powder
- ½ teaspoon salt
- 1 cup crushed panko breadcrumbs
- 1 large egg
- 2 tablespoons water
- oil for misting or cooking spray

Directions:

1. Peel and cut the eggplant into fat fries, ⅜- to ½-inch thick.
2. Preheat air fryer to 390°F.
3. In a small cup, mix together the coriander, cumin, garlic, and salt.
4. Combine 1 teaspoon of the seasoning mix and panko crumbs in a shallow dish.
5. Place eggplant fries in a large bowl, sprinkle with remaining seasoning, and stir well to combine.
6. Beat eggs and water together and pour over eggplant fries. Stir to coat.
7. Remove eggplant from egg wash, shaking off excess, and roll in panko crumbs.
8. Spray with oil.
9. Place half of the fries in air fryer basket. You should have only a single layer, but it's fine if they overlap a little.
10. Cook for 5minutes. Shake basket, mist lightly with oil, and cook 3 minutes longer, until browned and crispy.
11. Repeat step 10 to cook remaining eggplant.

Broccoli Florets

Servings: 4
Cooking Time: 20 Minutes
Ingredients:

- 1 lb. broccoli, cut into florets
- 1 tbsp. lemon juice
- 1 tbsp. olive oil
- 1 tbsp. sesame seeds
- 3 garlic cloves, minced

Directions:

1. In a bowl, combine all of the ingredients, coating the broccoli well.
2. Transfer to the Air Fryer basket and air fry at 400°F for 13 minutes.

Smoked Whitefish Spread

Servings: 1
Cooking Time: 10 Minutes
Ingredients:

- ¾ pound Boneless skinless white-flesh fish fillets, such as hake or trout
- 3 tablespoons Liquid smoke
- 3 tablespoons Regular, low-fat, or fat-free mayonnaise (gluten-free, if a concern)
- 2 teaspoons Jarred prepared white horseradish (optional)
- ¼ teaspoon Onion powder
- ¼ teaspoon Celery seeds
- ¼ teaspoon Table salt
- ¼ teaspoon Ground black pepper

Directions:

1. Put the fish fillets in a zip-closed bag, add the liquid smoke, and seal closed. Rub the liquid smoke all over the fish , then refrigerate the sealed bag for 2 hours.
2. Preheat the air fryer to 400°F.
3. Set a 12-inch piece of aluminum foil on your work surface. Remove the fish fillets from the bag and set them in the center of this piece of foil (the fillets can overlap). Fold the long sides of the foil together and crimp them closed. Make a tight seam so no steam can escape. Fold up the ends and crimp to seal well.
4. Set the packet in the basket and air-fry undisturbed for 10 minutes.
5. Use kitchen tongs to transfer the foil packet to a wire rack. Cool for a minute or so. Open the packet, transfer the fish to a plate, and refrigerate for 30 minutes.
6. Put the cold fish in a food processor. Add the mayonnaise, horseradish (if using), onion powder, celery seeds, salt, and pepper. Cover and pulse to a slightly coarse spread, certainly not fully smooth.
7. For a more traditional texture, put the fish fillets in a bowl, add the other ingredients, and stir with a wooden spoon, mashing the fish with everything else to make a coarse paste.
8. Scrape the spread into a bowl and serve at once, or cover with plastic wrap and store in the fridge for up to 4 days.

Chili Black Bean Empanadas

Servings: 4
Cooking Time: 20 Minutes
Ingredients:
- ½ cup cooked black beans
- ¼ cup white onions, diced
- 1 tsp red chili powder
- ½ tsp paprika
- ½ tsp garlic salt
- ½ tsp ground cumin
- ½ tsp ground cinnamon
- 4 empanada dough shells

Directions:
1. Preheat air fryer to 350°F. Stir-fry black beans and onions in a pan over medium heat for 5 minutes. Add chili, paprika, garlic salt, cumin, and cinnamon. Set aside covered when onions are soft and the beans are hot.
2. On a clean workspace, lay the empanada shells. Spoon bean mixture onto shells without spilling. Fold the shells over to cover fully. Seal the edges with water and press with a fork. Transfer the empanadas to the foil-lined frying basket and Bake for 15 minutes, flipping once halfway through cooking. Cook until golden. Serve.

Garlicky Eggplant Chips

Servings: 4
Cooking Time: 13 Minutes
Ingredients:
- 2 eggplants, peeled and thinly sliced
- Salt
- ½ cup tapioca starch
- ¼ cup canola oil
- ½ cup water
- 1 teaspoon garlic powder
- ½ teaspoon dried dill weed
- ½ teaspoon black pepper, to taste

Directions:
1. Season and rub the eggplant slices with salt and leave for ½ an hour.
2. Run them under cold water to rinse off any excess salt.
3. In a suitable bowl, coat the eggplant slices with all of the other ingredients.
4. Cook at almost 390 degrees F/ 200 degrees C for 13 minutes.
5. Serve.

Cheesy Apple Roll-ups

Servings:8
Cooking Time: 4 To 5 Minutes
Ingredients:
- 8 slices whole wheat sandwich bread
- 4 ounces (113 g) Colby Jack cheese, grated
- ½ small apple, chopped
- 2 tablespoons butter, melted

Directions:
1. Preheat the air fryer to 390ºF (199ºC).

2. Remove the crusts from the bread and flatten the slices with a rolling pin. Don't be gentle. Press hard so that bread will be very thin.
3. Top bread slices with cheese and chopped apple, dividing the ingredients evenly.
4. Roll up each slice tightly and secure each with one or two toothpicks.
5. Brush outside of rolls with melted butter.
6. Place in air fryer basket and air fry for 4 to 5 minutes, or until outside is crisp and nicely browned.
7. Serve hot.

Cauliflower Wings With Buffalo Sauce

Servings: 4
Cooking Time: 14 Minutes
Ingredients:
- 1 cauliflower head, cut into florets
- 1 tablespoon butter, melted
- ½ cup buffalo sauce
- Black pepper
- Salt

Directions:
1. Grease its air fryer basket with cooking spray.
2. In a suitable bowl, mix together buffalo sauce, butter, black pepper, and salt.
3. Add cauliflower florets into the air fryer basket and cook at almost 400 degrees F/ 205 degrees C for 7 minutes.
4. Transfer cauliflower florets into the buffalo sauce mixture and toss well.
5. Again, add cauliflower florets into the air fryer basket and cook for 7 minutes more at 400 degrees F/ 205 degrees C.
6. Serve and enjoy.

Spiced Sweet Potato Fries

Servings:2
Cooking Time: 15 Minutes
Ingredients:
- 2 tablespoons olive oil
- 1½ teaspoons smoked paprika
- 1½ teaspoons kosher salt, plus more as needed
- 1 teaspoon chili powder
- ½ teaspoon ground cumin
- ½ teaspoon ground turmeric
- ½ teaspoon mustard powder
- ¼ teaspoon cayenne pepper
- 2 medium sweet potatoes (about 10 ounces / 284 g each), cut into wedges, ½ inch thick and 3 inches long
- Freshly ground black pepper, to taste
- ⅔ cup sour cream
- 1 garlic clove, grated

Directions:
1. Preheat the air fryer to 400ºF (204ºC).
2. In a large bowl, combine the olive oil, paprika, salt, chili powder, cumin, turmeric, mustard powder, and

cayenne. Add the sweet potatoes, season with black pepper, and toss to evenly coat.

3. Transfer the sweet potatoes to the air fryer (save the bowl with the leftover oil and spices) and air fry for 15 minutes, shaking the basket halfway through, or until golden brown and crisp. Return the potato wedges to the reserved bowl and toss again while they are hot.

4. Meanwhile, in a small bowl, stir together the sour cream and garlic. Season with salt and black pepper and transfer to a serving dish.

5. Serve the potato wedges hot with the garlic sour cream.

Poutine

Servings: 2
Cooking Time: 25 Minutes
Ingredients:
- 2 russet potatoes, scrubbed and cut into ½-inch sticks
- 2 teaspoons vegetable oil
- 2 tablespoons butter
- ¼ onion, minced (about ¼ cup)
- 1 clove garlic, smashed
- ¼ teaspoon dried thyme
- 3 tablespoons flour
- 1 teaspoon tomato paste
- 1½ cups strong beef stock
- salt and lots of freshly ground black pepper
- a few dashes of Worcestershire sauce
- ⅔ cup chopped string cheese or cheese curds

Directions:
1. Bring a large saucepan of salted water to a boil on the stovetop while you peel and cut the potatoes. Blanch the potatoes in the boiling salted water for 4 minutes while you Preheat the air fryer to 400°F. Strain the potatoes and rinse them with cold water. Dry them well with a clean kitchen towel.

2. Toss the dried potato sticks gently with the oil and place them in the air fryer basket. Air-fry for 25 minutes, shaking the basket a few times while the fries cook to help them brown evenly.

3. While the fries are cooking, make the gravy. Melt the butter in a small saucepan over medium heat. Add the onion, garlic and thyme and cook for five minutes, until soft and just starting to brown. Stir in the flour and cook for another two minutes, stirring regularly. Finally, add the tomato paste and continue to cook for another minute or two. Whisk in the beef stock and bring the mixture to a boil to thicken. Season to taste with salt, lots of freshly ground black pepper and a few dashes of Worcestershire sauce. Keep the gravy warm.

4. As soon as the fries are done, season them with salt and transfer to a plate or basket. Top the fries with the cheese curds or string cheese, and pour the warm gravy over the top.

Korean-style Wings

Servings: 4
Cooking Time: 10 Minutes
Ingredients:
- 1 pound chicken wings, drums and flats separated
- ½ teaspoon salt
- ¼ teaspoon ground black pepper
- ¼ cup gochujang sauce
- 2 tablespoons soy sauce
- 1 teaspoon ground ginger
- ¼ cup mayonnaise

Directions:
1. Preheat the air fryer to 350°F.
2. Sprinkle wings with salt and pepper. Place wings in the air fryer basket and cook 15 minutes, turning halfway through cooking time.
3. In a medium bowl, mix gochujang sauce, soy sauce, ginger, and mayonnaise.
4. Toss wings in sauce mixture and adjust the air fryer temperature to 400°F.
5. Place wings back in the air fryer basket and cook an additional 5 minutes until the internal temperature reaches at least 165°F. Serve warm.

Cinnamon Pita Chips

Servings: 4
Cooking Time: 6 Minutes
Ingredients:
- 2 tablespoons sugar
- 2 teaspoons cinnamon
- 2 whole 6-inch pitas, whole grain or white
- oil for misting or cooking spray

Directions:
1. Mix sugar and cinnamon together.
2. Cut each pita in half and each half into 4 wedges. Break apart each wedge at the fold.
3. Mist one side of pita wedges with oil or cooking spray. Sprinkle them all with half of the cinnamon sugar.
4. Turn the wedges over, mist the other side with oil or cooking spray, and sprinkle with the remaining cinnamon sugar.
5. Place pita wedges in air fryer basket and cook at 330°F for 2minutes.
6. Shake basket and cook 2 more minutes. Shake again, and if needed cook 2 more minutes, until crisp. Watch carefully because at this point they will cook very quickly.

Bbq Chips

Servings: 2
Cooking Time: 30 Minutes
Ingredients:
- 1 scrubbed russet potato, sliced
- ½ tsp smoked paprika
- ¼ tsp chili powder
- ¼ tsp garlic powder
- 1/8 tsp onion powder
- ¼ tbsp smoked paprika
- 1/8 tsp light brown sugar
- Salt and pepper to taste

- 2 tsp olive oil

Directions:

1. Preheat air fryer at 400ºF. Combine all seasoning in a bowl. Set aside. In another bowl, mix potato chips, olive oil, black pepper, and salt until coated. Place potato chips in the frying basket and Air Fry for 17 minutes, shaking 3 times. Transfer it into a bowl. Sprinkle with the bbq mixture and let sit for 15 minutes. Serve immediately.

Skinny Fries

Servings: 2
Cooking Time: 15 Minutes

Ingredients:

- 2 to 3 russet potatoes, peeled and cut into ¼-inch sticks
- 2 to 3 teaspoons olive or vegetable oil
- salt

Directions:

1. Cut the potatoes into ¼-inch strips. Rinse the potatoes with cold water several times and let them soak in cold water for at least 10 minutes or as long as overnight.
2. Preheat the air fryer to 380°F.
3. Drain and dry the potato sticks really well, using a clean kitchen towel. Toss the fries with the oil in a bowl and then air-fry the fries in two batches at 380°F for 15 minutes, shaking the basket a couple of times while they cook.
4. Add the first batch of French fries back into the air fryer basket with the finishing batch and let everything warm through for a few minutes. As soon as the fries are done, season them with salt and transfer to a plate or basket. Serve them warm with ketchup or your favorite dip.

Simple Pizza Bites

Servings:10
Cooking Time: 3 Minutes

Ingredients:

- 10 Mozzarella cheese slices
- 10 pepperoni slices

Directions:

1. Line the air fryer pan with baking paper and put Mozzarella cheese slices in it.
2. Cook them for 3 minutes at 400 degrees F/ 205 degrees C or until melted. Once cooked, remove the cheese from the air fryer and cool them to room temperature.
3. Put the pepperoni slices on the cheese and fold the cheese in the shape of turnovers.
4. Enjoy!

Avocado Egg Rolls

Servings: 8
Cooking Time: 8 Minutes

Ingredients:

- 8 full-size egg roll wrappers
- 1 medium avocado, sliced into 8 pieces

- 1 cup cooked black beans, divided
- ½ cup mild salsa, divided
- ½ cup shredded Mexican cheese, divided
- ⅓ cup filtered water, divided
- ½ cup sour cream
- 1 teaspoon chipotle hot sauce

Directions:

1. Preheat the air fryer to 400°F.
2. Place the egg roll wrapper on a flat surface and place 1 strip of avocado down in the center.
3. Top the avocado with 2 tablespoons of black beans, 1 tablespoon of salsa, and 1 tablespoon of shredded cheese.
4. Place two of your fingers into the water, and then moisten the four outside edges of the egg roll wrapper with water (so the outer edges will secure shut).
5. Fold the bottom corner up, covering the filling. Then secure the sides over the top, remembering to lightly moisten them so they stick. Tightly roll the egg roll up and moisten the final flap of the wrapper and firmly press it into the egg roll to secure it shut.
6. Repeat Steps 2–5 until all 8 egg rolls are complete.
7. When ready to cook, spray the air fryer basket with olive oil spray and place the egg rolls into the basket. Depending on the size and type of air fryer you have, you may need to do this in two sets.
8. Cook for 4 minutes, flip, and then cook the remaining 4 minutes.
9. Repeat until all the egg rolls are cooked. Meanwhile, mix the sour cream with the hot sauce to serve as a dipping sauce.
10. Serve warm.

Bruschetta With Basil Pesto

Servings:4
Cooking Time: 5 To 11 Minutes

Ingredients:

- 8 slices French bread, ½ inch thick
- 2 tablespoons softened butter
- 1 cup shredded Mozzarella cheese
- ½ cup basil pesto
- 1 cup chopped grape tomatoes
- 2 green onions, thinly sliced

Directions:

1. Preheat the air fryer to 350°F (177°C).
2. Spread the bread with the butter and place butter-side up in the air fryer basket. Bake for 3 to 5 minutes, or until the bread is light golden brown.
3. Remove the bread from the basket and top each piece with some of the cheese. Return to the basket in 2 batches and bake for 1 to 3 minutes, or until the cheese melts.
4. Meanwhile, combine the pesto, tomatoes, and green onions in a small bowl.
5. When the cheese has melted, remove the bread from the air fryer and place on a serving plate. Top each slice with some of the pesto mixture and serve.

Italian Bruschetta With Mushrooms & Cheese

Servings: 4
Cooking Time: 25 Minutes
Ingredients:
- ½ cup button mushrooms, chopped
- ½ baguette, sliced
- 1 garlic clove, minced
- 3 oz sliced Parmesan cheese
- 1 tbsp extra virgin olive oil
- Salt and pepper to taste

Directions:
1. Preheat air fryer to 350°F. Add the mushrooms, olive oil, salt, pepper, and garlic to a mixing bowl and stir thoroughly to combine. Divide the mushroom mixture between the bread slices, drizzling all over the surface with olive oil, then cover with Parmesan slices. Place the covered bread slices in the greased frying basket and Bake for 15 minutes. Serve and enjoy!

Curly Kale Chips With Greek Sauce

Servings: 4
Cooking Time: 15 Minutes
Ingredients:
- 1 cup Greek yogurt
- 3 tbsp lemon juice
- ½ tsp mustard powder
- ½ tsp dried dill
- 1 tbsp ground walnuts
- 1 bunch curly kale
- 2 tbsp olive oil
- Salt and pepper to taste

Directions:
1. Preheat air fryer to 390°F. Mix together yogurt, lemon juice, mustard powder, ground walnuts, and dill until well blended. Set aside. Cut off the stems and ribs from the kale, then cut the leaves into 3-inch pieces.
2. In a bowl, toss the kale with olive oil, salt and pepper. Arrange the kale in the fryer and Air Fry for 2-3 minutes. Shake the basket, then cook for another 2-3 minutes or until the kale is crisp. Serve the chips with Greek sauce.

Crispy Prosciutto-wrapped Asparagus

Servings:6
Cooking Time: 16 To 24 Minutes
Ingredients:
- 12 asparagus spears, woody ends trimmed
- 24 pieces thinly sliced prosciutto
- Cooking spray

Directions:
1. Preheat the air fryer to 360ºF (182ºC).
2. Wrap each asparagus spear with 2 slices of prosciutto, then repeat this process with the remaining asparagus and prosciutto.
3. Spray the air fryer basket with cooking spray, then place 2 to 3 bundles in the basket and air fry for 4 minutes. Repeat this process with the remaining asparagus bundles.
4. Remove the bundles and allow to cool on a wire rack for 5 minutes before serving.

Zucchini Fries With Roasted Garlic Aïoli

Servings: 4
Cooking Time: 12 Minutes
Ingredients:
- Roasted Garlic Aïoli:
- 1 teaspoon roasted garlic
- ½ cup mayonnaise
- 2 tablespoons olive oil
- juice of ½ lemon
- salt and pepper
- Zucchini Fries:
- ½ cup flour
- 2 eggs, beaten
- 1 cup seasoned breadcrumbs
- salt and pepper
- 1 large zucchini, cut into ½-inch sticks
- olive oil in a spray bottle, can or mister

Directions:
1. To make the aïoli, combine the roasted garlic, mayonnaise, olive oil and lemon juice in a bowl and whisk well. Season the aïoli with salt and pepper to taste.
2. Prepare the zucchini fries. Create a dredging station with three shallow dishes. Place the flour in the first shallow dish and season well with salt and freshly ground black pepper. Put the beaten eggs in the second shallow dish. In the third shallow dish, combine the breadcrumbs, salt and pepper. Dredge the zucchini sticks, coating with flour first, then dipping them into the eggs to coat, and finally tossing in breadcrumbs. Shake the dish with the breadcrumbs and pat the crumbs onto the zucchini sticks gently with your hands so they stick evenly.
3. Place the zucchini fries on a flat surface and let them sit at least 10 minutes before air-frying to let them dry out a little. Preheat the air fryer to 400°F.
4. Spray the zucchini sticks with olive oil, and place them into the air fryer basket. You can air-fry the zucchini in two layers, placing the second layer in the opposite direction to the first. Air-fry for 12 minutes turning and rotating the fries halfway through the cooking time. Spray with additional oil when you turn them over.
5. Serve zucchini fries warm with the roasted garlic aïoli.

Chapter 4: Bread And Breakfast Recipes

Morning Burrito

Servings: 4
Cooking Time: 15 Minutes
Ingredients:
- 2 oz cheddar cheese, torn into pieces
- 2 hard-boiled eggs, chopped
- 1 avocado, chopped
- 1 red bell pepper, chopped
- 3 tbsp salsa
- 4 flour tortillas

Directions:
1. Whisk the eggs, avocado, red bell pepper, salsa, and cheese. Pout the tortillas on a clean surface and divide the egg mix between them. Fold the edges and roll up; poke a toothpick through so they hold. Preheat air fryer to 390°F. Place the burritos in the frying basket and Air Fry for 3-5 minutes until crispy and golden. Serve hot.

Spinach-bacon Rollups

Servings: 4
Cooking Time: 9 Minutes
Ingredients:
- 4 flour tortillas
- 4 slices Swiss cheese
- 1 cup baby spinach leaves
- 4 slices turkey bacon

Directions:
1. Preheat air fryer to 390°F.
2. On each tortilla, place one slice of cheese and ¼ cup of spinach.
3. Roll up tortillas and wrap each with a strip of bacon. Secure each end with a toothpick.
4. Place rollups in air fryer basket, leaving a little space in between them.
5. Cook for 4minutes. Turn and rearrange rollups and cook for 5minutes longer, until bacon is crisp.

Sausage Egg Muffins

Servings: 4
Cooking Time: 30 Minutes
Ingredients:
- 6 oz Italian sausage
- 6 eggs
- 1/8 cup heavy cream
- 3 oz cheese

Directions:
1. Preheat the fryer to 350°F.
2. Grease a muffin pan.
3. Slice the sausage links and place them two to a tin.
4. Beat the eggs with the cream and season with salt and pepper.
5. Pour over the sausages in the tin.
6. Sprinkle with cheese and the remaining egg mixture.
7. Cook for 20 minutes or until the eggs are done and serve!

Soft Pretzels

Servings: 12

Cooking Time: 6 Minutes
Ingredients:
- 2 teaspoons yeast
- 1 cup water, warm
- 1 teaspoon sugar
- 1 teaspoon salt
- 2½ cups all-purpose flour
- 2 tablespoons butter, melted
- 1 cup boiling water
- 1 tablespoon baking soda
- coarse sea salt
- melted butter

Directions:
1. Combine the yeast and water in a small bowl. Combine the sugar, salt and flour in the bowl of a stand mixer. With the mixer running and using the dough hook, drizzle in the yeast mixture and melted butter and knead dough until smooth and elastic – about 10 minutes. Shape into a ball and let the dough rise for 1 hour.
2. Punch the dough down to release any air and decide what size pretzels you want to make.
3. a. To make large pretzels, divide the dough into 12 portions.
4. b. To make medium sized pretzels, divide the dough into 24 portions.
5. c. To make mini pretzel knots, divide the dough into 48 portions.
6. Roll each portion into a skinny rope using both hands on the counter and rolling from the center to the ends of the rope. Spin the rope into a pretzel shape (or tie the rope into a knot) and place the tied pretzels on a parchment lined baking sheet.
7. Preheat the air fryer to 350°F.
8. Combine the boiling water and baking soda in a shallow bowl and whisk to dissolve (this mixture will bubble, but it will settle down). Let the water cool so that you can put your hands in it. Working in batches, dip the pretzels (top side down) into the baking soda-water mixture and let them soak for 30 seconds to a minute. (This step is what gives pretzels their texture and helps them to brown faster.) Then, remove the pretzels carefully and return them (top side up) to the baking sheet. Sprinkle the coarse salt on the top.
9. Air-fry in batches for 3 minutes per side. When the pretzels are finished, brush them generously with the melted butter and enjoy them warm with some spicy mustard.

Spice Muffins

Servings:6
Cooking Time: 15 Minutes
Ingredients:
- 1 cup blanched finely ground almond flour
- ¼ cup granular erythritol
- 2 tablespoons salted butter, melted
- 1 large egg, whisked
- 2 teaspoons baking powder
- 1 teaspoon ground allspice

Directions:
1. In a large bowl, combine all ingredients. Evenly pour batter into six silicone muffin cups greased with cooking spray.
2. Place muffin cups into air fryer basket. Adjust the temperature to 320°F and set the timer for 15 minutes. Cooked muffins should be golden brown.
3. Let muffins cool in cups 15 minutes to avoid crumbling. Serve warm.

Banana-strawberry Cakecups

Servings: 6
Cooking Time: 25 Minutes
Ingredients:
- ½ cup mashed bananas
- ¼ cup maple syrup
- ½ cup Greek yogurt
- 1 tsp vanilla extract
- 1 egg
- 1 ½ cups flour
- 1 tbsp cornstarch
- ½ tsp baking soda
- ½ tsp baking powder
- ½ tsp salt
- ½ cup strawberries, sliced

Directions:
1. Preheat air fryer to 360°F. Place the mashed bananas, maple syrup, yogurt, vanilla, and egg in a large bowl and mix until smooth. Sift in 1 ½ cups of the flour, baking soda, baking powder, and salt, then stir to combine.
2. In a small bowl, toss the strawberries with the cornstarch. Fold the mixture into the muffin batter. Divide the mixture evenly between greased muffin cups and place into the air frying basket. Bake for 12-15 minutes until golden brown on top and a toothpick inserted into the middle of one of the muffins comes out clean. Leave to cool for 5 minutes. Serve and enjoy!

Dill Eggs In Wonton

Servings: 4
Cooking Time: 4 Minutes
Ingredients:
- 2 eggs, hard-boiled, peeled
- 1 tablespoon cream cheese
- 1 tablespoon fresh dill, chopped
- 1 teaspoon ground black pepper
- 4 wontons wrap
- 1 egg white, whisked
- 1 teaspoon sesame oil

Directions:
1. Before cooking, heat your air fryer to 395 degrees F/ 200 degrees C.
2. Grease the air fryer basket with sesame oil.
3. Chop the hard-boiled eggs and in a bowl, mix together with dill, ground pepper, and cream cheese.
4. Separate the egg mixture onto wonton wraps and roll them into rolls.
5. Use the whisked egg white to brush the wontons.

6. Arrange the wontons evenly on the greased air fryer basket.
7. Cook in your air fryer at 395 degrees F/ 200 degrees C for 2 minutes from each side or until golden brown flip to the other side.

Lush Vegetable Omelet

Servings:2
Cooking Time: 13 Minutes
Ingredients:
- 2 teaspoons canola oil
- 4 eggs, whisked
- 3 tablespoons plain milk
- 1 teaspoon melted butter
- 1 red bell pepper, seeded and chopped
- 1 green bell pepper, seeded and chopped
- 1 white onion, finely chopped
- ½ cup baby spinach leaves, roughly chopped
- ½ cup Halloumi cheese, shaved
- Kosher salt and freshly ground black pepper, to taste

Directions:
1. Preheat the air fryer to 350°F (177°C).
2. Grease a baking pan with canola oil.
3. Put the remaining ingredients in the baking pan and stir well.
4. Transfer to the air fryer and bake for 13 minutes.
5. Serve warm.

Breakfast Frittata

Servings:2
Cooking Time: 25 Minutes
Ingredients:
- 4 cooked pancetta slices, chopped
- 5 eggs
- Salt and pepper to taste
- ½ leek, thinly sliced
- ½ cup grated cheddar cheese
- 1 tomato, sliced
- 1 cup iceberg lettuce, torn
- 2 tbsp milk

Directions:
1. Preheat air fryer to 320°F. Beat the eggs, milk, salt, and pepper in a bowl. Mix in pancetta and cheddar. Transfer to a greased with olive oil baking pan. Top with tomato slices and leek and place it in the frying basket. Bake for 14 minutes. Let cool for 5 minutes. Serve with lettuce.

Jalapeño And Bacon Breakfast Pizza

Servings:2
Cooking Time: 10 Minutes
Ingredients:
- 1 cup shredded mozzarella cheese
- 1 ounce cream cheese, broken into small pieces
- 4 slices cooked sugar-free bacon, chopped
- ¼ cup chopped pickled jalapeños
- 1 large egg, whisked
- ¼ teaspoon salt

Directions:

1. Place mozzarella in a single layer on the bottom of an ungreased 6" round nonstick baking dish. Scatter cream cheese pieces, bacon, and jalapeños over mozzarella, then pour egg evenly around baking dish.
2. Sprinkle with salt and place into air fryer basket. Adjust the temperature to 330°F and set the timer for 10 minutes. When cheese is brown and egg is set, pizza will be done.
3. Let cool on a large plate 5 minutes before serving.

Spinach Eggs And Cheese

Servings: 2
Cooking Time: 40 Minutes
Ingredients:

- 3 whole eggs
- 3 oz cottage cheese
- 3-4 oz chopped spinach
- ¼ cup parmesan cheese
- ¼ cup of milk

Directions:

1. Preheat your fryer to 375°F.
2. In a large bowl, whisk the eggs, cottage cheese, the parmesan and the milk.
3. Mix in the spinach.
4. Transfer to a small, greased, fryer dish.
5. Sprinkle the cheese on top.
6. Bake for 25-30 minutes.
7. Let cool for 5 minutes and serve.

Fried Bacon With Pork Rinds

Servings: 4
Cooking Time: 12 Minutes
Ingredients:

- 10 ounces bacon
- 3 ounces pork rinds
- 2 eggs, beaten
- ½ teaspoon salt
- ½ teaspoon ground black pepper
- Cooking spray

Directions:

1. Before cooking, heat your air fryer to 395 degrees F/ 200 degrees C.
2. Spritz the cooking spray over an air fryer basket.
3. While the air fryer is preheating, cut the bacon into 4 cubes and season with salt and ground black pepper.
4. Then dip the bacon in the beaten egg and coat in the pork rinds.
5. Transfer to the greased basket.
6. Cook the fried bacon with pork rinds in the air fryer for 12 minutes and flip to the other side halfway through cooking. Cook for one or a few more minutes if necessary until it is light brown.
7. When cooked, transfer from the air fryer and serve.

Grilled Bbq Sausages

Servings:3
Cooking Time: 30 Minutes
Ingredients:

- 6 sausage links

- ½ cup prepared BBQ sauce

Directions:

1. Preheat the air fryer at 390°F.
2. Place the grill pan accessory in the air fryer.
3. Place the sausage links and grill for 30 minutes.
4. Flip halfway through the cooking time.
5. Before serving brush with prepared BBQ sauce.

Eggplant Parmesan Subs

Servings: 2
Cooking Time: 13 Minutes
Ingredients:

- 4 Peeled eggplant slices
- Olive oil spray
- 2 tablespoons plus 2 teaspoons Jarred pizza sauce, any variety except creamy
- ¼ cup (about ⅔ ounce) Finely grated Parmesan cheese
- 2 Small, long soft rolls, such as hero, hoagie, or Italian sub rolls (gluten-free, if a concern), split open lengthwise

Directions:

1. Preheat the air fryer to 350°F .
2. When the machine is at temperature, coat both sides of the eggplant slices with olive oil spray. Set them in the basket in one layer and air-fry undisturbed for 10 minutes, until lightly browned and softened.
3. Increase the machine's temperature to 375°F. Top each eggplant slice with 2 teaspoons pizza sauce, then 1 tablespoon cheese. Air-fry undisturbed for 2 minutes, or until the cheese has melted.
4. Use a nonstick-safe spatula, and perhaps a flatware fork for balance, to transfer the eggplant slices cheese side up to a cutting board. Set the roll(s) cut side down in the basket in one layer and air-fry undisturbed for 1 minute, to toast the rolls a bit and warm them up. Set 2 eggplant slices in each warm roll.

Creamy Soufflés

Servings: 8
Cooking Time: 20 Minutes
Ingredients:

- 6 large eggs, separated
- ¾ cup heavy cream
- ¼ teaspoon cayenne pepper
- ½ teaspoon xanthan gum
- ½ teaspoon black pepper
- ¼ teaspoon cream of tartar
- 2 tablespoons chives, chopped
- 2 cups cheddar cheese, shredded
- 1 teaspoon salt

Directions:

1. At 325 degrees F/ 160 degrees C, preheat your air fryer.
2. Spray eight ramekins with cooking spray. Set aside.
3. In a suitable bowl, whisk together almond flour, cayenne pepper, black pepper, salt, and xanthan gum.
4. Slowly add heavy cream and mix to combine.

5. Whisk in egg yolks, chives, and cheese until well combined.

6. In a suitable bowl, add egg whites and cream of tartar and beat until stiff peaks form.

7. Fold egg white mixture into the dry almond flour mixture until combined.

8. Pour mixture into the prepared ramekins. Divide ramekins in batches.

9. Place the first batch of ramekins into the air fryer basket.

10. Cook soufflé for 20 minutes.

11. Serve and enjoy.

Basil Tomato Bowls

Servings: 4
Cooking Time: 15 Minutes
Ingredients:
- 1 pound cherry tomatoes, halved
- 1 cup mozzarella, shredded
- Cooking spray
- Salt and black pepper to the taste
- 1 teaspoon basil, chopped

Directions:
1. Grease the tomatoes with the cooking spray, season with salt and pepper, sprinkle the mozzarella on top, place them all in your air fryer's basket, cook at 330°F for 15 minutes, divide into bowls, sprinkle the basil on top and serve.

English Pumpkin Egg Bake

Servings:2
Cooking Time: 10 Minutes
Ingredients:
- 2 eggs
- ½ cup milk
- 2 cups flour
- 2 tablespoons cider vinegar
- 2 teaspoons baking powder
- 1 tablespoon sugar
- 1 cup pumpkin purée
- 1 teaspoon cinnamon powder
- 1 teaspoon baking soda
- 1 tablespoon olive oil

Directions:
1. Preheat the air fryer to 300ºF (149ºC).
2. Crack the eggs into a bowl and beat with a whisk. Combine with the milk, flour, cider vinegar, baking powder, sugar, pumpkin purée, cinnamon powder, and baking soda, mixing well.
3. Grease a baking tray with oil. Add the mixture and transfer into the air fryer. Bake for 10 minutes.
4. Serve warm.

Fried Chicken And Waffles

Servings: 4
Cooking Time: 30 Minutes
Ingredients:
- 8 whole chicken wings
- 1 teaspoon garlic powder
- Chicken seasoning or rub
- Pepper
- ½ cup all-purpose flour
- Cooking oil
- 8 frozen waffles
- Maple syrup (optional)

Directions:
1. In a medium bowl, season the chicken with the garlic powder and chicken seasoning and pepper to taste.
2. Transfer the chicken to a sealable plastic bag and add the flour. Shake to thoroughly coat the chicken.
3. Spray the air fryer basket with cooking oil.
4. Using tongs, transfer the chicken from the bag to the air fryer. It is okay to stack the chicken wings on top of each other. Spray them with cooking oil. Cook for 5 minutes.
5. Open the air fryer and shake the basket. Continue to cook the chicken. Repeat shaking every 5 minutes until 20 minutes has passed and the chicken is fully cooked.
6. Remove the cooked chicken from the air fryer and set aside.
7. Rinse the basket and base out with warm water. Return them to the air fryer.
8. Reduce the temperature of the air fryer to 370ºF.
9. Place the frozen waffles in the air fryer. Do not stack. Depending on the size of your air fryer, you may need to cook the waffles in batches. Spray the waffles with cooking oil. Cook for 6 minutes.
10. If necessary, remove the cooked waffles from the air fryer, then repeat step 9 for the remaining waffles.
11. Serve the waffles with the chicken and a touch of maple syrup if desired.

Garlic Bread Knots

Servings: 8
Cooking Time: 5 Minutes
Ingredients:
- ¼ cup melted butter
- 2 teaspoons garlic powder
- 1 teaspoon dried parsley
- 1 tube of refrigerated French bread dough

Directions:
1. Mix the melted butter, garlic powder and dried parsley in a small bowl and set it aside.
2. To make smaller knots, cut the long tube of bread dough into 16 slices. If you want to make bigger knots, slice the dough into 8 slices. Shape each slice into a long rope about 6 inches long by rolling it on a flat surface with the palm of your hands. Tie each rope into a knot and place them on a plate.
3. Preheat the air fryer to 350°F.
4. Transfer half of the bread knots into the air fryer basket, leaving space in between each knot. Brush each knot with the butter mixture using a pastry brush.
5. Air-fry for 5 minutes. Remove the baked knots and brush a little more of the garlic butter mixture on each. Repeat with the remaining bread knots and serve warm.

Creamy Parsley Soufflé

Servings:2

Cooking Time:10 Minutes

Ingredients:

- 2 eggs
- 1 tablespoon fresh parsley, chopped
- 1 fresh red chili pepper, chopped
- 2 tablespoons light cream
- Salt, to taste

Directions:

1. Preheat the Air fryer to 390°F and grease 2 soufflé dishes.
2. Mix together all the ingredients in a bowl until well combined.
3. Transfer the mixture into prepared soufflé dishes and place in the Air fryer.
4. Cook for about 10 minutes and dish out to serve warm.

Denver Eggs

Servings:2

Cooking Time: 15 Minutes

Ingredients:

- 3 large eggs
- 1 tablespoon salted butter, melted
- ¼ cup seeded and chopped green bell pepper
- 2 tablespoons peeled and chopped yellow onion
- ¼ cup chopped cooked no-sugar-added ham
- ¼ teaspoon salt
- ¼ teaspoon ground black pepper

Directions:

1. Crack eggs into an ungreased 6" round nonstick baking dish. Mix in butter, bell pepper, onion, ham, salt, and black pepper.
2. Place dish into air fryer basket. Adjust the temperature to 320°F and set the timer for 15 minutes. The eggs will be fully cooked and firm in the middle when done.
3. Slice in half and serve warm on two medium plates.

Breakfast Cobbler With Blueberries

Servings: 4

Cooking Time: 15 Minutes

Ingredients:

- ⅓ cup whole-wheat pastry flour
- ¾ teaspoon baking powder
- Dash salt
- ½ cup milk
- 2 tablespoons pure maple syrup
- ½ teaspoon vanilla extract
- Cooking oil spray
- ½ cup fresh blueberries
- ¼ cup Granola, or plain store-bought granola

Directions:

1. In a suitable bowl, whisk the flour, baking powder, and salt.
2. Add maple syrup, the milk, and vanilla and gently whisk.

3. Spray a suitable 6-by-2-inch round baking pan with cooking oil and pour the prepared batter into the pan.
4. Top evenly with the blueberries and granola.
5. At 350 degrees F/ 175 degrees C, preheat your air fryer and cook for almost 15 minutes.
6. Garnish and serve.

Scrambled Eggs

Servings: 2

Cooking Time: 6 Minutes

Ingredients:

- 4 eggs
- 1/4 tsp garlic powder
- 1/4 tsp onion powder
- 1 tbsp parmesan cheese
- Pepper
- Salt

Directions:

1. Whisk eggs with garlic powder, onion powder, parmesan cheese, pepper, and salt.
2. Pour egg mixture into the air fryer baking dish.
3. Place dish in the air fryer and cook at 360°F for 2 minutes. Stir quickly and cook for 3-4 minutes more.
4. Stir well and serve.

Banana Baked Oatmeal

Servings:2

Cooking Time:10 Minutes

Ingredients:

- 1 cup quick-cooking oats
- 1 cup whole milk
- 2 tablespoons unsalted butter, melted
- 1 medium banana, peeled and mashed
- 2 tablespoons brown sugar
- ½ teaspoon vanilla extract
- ½ teaspoon salt

Directions:

1. Preheat the air fryer to 360°F.
2. In a 6" round pan, add oats. Pour in milk and butter.
3. In a medium bowl, mix banana, brown sugar, vanilla, and salt until combined. Add to pan and mix until well combined.
4. Place in the air fryer and cook 10 minutes until the top is brown and oats feel firm to the touch. Serve warm.

Roasted Vegetable Frittata

Servings: 1

Cooking Time: 19 Minutes

Ingredients:

- ½ red or green bell pepper, cut into ½-inch chunks
- 4 button mushrooms, sliced
- ½ cup diced zucchini
- ½ teaspoon chopped fresh oregano or thyme
- 1 teaspoon olive oil
- 3 eggs, beaten
- ½ cup grated Cheddar cheese
- salt and freshly ground black pepper, to taste
- 1 teaspoon butter

- 1 teaspoon chopped fresh parsley

Directions:

1. Preheat the air fryer to 400°F.

2. Toss the peppers, mushrooms, zucchini and oregano with the olive oil and air-fry for 6 minutes, shaking the basket once or twice during the cooking process to redistribute the ingredients.

3. While the vegetables are cooking, beat the eggs well in a bowl, stir in the Cheddar cheese and season with salt and freshly ground black pepper. Add the air-fried vegetables to this bowl when they have finished cooking.

4. Place a 6- or 7-inch non-stick metal cake pan into the air fryer basket with the butter using an aluminum sling to lower the pan into the basket. (Fold a piece of aluminum foil into a strip about 2-inches wide by 24-inches long.) Air-fry for 1 minute at 380°F to melt the butter. Remove the cake pan and rotate the pan to distribute the butter and grease the pan. Pour the egg mixture into the cake pan and return the pan to the air fryer, using the aluminum sling.

5. Air-fry at 380°F for 12 minutes, or until the frittata has puffed up and is lightly browned. Let the frittata sit in the air fryer for 5 minutes to cool to an edible temperature and set up. Remove the cake pan from the air fryer, sprinkle with parsley and serve immediately.

Classical Eggs Ramekins

Servings: 5
Cooking Time: 6 Minutes
Ingredients:
- 5 eggs
- 1 teaspoon coconut oil, melted
- ¼ teaspoon ground black pepper

Directions:

1. Using coconut oil, grease the ramekins and whisk in eggs.

2. Sprinkle on the top with ground black pepper.

3. Then place in your air fryer and cook at 355 degrees F/ 180 degrees C for 6 minutes.

Hole In One

Servings: 1
Cooking Time: 7 Minutes
Ingredients:
- 1 slice bread
- 1 teaspoon soft butter
- 1 egg
- salt and pepper
- 1 tablespoon shredded Cheddar cheese
- 2 teaspoons diced ham

Directions:

1. Place a 6 x 6-inch baking dish inside air fryer basket and preheat fryer to 330°F.

2. Using a 2½-inch-diameter biscuit cutter, cut a hole in center of bread slice.

3. Spread softened butter on both sides of bread.

4. Lay bread slice in baking dish and crack egg into the hole. Sprinkle egg with salt and pepper to taste.

5. Cook for 5minutes.

6. Turn toast over and top it with shredded cheese and diced ham.

7. Cook for 2 more minutes or until yolk is done to your liking.

Easy Caprese Flatbread

Servings: 2
Cooking Time: 15 Minutes
Ingredients:
- 1 fresh mozzarella ball, sliced
- 1 flatbread
- 2 tsp olive oil
- ¼ garlic clove, minced
- 1 egg
- ⅛ tsp salt
- ¼ cup diced tomato
- 6 basil leaves
- ½ tsp dried oregano
- ½ tsp balsamic vinegar

Directions:

1. Preheat air fryer to 380°F. Lightly brush the top of the bread with olive oil, then top with garlic. Crack the egg into a small bowl and sprinkle with salt. Place the bread into the frying basket and gently pour the egg onto the top of the pita. Top with tomato, mozzarella, oregano and basil. Bake for 6 minutes. When ready, remove the pita pizza and drizzle with balsamic vinegar. Let it cool for 5 minutes. Slice and serve.

Mushroom And Squash Toast

Servings:4
Cooking Time: 10 Minutes
Ingredients:
- 1 tablespoon olive oil
- 1 red bell pepper, cut into strips
- 2 green onions, sliced
- 1 cup sliced button or cremini mushrooms
- 1 small yellow squash, sliced
- 2 tablespoons softened butter
- 4 slices bread
- ½ cup soft goat cheese

Directions:

1. Brush the air fryer basket with the olive oil and preheat the air fryer to 350°F (177°C).

2. Put the red pepper, green onions, mushrooms, and squash inside the air fryer, give them a stir and air fry for 7 minutes or the vegetables are tender, shaking the basket once throughout the cooking time.

3. Remove the vegetables and set them aside.

4. Spread the butter on the slices of bread and transfer to the air fryer, butter-side up. Brown for 3 minutes.

5. Remove the toast from the air fryer and top with goat cheese and vegetables. Serve warm.

Sweet Potato & Mushroom Hash

Servings: 6
Cooking Time: 35 Minutes
Ingredients:
- 2 peeled sweet potatoes, cubed
- 4 oz baby Bella mushrooms, diced
- ½ red bell pepper, diced
- ½ red onion, diced
- 2 tbsp olive oil
- 1 garlic clove, minced
- Salt and pepper to taste
- ½ tbsp chopped marjoram

Directions:
1. Preheat air fryer to 380°F. Place all ingredients in a large bowl and toss until the vegetables are well coated. Pour the vegetables into the frying basket. Bake for 8-10 minutes, then shake the vegetables. Cook for 8-10 more minutes. Serve and enjoy!

Cheese Taquitos With Cilantro

Servings: 3
Cooking Time: 10 Minutes
Ingredients:
- 3 white corn tortillas
- 3 teaspoons of roasted green chilies
- 1 teaspoon of crumbled cheese
- 3 cheese sticks
- 1 tablespoon of cilantro
- 1 teaspoon of olive oil

Directions:
1. At 400 degrees F/ 205 degrees C, preheat your air fryer.
2. Lightly grease corn tortillas with olive oil on per side.
3. Cut a small pocket at the center of cheese sticks and put chilies in the pockets.
4. Put the stuffed cheese on the tortillas and roll them up.
5. Put them in the preheated air fryer, seam side down.
6. Cook the tortillas at 400 degrees F/ 205 degrees C for 7–10 minutes.
7. Top with cilantro and crumbled cheese.
8. Serve warm and enjoy your Cheesy Taquitos!

Baked Pancakes With Caramelized Apples

Servings: 2
Cooking Time: 4 Minutes
Ingredients:
- 1 tablespoon milk
- 1 cup flour
- 1 ½ tablespoons of sugar
- 1 egg
- ½ teaspoon salt
- ½ teaspoon baking soda
- 1 tablespoon olive oil or another

Directions:

1. Mix all dry ingredients. And mix all the liquid ingredients separately.
2. Add rest of the liquid ingredients to dry ingredients and mix well with a whisk.
3. At 370 degrees F/ 185 degrees C, preheat your air fryer.
4. Grease its air fryer basket or special dish with a little olive oil.
5. Cook in portions for 2 minutes on each side.
6. To make the caramelized Apples: peel the apples, cut into cubes and place in the pan. Sprinkle with sugar and cinnamon, cook until the apples are golden and soft.

Oat Muffins With Blueberries

Servings: 6
Cooking Time: 25 Minutes
Ingredients:
- ¾ cup old-fashioned rolled oats
- 1 ½ cups flour
- ½ cup evaporated cane sugar
- 1 tbsp baking powder
- 1 tsp ground cinnamon
- ¼ tsp ground chia seeds
- ¼ tsp ground sesame seeds
- ½ tsp salt
- 1 cup vanilla almond milk
- 4 tbsp butter, softened
- 2 eggs
- 1 tsp vanilla extract
- 1 cup blueberries
- 2 tbsp powdered sugar

Directions:
1. Preheat air fryer to 350°F. Combine flour oats, sugar, baking powder, chia seeds, sesame seeds, cinnamon, and salt in a bowl. Mix the almond milk, butter, eggs, and vanilla in another bowl until smooth. Pour in dry ingredients and stir to combine. Fold in blueberries.Fill 12 silicone muffin cups about halfway and place them in the frying basket. Bake for 12-15 minutes until just browned, and a toothpick in the center comes out clean. Cool for 5 minutes. Serve topped with powdered sugar.

Coconut Pudding

Servings: 4
Cooking Time: 20 Minutes
Ingredients:
- 1 cup cauliflower rice
- ½ cup coconut, shredded
- 3 cups coconut milk
- 2 tablespoons stevia

Directions:
1. In a pan that fits the air fryer, combine all the ingredients and whisk well. Introduce the in your air fryer and cook at 360°F for 20 minutes. Divide into bowls and serve for breakfast.

Breakfast Chimichangas

Servings: 4
Cooking Time: 8 Minutes
Ingredients:
- Four 8-inch flour tortillas
- ½ cup canned refried beans
- 1 cup scrambled eggs
- ½ cup grated cheddar or Monterey jack cheese
- 1 tablespoon vegetable oil
- 1 cup salsa

Directions:
1. Lay the flour tortillas out flat on a cutting board. In the center of each tortilla, spread 2 tablespoons refried beans. Next, add ¼ cup eggs and 2 tablespoons cheese to each tortilla.
2. To fold the tortillas, begin on the left side and fold to the center. Then fold the right side into the center. Next fold the bottom and top down and roll over to completely seal the chimichanga. Using a pastry brush or oil mister, brush the tops of the tortilla packages with oil.
3. Preheat the air fryer to 400°F for 4 minutes. Place the chimichangas into the air fryer basket, seam side down, and air fry for 4 minutes. Using tongs, turn over the chimichangas and cook for an additional 2 to 3 minutes or until light golden brown.

Pumpkin Donut Holes

Servings:12
Cooking Time:14 Minutes
Ingredients:
- 1 cup whole-wheat pastry flour, plus more as needed
- 3 tablespoons packed brown sugar
- ½ teaspoon ground cinnamon
- 1 teaspoon low-sodium baking powder
- ⅓ cup canned no-salt-added pumpkin purée (not pumpkin pie filling; see Tip)
- 3 tablespoons 2 percent milk, plus more as needed
- 2 tablespoons unsalted butter, melted
- 1 egg white
- Powdered sugar (optional)

Directions:
1. In a medium bowl, mix the pastry flour, brown sugar, cinnamon, and baking powder.
2. In a small bowl, beat the pumpkin, milk, butter, and egg white until combined. Add the pumpkin mixture to the dry ingredients and mix until combined. You may need to add more flour or milk to form a soft dough.
3. Divide the dough into 12 pieces. With floured hands, form each piece into a ball.
4. Cut a piece of parchment paper or aluminum foil to fit inside the air fryer basket but about 1 inch smaller in diameter. Poke holes in the paper or foil and place it in the basket.
5. Put 6 donut holes into the basket, leaving some space around each. Air-fry for 5 to 7 minutes, or until the donut holes reach an internal temperature of 200°F and are firm and light golden brown.

6. Let cool for 5 minutes. Remove from the basket and roll in powdered sugar, if desired. Repeat with the remaining donut holes and serve.

Egg & Bacon Toasts

Servings: 4
Cooking Time: 25 Minutes
Ingredients:
- 4 French bread slices, cut diagonally
- 1 + tsp butter
- 4 eggs
- 2 tbsp milk
- ½ tsp dried thyme
- Salt and pepper to taste
- 4 oz cooked bacon, crumbled
- 2/3 cup grated Colby cheese

Directions:
1. Preheat the air fryer to 350°F. Spray each slice of bread with oil and Bake in the frying basket for 2-3 minutes until light brown; set aside. Beat together the eggs, milk, thyme, salt, and pepper in a bowl and add the melted butter. Transfer to a 6-inch cake pan and place the pan into the fryer. Bake for 7-8 minutes, stirring once or until the eggs are set. Transfer the egg mixture into a bowl.
2. Top the bread slices with egg mixture, bacon, and cheese. Return to the fryer and Bake for 4-8 minutes or until the cheese melts and browns in spots. Serve.

Mashed Potato Taquitos With Hot Sauce

Servings: 4
Cooking Time: 30 Minutes
Ingredients:
- 1 potato, peeled and cubed
- 2 tbsp milk
- 2 garlic cloves, minced
- Salt and pepper to taste
- ½ tsp ground cumin
- 2 tbsp minced scallions
- 4 corn tortillas
- 1 cup red chili sauce
- 1 avocado, sliced
- 2 tbsp cilantro, chopped

Directions:
1. In a pot fitted with a steamer basket, cook the potato cubes for 15 minutes on the stovetop. Pour the potato cubes into a bowl and mash with a potato masher. Add the milk, garlic, salt, pepper, and cumin and stir. Add the scallions and cilantro and stir them into the mixture.
2. Preheat air fryer to 390°F. Run the tortillas under water for a second, then place them in the greased frying basket. Air Fry for 1 minute. Lay the tortillas on a flat surface. Place an equal amount of the potato filling in the center of each. Roll the tortilla sides over the filling and place seam-side down in the frying basket. Fry for 7 minutes or until the tortillas are golden and slightly crisp. Serve with chili sauce and avocado slices. Enjoy!

Puffed Egg Tarts

Servings:4
Cooking Time:42 Minutes
Ingredients:
- 1 sheet frozen puff pastry half, thawed and cut into 4 squares
- ¾ cup Monterey Jack cheese, shredded and divided
- 4 large eggs
- 1 tablespoon fresh parsley, minced
- 1 tablespoon olive oil

Directions:
1. Preheat the Air fryer to 390°F
2. Place 2 pastry squares in the air fryer basket and cook for about 10 minutes.
3. Remove Air fryer basket from the Air fryer and press each square gently with a metal tablespoon to form an indentation.
4. Place 3 tablespoons of cheese in each hole and top with 1 egg each.
5. Return Air fryer basket to Air fryer and cook for about 11 minutes.
6. Remove tarts from the Air fryer basket and sprinkle with half the parsley.
7. Repeat with remaining pastry squares, cheese and eggs.
8. Dish out and serve warm.

Onion Marinated Skirt Steak

Servings:3
Cooking Time: 45 Minutes
Ingredients:
- 1 large red onion, grated or pureed
- 2 tablespoons brown sugar
- 1 tablespoon vinegar
- 1 ½ pounds skirt steak
- Salt and pepper to taste

Directions:
1. Place all ingredients in a Ziploc bag and allow to marinate in the fridge for at least 2 hours.
2. Preheat the air fryer at 390°F.
3. Place the grill pan accessory in the air fryer.
4. Grill for 15 minutes per batch.
5. Flip every 8 minutes for even grilling.

Zoodles With Cheese

Servings: 3
Cooking Time: 45 Minutes
Ingredients:
- 1 egg
- ½ cup parmesan cheese, grated
- ½ cup feta cheese, crumbled
- 1 tablespoon thyme
- 1 garlic clove, chopped
- 1 onion, chopped
- 2 medium zucchinis, trimmed and spiralized
- 2 tablespoon olive oil
- 1 cup mozzarella cheese, grated
- ½ teaspoon black pepper

- ½ teaspoon salt

Directions:
1. At 350 degrees F/ 175 degrees C, preheat your air fryer.
2. Add spiralized zucchini and salt in a colander and set aside for almost 10 minutes.
3. Wash zucchini noodles and pat dry with a paper towel.
4. Set a suitable pan with oil over medium heat.
5. Add garlic and onion and sauté for 3-4 minutes
6. Stir in zucchini noodles and cook for 4-5 minutes or until softened.
7. Add zucchini mixture into the air fryer basket.
8. Stir in egg, thyme, cheeses. Mix well and season.
9. Place pan in the preheated air fryer and cook for 30-35 minutes.
10. Serve and enjoy.

Breakfast Muffins With Bacon And Cheese

Servings: 4
Cooking Time: 15 Minutes
Ingredients:
- 1 ½ cup of all-purpose flour
- 2 teaspoons of baking powder
- ½ cup of milk
- 2 eggs
- 1 tablespoon of freshly chopped parsley
- 4 cooked and chopped bacon slices
- 1 thinly chopped onion
- ½ cup of shredded cheddar cheese
- ½ teaspoon of onion powder
- 1 teaspoon of salt
- 1 teaspoon of black pepper

Directions:
1. At 360 degrees F/ 180 degrees C, preheat your air fryer.
2. Using a suitable bowl, add and stir all the recipe ingredients until it mixes properly.
3. Then grease the muffin cups with a nonstick cooking spray or line it with a parchment paper. Pour the batter proportionally into each muffin cup.
4. Place it inside your air fryer and air fry it for almost 15 minutes.
5. Thereafter, carefully remove it from your air fryer and allow it to chill.
6. Serve and enjoy!

Mozzarella Eggs With Basil Pesto

Servings: 4
Cooking Time: 20 Minutes
Ingredients:
- 2 tablespoons butter, melted
- 6 teaspoons basil pesto
- 1 cup mozzarella cheese, grated
- 6 eggs, whisked
- 1 tablespoons basil, chopped
- A pinch of salt and black pepper

Directions:

1. Before cooking, heat your air fryer to 360 degrees F/ 180 degrees C.
2. Mix the basil pesto, mozzarella cheese, the whisked egg, basil, salt, and black pepper together in a bowl. Whisk.
3. Drizzle the baking pan with butter and then add the mixture.
4. Cook in your air fryer at 360 degrees F/ 180 degrees C for 20 minutes.
5. When the cooking time is up, transfer from the air fryer and serve on plates.
6. Enjoy your breakfast.

Pigs In A Blanket

Servings: 10
Cooking Time: 8 Minutes
Ingredients:

- 1 cup all-purpose flour, plus more for rolling
- 1 teaspoon baking powder
- ¼ cup salted butter, cut into small pieces
- ½ cup buttermilk
- 10 fully cooked breakfast sausage links

Directions:

1. In a large mixing bowl, whisk together the flour and baking powder. Using your fingers or a pastry blender, cut in the butter until you have small pea-size crumbles.
2. Using a rubber spatula, make a well in the center of the flour mixture. Pour the buttermilk into the well, and fold the mixture together until you form a dough ball.
3. Place the sticky dough onto a floured surface and, using a floured rolling pin, roll out until ½-inch thick. Using a round biscuit cutter, cut out 10 rounds, reshaping the dough and rolling out, as needed.
4. Place 1 fully cooked breakfast sausage link on the left edge of each biscuit and roll up, leaving the ends slightly exposed.
5. Using a pastry brush, brush the biscuits with the whisked eggs, and spray them with cooking spray.
6. Place the pigs in a blanket into the air fryer basket with at least 1 inch between each biscuit. Set the air fryer to 340°F and cook for 8 minutes.

Oat & Nut Granola

Servings: 6
Cooking Time: 25 Minutes
Ingredients:

- 2 cups rolled oats
- ¼ cup pistachios
- ¼ cup chopped almonds
- ¼ cup chopped cashews
- ¼ cup honey
- 2 tbsp light brown sugar
- 3 tbsp butter
- ½ tsp ground cinnamon
- ½ cup dried figs

Directions:

1. Preheat the air fryer to 325°F. Combine the oats, pistachios, almonds, and cashews in a bowl and toss,

then set aside. In a saucepan, cook the honey, brown sugar, butter, and cinnamon and over low heat, stirring frequently, 4 minutes. Melt the butter completely and make sure the mixture is smooth, then pour over the oat mix and stir.
2. Scoop the granola mixture in a greased baking pan. Put the pan in the frying basket and Bake for 7 minutes, then remove the pan and stir. Cook for another 6-9 minutes or until the granola is golden, then add the dried figs and stir. Remove the pan and let cool. Store in a covered container at room temperature for up to 3 days.

Garlic Parmesan Bread Ring

Servings: 6
Cooking Time: 30 Minutes
Ingredients:

- ½ cup unsalted butter, melted
- ¼ teaspoon salt (omit if using salted butter)
- ¾ cup grated Parmesan cheese
- 3 to 4 cloves garlic, minced
- 1 tablespoon chopped fresh parsley
- 1 pound frozen bread dough, defrosted
- olive oil
- 1 egg, beaten

Directions:

1. Combine the melted butter, salt, Parmesan cheese, garlic and chopped parsley in a small bowl.
2. Roll the dough out into a rectangle that measures 8 inches by 17 inches. Spread the butter mixture over the dough, leaving a half-inch border un-buttered along one of the long edges. Roll the dough from one long edge to the other, ending with the un-buttered border. Pinch the seam shut tightly. Shape the log into a circle sealing the ends together by pushing one end into the other and stretching the dough around it.
3. Cut out a circle of aluminum foil that is the same size as the air fryer basket. Brush the foil circle with oil and place an oven safe ramekin or glass in the center. Transfer the dough ring to the aluminum foil circle, around the ramekin. This will help you make sure the dough will fit in the basket and maintain its ring shape. Use kitchen shears to cut 8 slits around the outer edge of the dough ring halfway to the center. Brush the dough ring with egg wash.
4. Preheat the air fryer to 400°F for 4 minutes. When it has Preheated, brush the sides of the basket with oil and transfer the dough ring, foil circle and ramekin into the basket. Slide the drawer back into the air fryer, but do not turn the air fryer on. Let the dough rise inside the warm air fryer for 30 minutes.
5. After the bread has proofed in the air fryer for 30 minutes, set the temperature to 340°F and air-fry the bread ring for 15 minutes. Flip the bread over by inverting it onto a plate or cutting board and sliding it back into the air fryer basket. Air-fry for another 15 minutes. Let the bread cool for a few minutes before slicing the bread ring in between the slits and serving warm.

Huevos Rancheros

Servings: 4
Cooking Time: 45 Minutes + Cooling Time
Ingredients:
- 1 tbsp olive oil
- 20 cherry tomatoes, halved
- 2 chopped plum tomatoes
- ¼ cup tomato sauce
- 2 scallions, sliced
- 2 garlic cloves, minced
- 1 tsp honey
- ½ tsp salt
- ⅛ tsp cayenne pepper
- ¼ tsp grated nutmeg
- ¼ tsp paprika
- 4 eggs

Directions:
1. Preheat the air fryer to 370°F. Combine the olive oil, cherry tomatoes, plum tomatoes, tomato sauce, scallions, garlic, nutmeg, honey, salt, paprika and cayenne in a 7-inch springform pan that has been wrapped in foil to prevent leaks. Put the pan in the frying basket and
2. Bake the mix for 15-20 minutes, stirring twice until the tomatoes are soft. Mash some of the tomatoes in the pan with a fork, then stir them into the sauce. Also, break the eggs into the sauce, then return the pan to the fryer and Bake for 2 minutes. Remove the pan from the fryer and stir the eggs into the sauce, whisking them through the sauce. Don't mix in completely. Cook for 4-8 minutes more or until the eggs are set. Let cool, then serve.

Parmesan Breakfast Casserole

Servings: 3
Cooking Time: 20 Minutes
Ingredients:
- 5 eggs
- 2 tbsp heavy cream
- 3 tbsp chunky tomato sauce
- 2 tbsp parmesan cheese, grated

Directions:
1. Preheat the air fryer to 325°F.
2. In mixing bowl, combine together cream and eggs.
3. Add cheese and tomato sauce and mix well.
4. Spray air fryer baking dish with cooking spray.
5. Pour mixture into baking dish and place in the air fryer basket.

6. Cook for 20 minutes.
7. Serve and enjoy.

Asparagus And Bell Pepper Strata

Servings: 4
Cooking Time:14 To 20 Minutes
Ingredients:
- 8 large asparagus spears, trimmed and cut into 2-inch pieces
- ⅓ cup shredded carrot (see Tip)
- ½ cup chopped red bell pepper
- 2 slices low-sodium whole-wheat bread, cut into ½-inch cubes
- 3 egg whites
- 1 egg
- 3 tablespoons 1 percent milk
- ½ teaspoon dried thyme

Directions:
1. In a 6-by-2-inch pan, combine the asparagus, carrot, red bell pepper, and 1 tablespoon of water. Bake in the air fryer for 3 to 5 minutes, or until crisp-tender. Drain well.
2. Add the bread cubes to the vegetables and gently toss.
3. In a medium bowl, whisk the egg whites, egg, milk, and thyme until frothy.
4. Pour the egg mixture into the pan. Bake for 11 to 15 minutes, or until the strata is slightly puffy and set and the top starts to brown. Serve.

Gold Avocado

Servings:4
Cooking Time: 6 Minutes
Ingredients:
- 2 large avocados, sliced
- ¼ teaspoon paprika
- Salt and ground black pepper, to taste
- ½ cup flour
- 2 eggs, beaten
- 1 cup bread crumbs

Directions:
1. Preheat the air fryer to 400ºF (204ºC).
2. Sprinkle paprika, salt and pepper on the slices of avocado.
3. Lightly coat the avocados with flour. Dredge them in the eggs, before covering with bread crumbs.
4. Transfer to the air fryer and air fry for 6 minutes.
5. Serve warm.

Chapter 5: Beef, pork & Lamb Recipes

Maple'n Soy Marinated Beef

Servings:4
Cooking Time: 45 Minutes
Ingredients:
- 2 pounds sirloin flap steaks, pounded
- 3 tablespoons balsamic vinegar
- 3 tablespoons maple syrup
- 3 tablespoons soy sauce
- 4 cloves of garlic, minced

Directions:
1. Preheat the air fryer to 390°F.
2. Place the grill pan accessory in the air fryer.
3. On a deep dish, place the flap steaks and season with soy sauce, balsamic vinegar, and maple syrup, and garlic.
4. Place on the grill pan and cook for 15 minutes in batches.

Beef And Cheese Empanadas

Servings:15
Cooking Time: 25 Minutes
Ingredients:
- Cooking oil
- 2 garlic cloves, chopped
- ⅓ cup chopped green bell pepper
- ⅓ medium onion, chopped
- 8 ounces 93% lean ground beef
- 1 teaspoon burger seasoning
- Salt
- Pepper
- 15 empanada wrappers
- 1 cup shredded mozzarella cheese
- 1 cup shredded Pepper Jack cheese
- 1 tablespoon butter

Directions:
1. Spray a skillet with cooking oil and place over medium-high heat. Add the garlic, green bell pepper, and onion. Cook until fragrant, about 2 minutes.
2. Add the ground beef to the skillet. Season the beef with the hamburger seasoning and salt and pepper to taste. Using a spatula, break up the beef into small pieces. Cook the beef until browned. Drain any excess fat.
3. Lay the empanada wrappers on a flat surface.
4. Dip a basting brush in water. Glaze each of the empanada wrappers with the wet brush along the edges. This will soften the crust and make it easier to roll. You can also dip your fingers in water to moisten the edges.
5. Scoop 2 to 3 tablespoons of ground beef mixture onto each empanada wrapper. Sprinkle the mozzarella and Pepper Jack cheeses over the beef mixture.
6. Close the empanadas by folding the empanada in half. Using the back of a fork, press along the edges to seal.
7. Place 7 or 8 of the empanadas in the air fryer. Spray each with cooking oil. Cook for 8 minutes.
8. Open the air fryer and flip the empanadas. Cook for an additional 4 minutes.
9. Remove the cooked empanadas from the air fryer, then repeat steps 7 and 8 for the remaining 7 or 8 empanadas.
10. For added flavor, melt the butter in the microwave for 20 seconds. Using a cooking brush, spread the melted butter over the top of each.
11. Cool before serving.

Glazed Tender Pork Chops

Servings: 3
Cooking Time: 14 Minutes
Ingredients:
- 3 pork chops, rinsed and pat dry
- ¼ teaspoon smoked paprika
- ½ teaspoon garlic powder
- 2 teaspoons olive oil
- Black pepper
- Salt

Directions:
1. Coat pork chops with paprika, olive oil, garlic powder, black pepper, and salt.
2. Place the prepared pork chops in air fryer basket and cook at almost 380 degrees F/ 195 degrees C for almost 10-14 minutes. Turn halfway through the cooking time.
3. Serve and enjoy.

Beef And Mushroom Calzones

Servings:6
Cooking Time: 20 Minutes
Ingredients:
- Cooking oil
- ½ cup chopped onion
- 2 garlic cloves, minced
- ¼ cup chopped mushrooms
- 1 pound 93% lean ground beef
- 1 tablespoon Italian seasoning
- Salt
- Pepper
- 1½ cups pizza sauce
- 1 teaspoon all-purpose flour
- 1 (13-ounce) can refrigerated pizza dough
- 1 cup shredded Cheddar cheese

Directions:
1. Spray a skillet with cooking oil and place over medium-high heat. Add the chopped onion, garlic, and mushrooms. Cook for 2 to 3 minutes, until fragrant.
2. Add the ground beef, Italian seasoning, and salt and pepper to taste. Use a large spoon or spatula to break up the beef into small pieces. Cook for 2 to 4 minutes, until browned.
3. Add the pizza sauce. Stir to combine.
4. Sprinkle the flour on a flat work surface. Roll out the pizza dough. Cut the dough into 6 equal-sized rectangles.
5. Mound ½ cup of the ground beef mixture on each of the rectangles. Sprinkle 1 tablespoon of shredded cheese over the beef mixture.

6. Fold each crust up to close the calzones. Using the back of a fork, press along the open edges of each calzone to seal.

7. Place the calzones in the air fryer. Do not stack. Cook in batches. Spray the calzones with cooking oil. Cook for 10 minutes.

8. Remove the cooked calzones from the air fryer, then repeat step 7 for the remaining calzones.

9. Cool before serving.

Cheese Ground Pork

Servings: 4
Cooking Time: 40 Minutes
Ingredients:
- 1 tablespoon olive oil
- 1 ½ pounds pork, ground
- Salt and black pepper, to taste
- 1 medium-sized leek, sliced
- 1 teaspoon fresh garlic, minced
- 2 carrots, trimmed and sliced
- 1 (2-ounce) jar pimiento, drained and chopped
- 1 can (10 ¾-ounces) condensed cream of mushroom soup
- 1 cup water
- ½ cup ale
- 1 cup cream cheese
- ½ cup soft fresh breadcrumbs
- 1 tablespoon fresh cilantro, chopped

Directions:
1. At 320 degrees F/ 160 degrees C, preheat your Air Fryer.
2. Spread the olive oil in a suitable baking dish and heat for 1 to 2 minutes.
3. Add the pork, salt, black pepper and cook for 6 minutes, crumbling with a fork.
4. Then stir in the leeks and cook for 4 to 5 minutes, with occasional stirring.
5. Add the garlic, carrots, pimiento, mushroom soup, water, ale, and cream cheese.
6. Gently stir to combine.
7. Turn the temperature to 370 degrees F/ 185 degrees C.
8. Top with the breadcrumbs.
9. Place the stuffed baking dish in the cooking basket and cook approximately 30 minutes or until everything is thoroughly cooked.
10. Serve garnished with fresh cilantro.

Italian-style Honey Pork

Servings: 3
Cooking Time: 50 Minutes
Ingredients:
- 1 teaspoon Celtic sea salt
- ½-teaspoon black pepper, freshly cracked
- ¼ cup red wine
- 1 tablespoon mustard
- 1 tablespoon honey
- 2 garlic cloves, minced

- 1 lb. pork top loin
- 1 tablespoon Italian herb seasoning blend

Directions:
1. Prepare a suitable bowl, mix up the salt, black pepper, red wine, mustard, honey, garlic and the pork top loin, then marinate the pork top loin at least 30 minutes.
2. Spray the cooking basket of your air fryer with the non-stick cooking spray.
3. Sprinkle the Italian herb on the top of the pork top loin after transfer it to the basket.
4. Cook the pork top loin at 370 degrees F/ 185 degrees C for 10 minutes, flipping and spraying with cooking oil halfway through.
5. When cooked, serve and enjoy.

Broccoli & Mushroom Beef

Servings: 4
Cooking Time: 30 Minutes
Ingredients:
- 1 lb sirloin strip steak, cubed
- 1 cup sliced cremini mushrooms
- 2 tbsp potato starch
- ½ cup beef broth
- 1 tsp soy sauce
- 2 ½ cups broccoli florets
- 1 onion, chopped
- 1 tbsp grated fresh ginger
- 1 cup cooked quinoa

Directions:
1. Add potato starch, broth, and soy sauce to a bowl and mix, then add in the beef and coat thoroughly. Marinate for 5 minutes. Preheat air fryer to 400°F. Set aside the broth and move the beef to a bowl. Add broccoli, onion, mushrooms, and ginger and transfer the bowl to the air fryer. Bake for 12-15 minutes until the beef is golden brown and the veggies soft. Pour the reserved broth over the beef and cook for 2-3 more minutes until the sauce is bubbling. Serve warm over cooked quinoa.

Italian Sausage & Peppers

Servings: 6
Cooking Time: 25 Minutes
Ingredients:
- 1 6-ounce can tomato paste
- ⅔ cup water
- 1 8-ounce can tomato sauce
- 1 teaspoon dried parsley flakes
- ½ teaspoon garlic powder
- ⅛ teaspoon oregano
- ½ pound mild Italian bulk sausage
- 1 tablespoon extra virgin olive oil
- ½ large onion, cut in 1-inch chunks
- 4 ounces fresh mushrooms, sliced
- 1 large green bell pepper, cut in 1-inch chunks
- 8 ounces spaghetti, cooked
- Parmesan cheese for serving

Directions:

1. In a large saucepan or skillet, stir together the tomato paste, water, tomato sauce, parsley, garlic, and oregano. Heat on stovetop over very low heat while preparing meat and vegetables.
2. Break sausage into small chunks, about ½-inch pieces. Place in air fryer baking pan.
3. Cook at 390°F for 5minutes. Stir. Cook 7 minutes longer or until sausage is well done. Remove from pan, drain on paper towels, and add to the sauce mixture.
4. If any sausage grease remains in baking pan, pour it off or use paper towels to soak it up. (Be careful handling that hot pan!)
5. Place olive oil, onions, and mushrooms in pan and stir. Cook for 5minutes or just until tender. Using a slotted spoon, transfer onions and mushrooms from baking pan into the sauce and sausage mixture.
6. Place bell pepper chunks in air fryer baking pan and cook for 8 minutes or until tender. When done, stir into sauce with sausage and other vegetables.
7. Serve over cooked spaghetti with plenty of Parmesan cheese.

Beef And Spinach Rolls

Servings:2
Cooking Time: 14 Minutes
Ingredients:
- 3 teaspoons pesto
- 2 pounds (907 g) beef flank steak
- 6 slices provolone cheese
- 3 ounces (85 g) roasted red bell peppers
- ¾ cup baby spinach
- 1 teaspoon sea salt
- 1 teaspoon black pepper

Directions:
1. Preheat the air fryer to 400°F (204°C).
2. Spoon equal amounts of the pesto onto each flank steak and spread it across evenly.
3. Put the cheese, roasted red peppers and spinach on top of the meat, about three-quarters of the way down.
4. Roll the steak up, holding it in place with toothpicks. Sprinkle with the sea salt and pepper.
5. Put inside the air fryer and air fry for 14 minutes, turning halfway through the cooking time.
6. Allow the beef to rest for 10 minutes before slicing up and serving.

Unique Beef Cheeseburgers

Servings: 4
Cooking Time: 15 Minutes
Ingredients:
- ½ lb. ground beef
- ⅓ cup breadcrumbs
- 2 tablespoons parsley, finely chopped
- 3 tablespoons parmesan cheese, shredded
- ½ teaspoon salt
- ⅓ teaspoon pepper
- 4 slices Cheddar cheese
- 4 burger buns

- 1 red onion, sliced
- 4 romaine lettuce leaves
- 4 teaspoons mayonnaise
- 1cup pickles, sliced

Directions:
1. Mix the ground beef with breadcrumbs, parmesan cheese, parsley, salt and pepper well in a suitable dish.
2. Form 4 patties from the meat mixture.
3. Cook the patties in your air fryer at 390 degrees F/ 200 degrees C for 13 minutes.
4. After that, place the cheese slices on the top and cook for 1 minute more.
5. When cooked, top with pickles, red onion, lettuce leaves, and mayonnaise.
6. Enjoy!

Pork And Pinto Bean Gorditas

Servings:4
Cooking Time: 21 Minutes
Ingredients:
- 1 pound (454 g) lean ground pork
- 2 tablespoons chili powder
- 2 tablespoons ground cumin
- 1 teaspoon dried oregano
- 2 teaspoons paprika
- 1 teaspoon garlic powder
- ½ cup water
- 1 (15-ounce / 425-g) can pinto beans, drained and rinsed
- ½ cup taco sauce
- Salt and freshly ground black pepper, to taste
- 2 cups grated Cheddar cheese
- 5 (12-inch) flour tortillas
- 4 (8-inch) crispy corn tortilla shells
- 4 cups shredded lettuce
- 1 tomato, diced
- ⅓ cup sliced black olives
- Sour cream, for serving
- Tomato salsa, for serving
- Cooking spray

Directions:
1. Preheat the air fryer to 400°F (204°C). Spritz the air fryer basket with cooking spray.
2. Put the ground pork in the air fryer basket and air fry at 400°F (204°C) for 10 minutes, stirring a few times to gently break up the meat. Combine the chili powder, cumin, oregano, paprika, garlic powder and water in a small bowl. Stir the spice mixture into the browned pork. Stir in the beans and taco sauce and air fry for an additional minute. Transfer the pork mixture to a bowl. Season with salt and freshly ground black pepper.
3. Sprinkle ½ cup of the grated cheese in the center of the flour tortillas, leaving a 2-inch border around the edge free of cheese and filling. Divide the pork mixture among the four tortillas, placing it on top of the cheese. Put a crunchy corn tortilla on top of the pork and top with shredded lettuce, diced tomatoes, and black olives.

Cut the remaining flour tortilla into 4 quarters. These quarters of tortilla will serve as the bottom of the gordita. Put one quarter tortilla on top of each gordita and fold the edges of the bottom flour tortilla up over the sides, enclosing the filling. While holding the seams down, brush the bottom of the gordita with olive oil and place the seam side down on the countertop while you finish the remaining three gorditas.

4.   Preheat the air fryer to 380ºF (193ºC).

5.   Air fry one gordita at a time. Transfer the gordita carefully to the air fryer basket, seam side down. Brush or spray the top tortilla with oil and air fry for 5 minutes. Carefully turn the gordita over and air fry for an additional 4 to 5 minutes until both sides are browned. When finished air frying all four gorditas, layer them back into the air fryer for an additional minute to make sure they are all warm before serving with sour cream and salsa.

Simple Air Fryer Steak

Servings: 2
Cooking Time: 18 Minutes
Ingredients:
- 12 oz steaks, 3/4-inch thick
- 1 tsp garlic powder
- 1 tsp olive oil
- Pepper
- Salt

Directions:
1.   Coat steaks with oil and season with garlic powder, pepper, and salt.
2.   Preheat the air fryer to 400°F.
3.   Place steaks in air fryer basket and cook for 15-18 minutes. Turn halfway through.
4.   Serve and enjoy.

Crispy Mustard Pork Tenderloin

Servings:4
Cooking Time: 14 Minutes
Ingredients:
- 1 pound pork tenderloin, cut into 1-inch slices
- Pinch salt
- Freshly ground black pepper
- 2 tablespoons Dijon mustard
- 1 clove garlic, minced
- ½ teaspoon dried basil
- 1 cup soft bread crumbs
- 2 tablespoons olive oil

Directions:
1.   Slightly pound the pork slices until they are about ¾-inch thick. Sprinkle with salt and pepper on both sides.
2.   Coat the pork with the Dijon mustard and sprinkle with the garlic and basil.
3.   On a plate, combine the bread crumbs and olive oil and mix well. Coat the pork slices with the bread crumb mixture, patting so the crumbs adhere.
4.   Place the pork in the air fryer basket, leaving a little space between each piece. Air-fry for 12 to 14 minutes

or until the pork reaches at least 145°F on a meat thermometer and the coating is crisp and brown. Serve immediately.

Beef & Barley Stuffed Bell Peppers

Servings: 4
Cooking Time: 30 Minutes
Ingredients:
- 1 cup pulled cooked roast beef
- 4 bell peppers, tops removed
- 1 onion, chopped
- ½ cup grated carrot
- 2 tsp olive oil
- 2 tomatoes, chopped
- 1 cup cooked barley
- 1 tsp dried marjoram

Directions:
1.   Preheat air fryer to 400°F. Cut the tops of the bell peppers, then remove the stems. Put the onion, carrots, and olive oil in a baking pan and cook for 2-4 minutes. The veggies should be crispy but soft. Put the veggies in a bowl, toss in the tomatoes, barley, roast beef, and marjoram, and mix to combine. Spoon the veggie mix into the cleaned bell peppers and put them in the frying basket. Bake for 12-16 minutes or until the peppers are tender. Serve warm.

Parmesan Sausage Meatballs

Servings: 8
Cooking Time: 15 Minutes
Ingredients:
- 1 pound Italian sausage
- 1-pound ground beef
- ½ teaspoon Italian seasoning
- ½ teaspoon red pepper flakes
- 1 ½ cups Parmesan cheese, grated
- 2 egg, lightly beaten
- 2 tablespoons parsley, chopped
- 2 garlic cloves, minced
- ¼ cup onion, minced
- Black pepper
- Salt

Directions:
1.   Add all the recipe ingredients into the suitable mixing bowl and mix until well combined.
2.   Grease its air fryer basket with cooking spray.
3.   Make meatballs from bowl mixture and place into the air fryer basket.
4.   Cook at almost 350 degrees F/ 175 degrees C for almost 15 minutes.
5.   Serve and enjoy.

Stuffed Cabbage Rolls

Servings: 4
Cooking Time: 50 Minutes
Ingredients:
- ½ cup long-grain brown rice
- 12 green cabbage leaves

- 1 lb ground beef
- 4 garlic cloves, minced
- Salt and pepper to taste
- 1 tsp ground cinnamon
- ½ tsp ground cumin
- 2 tbsp chopped mint
- 1 lemon, juiced and zested
- ½ cup beef broth
- 1 tbsp olive oil
- 2 tbsp parsley, chopped

Directions:
1. Place a large pot of salted water over medium heat and bring to a boil. Add the cabbage leaves and boil them for 3 minutes. Remove from the water and set aside. Combine the ground beef, rice, garlic, salt, pepper, cinnamon, cumin, mint, lemon juice and zest in a bowl.
2. Preheat air fryer to 360°F. Divide the beef mixture between the cabbage leaves and roll them up. Place the finished rolls into a greased baking dish. Pour the beef broth over the cabbage rolls and then brush the tops with olive oil. Put the casserole dish into the frying basket and Bake for 30 minutes. Top with parsley and enjoy!

Jerk Pork Butt Pieces
Servings: 4
Cooking Time: 20 Minutes
Ingredients:
- 1 ½ pounds pork butt, chopped into pieces
- 3 tablespoons jerk paste

Directions:
1. Add meat and jerk paste into the bowl and coat well. Place in the fridge for overnight.
2. Grease its air fryer basket with cooking spray.
3. At 390 degrees F/ 200 degrees C, preheat your air fryer.
4. Add marinated meat into the air fryer and cook for 20 minutes. Turn halfway through the cooking time.
5. Serve and enjoy.

Italian Lamb Chops With Avocado Mayo
Servings:2
Cooking Time: 12 Minutes
Ingredients:
- 2 lamp chops
- 2 teaspoons Italian herbs
- 2 avocados
- ½ cup mayonnaise
- 1 tablespoon lemon juice

Directions:
1. Season the lamb chops with the Italian herbs, then set aside for 5 minutes.
2. Preheat the air fryer to 400°F (204°C) and place the rack inside.
3. Put the chops on the rack and air fry for 12 minutes.
4. In the meantime, halve the avocados and open to remove the pits. Spoon the flesh into a blender.

5. Add the mayonnaise and lemon juice and pulse until a smooth consistency is achieved.
6. Take care when removing the chops from the air fryer, then plate up and serve with the avocado mayo.

Kawaii Pork Roast
Servings: 6
Cooking Time: 50 Minutes
Ingredients:
- Salt and white pepper to taste
- 2 tbsp soy sauce
- 2 tbsp honey
- 1 tbsp sesame oil
- ¼ tsp ground ginger
- 1 tsp oregano
- 2 cloves garlic, minced
- 1 boneless pork loin

Directions:
1. Preheat air fryer at 350ºF. Mix all ingredients in a bowl. Massage mixture into all sides of pork loin. Place pork loin in the greased frying basket and Roast for 40 minutes, flipping once. Let rest onto a cutting board for 5 minutes before slicing. Serve right away.

Minted Lamb Chops
Servings: 4
Cooking Time: 20 Minutes
Ingredients:
- 8 lamb chops
- 2 tsp olive oil
- 1 ½ tsp chopped mint leaves
- 1 tsp ground coriander
- 1 lemon, zested
- ½ tsp baharat seasoning
- 1 garlic clove, minced
- Salt and pepper to taste

Directions:
1. Preheat air fryer to 390°F. Coat the lamb chops with olive oil. Set aside. Mix mint, coriander, baharat, zest, garlic, salt and pepper in a bowl. Rub the seasoning onto both sides of the chops. Place the chops in the greased frying basket and Air Fry for 10 minutes. Flip the lamb chops and cook for another 5 minutes. Let the lamb chops rest for a few minutes. Serve right away.

Air Fried London Broil
Servings:8
Cooking Time: 25 Minutes
Ingredients:
- 2 pounds (907 g) London broil
- 3 large garlic cloves, minced
- 3 tablespoons balsamic vinegar
- 3 tablespoons whole-grain mustard
- 2 tablespoons olive oil
- Sea salt and ground black pepper, to taste
- ½ teaspoons dried hot red pepper flakes

Directions:

1. Wash and dry the London broil. Score its sides with a knife.
2. Mix the remaining ingredients. Rub this mixture into the broil, coating it well. Allow to marinate for a minimum of 3 hours.
3. Preheat the air fryer to 400ºF (204ºC).
4. Air fry the meat for 15 minutes. Turn it over and air fry for an additional 10 minutes before serving.

Quick & Simple Bratwurst With Vegetables

Servings: 6
Cooking Time: 20 Minutes
Ingredients:
- 1 package bratwurst, sliced 1/2-inch rounds
- 1/2 tbsp Cajun seasoning
- 1/4 cup onion, diced
- 2 bell pepper, sliced

Directions:
1. Add all ingredients into the large mixing bowl and toss well.
2. Line air fryer basket with foil.
3. Add vegetable and bratwurst mixture into the air fryer basket and cook at 390°F for 10 minutes.
4. Toss well and cook for 10 minutes more.
5. Serve and enjoy.

Mayonnaise Tomato Beef Patties

Servings: 4
Cooking Time: 20 Minutes
Ingredients:
- ¾ pound ground beef
- 1 smoked beef sausage, chopped
- 4 scallions, chopped
- 1 garlic clove, minced
- 2 tablespoons fresh coriander, chopped
- 4 tablespoons rolled oats
- 2 tablespoons tomato paste
- Himalayan salt and black pepper, to taste
- 8 small pretzel rolls
- 4 tablespoons mayonnaise
- 8 thin slices of tomato

Directions:
1. At 370 degrees F/ 185 degrees C, preheat your Air Fryer.
2. In a suitable mixing bowl, thoroughly combine the ground beef, sausage, scallions, garlic, coriander, oats, tomato paste, salt, and black pepper.
3. Knead with the prepared mixture until well combined.
4. Form the mixture into eight patties and cook them for almost 18 to 20 minutes.
5. Place the burgers on slider buns; top with mayonnaise and tomato slices.
6. Serve.

Spiced Pork Chops

Servings: 2
Cooking Time: 20 Minutes
Ingredients:
- 1 tablespoon olive oil
- ½ lb. pork chops
- ½ teaspoon dried oregano
- ¼ teaspoon red pepper flakes
- 1 teaspoon dried thyme
- ½ teaspoon salt
- ½ teaspoon pepper
- 6 large mushrooms, cleaned and sliced
- 1 large yellow onion, chopped
- 1 ½ tablespoons soy sauce
- 2 tablespoons fresh parsley, finely chopped

Directions:
1. Mix the pork chops with the onion, mushrooms, pepper, red pepper flakes, thyme, oregano, olive oil, soy sauce, and olive oil in a large bowl.
2. When coated, cook the pork chops and clean mushrooms in your air fryer at 390 degrees F/ 200 degrees C for 20 minutes.
3. Sprinkle with the fresh parsley, serve and enjoy!

Classic Salisbury Steak Burgers

Servings: 4
Cooking Time: 35 Minutes
Ingredients:
- ¼ cup bread crumbs
- 2 tbsp beef broth
- 1 tbsp cooking sherry
- 1 tbsp ketchup
- 1tbsp Dijon mustard
- 2 tsp Worcestershire sauce
- ½ tsp onion powder
- ½ tsp garlic powder
- 1 lb ground beef
- 1 cup sliced mushrooms
- 1 tbsp butter
- 4 buns, split and toasted

Directions:
1. Preheat the air fryer to 375°F. Combine the bread crumbs, broth, cooking sherry, ketchup, mustard, Worcestershire sauce, garlic and onion powder and mix well. Add the beef and mix with hands, then form into 4 patties and refrigerate while preparing the mushrooms. Mix the mushrooms and butter in a 6-inch pan. Place the pan in the air fryer and Bake for 8-10 minutes, stirring once until the mushrooms are brown and tender. Remove and set aside. Line the frying basket with round parchment paper and punch holes in it. Lay the burgers in a single layer and cook for 11-14 minutes or until cooked through. Put the burgers on the bun bottoms, top with the mushrooms, then the bun tops.

Spice Meatloaf

Servings: 8
Cooking Time: 20 Minutes
Ingredients:
- 1-pound ground beef
- ½ teaspoon dried tarragon
- 1 teaspoon Italian seasoning
- 1 tablespoon Worcestershire sauce
- ¼ cup ketchup
- ¼ cup coconut flour
- ½ cup almond flour
- 1 garlic clove, minced
- ¼ cup onion, chopped
- 2 eggs, lightly beaten
- ¼ teaspoon black pepper
- ½ teaspoon salt

Directions:
1. Add all the recipe ingredients into the mixing bowl and mix until well combined.
2. Make the equal shape of patties from mixture and place on a plate. Place in refrigerator for 10 minutes.
3. Grease its air fryer basket with cooking spray.
4. At 360 degrees F/ 180 degrees C, preheat your air fryer.
5. Place prepared patties in air fryer basket and cook for 10 minutes.
6. Serve and enjoy.

Salted 'n Peppered Scored Beef Chuck

Servings:6
Cooking Time: 1 Hour And 30 Minutes
Ingredients:
- 2 ounces black peppercorns
- 2 tablespoons olive oil
- 3 pounds beef chuck roll, scored with knife
- 3 tablespoons salt

Directions:
1. Preheat the air fryer to 390°F.
2. Place the grill pan accessory in the air fryer.
3. Season the beef chuck roll with black peppercorns and salt.
4. Brush with olive oil and cover top with foil.
5. Grill for 1 hour and 30 minutes.
6. Flip the beef every 30 minutes for even grilling on all sides.

Tender Country Ribs

Servings:4
Cooking Time: 20 To 25 Minutes
Ingredients:
- 12 country-style pork ribs, trimmed of excess fat
- 2 tablespoons cornstarch
- 2 tablespoons olive oil
- 1 teaspoon dry mustard
- ½ teaspoon thyme
- ½ teaspoon garlic powder

- 1 teaspoon dried marjoram
- Pinch salt
- Freshly ground black pepper

Directions:
1. Place the ribs on a clean work surface.
2. In a small bowl, combine the cornstarch, olive oil, mustard, thyme, garlic powder, marjoram, salt, and pepper, and rub into the ribs.
3. Place the ribs in the air fryer basket and roast for 10 minutes.
4. Carefully turn the ribs using tongs and roast for 10 to 15 minutes or until the ribs are crisp and register an internal temperature of at least 150°F.

Creamy Horseradish Roast Beef

Servings: 6
Cooking Time: 65 Minutes + Chilling Time
Ingredients:
- 1 topside roast, tied
- Salt to taste
- 1 tsp butter, melted
- 2 tbsp Dijon mustard
- 3 tbsp prepared horseradish
- 1 garlic clove, minced
- 2/3 cup buttermilk
- 2 tsp red wine
- 1 tbsp minced chives
- Salt and pepper to taste

Directions:
1. Preheat air fryer to 320°F. Mix salt, butter, half of the mustard, 1 tsp of horseradish, and garlic until blended. Rub all over the roast. Bake the roast in the air fryer for 30-35 minutes, flipping once until browned. Transfer to a cutting board and cover with foil. Let rest for 15 minutes.
2. In a bowl, mix buttermilk, horseradish, remaining mustard, chives, wine, salt, and pepper until smooth. Refrigerate. When ready to serve, carve the roast into thin slices and serve with horseradish cream on the side.

Spaghetti Squash Lasagna

Servings:6
Cooking Time: 1 Hour 15 Minutes
Ingredients:
- 2 large spaghetti squash, cooked (about 2¾ pounds / 1.2 kg)
- 4 pounds (1.8 kg) ground beef
- 1 (2½-pound / 1.1-kg) large jar Marinara sauce
- 25 slices Mozzarella cheese
- 30 ounces whole-milk ricotta cheese

Directions:
1. Preheat the air fryer to 375ºF (191ºC).
2. Slice the spaghetti squash and place it face down inside a baking dish. Fill with water until covered.
3. Bake in the preheated air fryer for 45 minutes until skin is soft.

4. Sear the ground beef in a skillet over medium-high heat for 5 minutes or until browned, then add the marinara sauce and heat until warm. Set aside.

5. Scrape the flesh off the cooked squash to resemble strands of spaghetti.

6. Layer the lasagna in a large greased pan in alternating layers of spaghetti squash, beef sauce, Mozzarella, ricotta. Repeat until all the ingredients have been used.

7. Bake for 30 minutes and serve!

Pork Cutlets With Aloha Salsa

Servings: 4
Cooking Time: 9 Minutes
Ingredients:
- Aloha Salsa
- 1 cup fresh pineapple, chopped in small pieces
- ¼ cup red onion, finely chopped
- ¼ cup green or red bell pepper, chopped
- ½ teaspoon ground cinnamon
- 1 teaspoon low-sodium soy sauce
- ⅛ teaspoon crushed red pepper
- ⅛ teaspoon ground black pepper
- 2 eggs
- 2 tablespoons milk
- ¼ cup flour
- ¼ cup panko breadcrumbs
- 4 teaspoons sesame seeds
- 1 pound boneless, thin pork cutlets (⅜- to ½-inch thick)
- lemon pepper and salt
- ¼ cup cornstarch
- oil for misting or cooking spray

Directions:
1. In a medium bowl, stir together all ingredients for salsa. Cover and refrigerate while cooking pork.
2. Preheat air fryer to 390°F.
3. Beat together eggs and milk in shallow dish.
4. In another shallow dish, mix together the flour, panko, and sesame seeds.
5. Sprinkle pork cutlets with lemon pepper and salt to taste. Most lemon pepper seasoning contains salt, so go easy adding extra.
6. Dip pork cutlets in cornstarch, egg mixture, and then panko coating. Spray both sides with oil or cooking spray.
7. Cook cutlets for 3 minutes. Turn cutlets over, spraying both sides, and continue cooking for 6 minutes or until well done.
8. Serve fried cutlets with salsa on the side.

Porterhouse Steak With Mustard And Butter

Servings: 2
Cooking Time: 15 Minutes
Ingredients:
- 1 lb. porterhouse steak, cut meat from bone in 2 pieces
- ½-teaspoon ground black pepper
- ½ teaspoon cayenne pepper
- ½-teaspoon salt
- ½ teaspoon garlic powder
- ½-teaspoon dried thyme
- ½-teaspoon dried marjoram
- ½ teaspoon Dijon mustard
- 1 tablespoon butter, melted

Directions:
1. Sprinkle all the seasonings on the top of the porterhouse steak.
2. Evenly coat the steak with the mustard and butter.
3. Cook the processed steak at 390 degrees F/ 200 degrees C for 12 to 14 minutes.
4. When done, serve and enjoy.

Bourbon-bbq Sauce Marinated Beef Bbq

Servings:4
Cooking Time: 60 Minutes
Ingredients:
- ¼ cup bourbon
- ¼ cup barbecue sauce
- 1 tablespoon Worcestershire sauce
- 2 pounds beef steak, pounded
- Salt and pepper to taste

Directions:
1. Place all ingredients in a Ziploc bag and allow to marinate in the fridge for at least 2 hours.
2. Preheat the air fryer to 390°F.
3. Place the grill pan accessory in the air fryer.
4. Place on the grill pan and cook for 20 minutes per batch.
5. Halfway through the cooking time, give a stir to cook evenly.
6. Meanwhile, pour the marinade on a saucepan and allow to simmer until the sauce thickens.
7. Serve beef with the bourbon sauce.

Ground Beef

Servings:4
Cooking Time: 9 Minutes
Ingredients:
- 1 pound 70/30 ground beef
- ¼ cup water
- 1 teaspoon salt
- ½ teaspoon ground black pepper
- 1 teaspoon garlic powder

Directions:
1. Preheat the air fryer to 400°F.
2. In a medium bowl, mix beef with remaining ingredients. Place beef in a 6" round cake pan and press into an even layer.
3. Place in the air fryer basket and set the timer to 10 minutes. After 5 minutes, open the air fryer and stir ground beef with a spatula. Return to the air fryer.
4. After 2 more minutes, open the air fryer, remove the pan and drain any excess fat from the ground beef. Return to the air fryer for and cook 2 more minutes until beef is brown and no pink remains.

Juicy Beef Kabobs With Sour Cream

Servings: 4

Cooking Time: 10 Minutes

Ingredients:

- 1-pound beef, cut into chunks
- 1 bell pepper, cut into 1-inch pieces
- 2 tablespoons soy sauce
- ⅓ cup sour cream
- ½ onion, cut into 1-inch pieces

Directions:

1. In a suitable bowl, mix together soy sauce and sour cream.
2. Add beef into the bowl and coat well and place in the refrigerator for overnight.
3. Thread marinated beef, bell peppers, and onions onto the soaked wooden skewers.
4. Place in your air fryer basket and cook at almost 400 degrees F/ 205 degrees C for almost 10 minutes. Turn halfway through the cooking time.
5. Serve and enjoy.

Beef Ribeye Steak

Servings: 4

Cooking Time: 20 Minutes

Ingredients:

- 4 (8-ounce) ribeye steaks
- 1 tablespoon McCormick Grill Mates Montreal Steak Seasoning
- Salt
- Pepper

Directions:

1. Season the steaks with the steak seasoning and salt and pepper to taste.
2. Place 2 steaks in the air fryer. You can use an accessory grill pan, a layer rack, or the standard air fryer basket. Cook for 4 minutes.
3. Open the air fryer and flip the steaks. Cook for an additional 4 to 5 minutes.
4. Check for doneness to determine how much additional cook time is need. (See Cooking tip.)
5. Remove the cooked steaks from the air fryer, then repeat steps 2 through 4 for the remaining 2 steaks.
6. Cool before serving.

Sriracha Pork Strips With Rice

Servings: 4

Cooking Time: 30 Minutes + Chilling Time

Ingredients:

- ½ cup lemon juice
- 2 tbsp lemon marmalade
- 1 tbsp avocado oil
- 1 tbsp tamari
- 2 tsp sriracha
- 1 tsp yellow mustard
- 1 lb pork shoulder strips
- 4 cups cooked white rice
- ¼ cup chopped cilantro
- 1 tsp black pepper

Directions:

1. Whisk the lemon juice, lemon marmalade, avocado oil, tamari, sriracha, and mustard in a bowl. Reserve half of the marinade. Toss pork strips with half of the marinade and let marinate covered in the fridge for 30 minutes.
2. Preheat air fryer at 350ºF. Place pork strips in the frying basket and Air Fry for 17 minutes, tossing twice. Transfer them to a bowl and stir in the remaining marinade. Serve over cooked rice and scatter with cilantro and pepper.

Pork Kabobs With Pineapple

Servings: 4

Cooking Time: 30 Minutes

Ingredients:

- 2 cans juice-packed pineapple chunks, juice reserved
- 1 green bell pepper, cut into ½-inch chunks
- 1 red bell pepper, cut into ½-inch chunks
- 1 lb pork tenderloin, cubed
- Salt and pepper to taste
- 1 tbsp honey
- ½ tsp ground ginger
- ½ tsp ground coriander
- 1 red chili, minced

Directions:

1. Preheat the air fryer to 375°F. Mix the coriander, chili, salt, and pepper in a bowl. Add the pork and toss to coat. Then, thread the pork pieces, pineapple chunks, and bell peppers onto skewers. Combine the pineapple juice, honey, and ginger and mix well. Use all the mixture as you brush it on the kebabs. Put the kebabs in the greased frying basket and Air Fry for 10-14 minutes or until cooked through. Serve and enjoy!

Pork Meatloaf With Onion

Servings: 4

Cooking Time: 20 Minutes

Ingredients:

- 1 egg, lightly beaten
- 1 onion, chopped
- ½ tablespoon thyme, chopped
- 1 oz. chorizo, chopped
- 1 tablespoon almond flour
- 1 lb. ground pork
- Pepper
- Salt

Directions:

1. In a suitable bowl, mix up all of the ingredients, then transfer the mixture to the cooking pan of your air fryer.
2. Cook at 390 degrees F/ 200 degrees C for 20 minutes.
3. When cooked, slice to serve and enjoy.

Boneless Ribeyes

Servings: 2
Cooking Time: 10-15 Minutes
Ingredients:
- 2 8-ounce boneless ribeye steaks
- 4 teaspoons Worcestershire sauce
- ½ teaspoon garlic powder
- pepper
- 4 teaspoons extra virgin olive oil
- salt

Directions:
1. Season steaks on both sides with Worcestershire sauce. Use the back of a spoon to spread evenly.
2. Sprinkle both sides of steaks with garlic powder and coarsely ground black pepper to taste.
3. Drizzle both sides of steaks with olive oil, again using the back of a spoon to spread evenly over surfaces.
4. Allow steaks to marinate for 30minutes.
5. Place both steaks in air fryer basket and cook at 390°F for 5minutes.
6. Turn steaks over and cook until done: medium rare: additional 5 minutes, medium: additional 7 minutes, well done: additional 10 minutes.
7. Remove steaks from air fryer basket and let sit 5minutes. Salt to taste and serve.

Ground Beef Calzones

Servings: 6
Cooking Time: 30 Minutes
Ingredients:
- 1 refrigerated pizza dough
- 1 cup shredded mozzarella
- ½ cup chopped onion
- 2 garlic cloves, minced
- ¼ cup chopped mushrooms
- 1 lb ground beef
- 1 tbsp pizza seasoning
- Salt and pepper to taste
- 1 ½ cups marinara sauce
- 1 tsp flour

Directions:
1. Warm 1 tbsp of oil in a skillet over medium heat. Stir-fry onion, garlic and mushrooms for 2-3 minutes or until aromatic. Add beef, pizza seasoning, salt and pepper. Use a large spoon to break up the beef. Cook for 3 minutes or until brown. Stir in marinara sauce and set aside.
2. On a floured work surface, roll out pizza dough and cut into 6 equal-sized rectangles. On each rectangle, add ½ cup of beef and top with 1 tbsp of shredded cheese. Fold one side of the dough over the filling to the opposite side. Press the edges using the back of a fork to seal them. Preheat air fryer to 400°F. Place the first batch of calzones in the air fryer and spray with cooking oil. Bake for 10 minutes. Let cool slightly and serve warm.

Unstuffed Cabbage

Servings:4
Cooking Time: 14 To 20 Minutes
Ingredients:
- 1 tablespoon olive oil
- 1 small onion, chopped
- 1½ cups chopped green cabbage
- 16 precooked frozen meatballs
- 1 cup frozen cooked rice
- 2 tomatoes, chopped
- ½ teaspoon dried marjoram
- Pinch salt
- Freshly ground black pepper

Directions:
1. In a 6-inch metal bowl, combine the oil and the onion. Bake for 2 to 4 minutes or until the onion is crisp and tender.
2. Add the cabbage, meatballs, rice, tomatoes, marjoram, salt, and pepper, and stir.
3. Bake for 12 to 16 minutes, stirring once during cooking time, until the meatballs are hot, the rice is warmed, and the vegetables are tender.

Easy & The Traditional Beef Roast Recipe

Servings:12
Cooking Time: 2 Hours
Ingredients:
- 1 cup organic beef broth
- 3 pounds beef round roast
- 4 tablespoons olive oil
- Salt and pepper to taste

Directions:
1. Place in a Ziploc bag all the ingredients and allow to marinate in the fridge for 2 hours.
2. Preheat the air fryer for 5 minutes.
3. Transfer all ingredients in a baking dish that will fit in the air fryer.
4. Place in the air fryer and cook for 2 hours for 400°F.

Barbecue-style Beef Cube Steak

Servings: 2
Cooking Time: 14 Minutes
Ingredients:
- 2 4-ounce beef cube steak(s)
- 2 cups Fritos (original flavor) or a generic corn chip equivalent, crushed to crumbs
- 6 tablespoons Purchased smooth barbecue sauce, any flavor (gluten-free, if a concern)

Directions:
1. Preheat the air fryer to 375°F.
2. Spread the Fritos crumbs in a shallow soup plate or a small pie plate. Rub the barbecue sauce onto both sides of the steak(s). Dredge the steak(s) in the Fritos crumbs to coat well and thoroughly, turning several times and pressing down to get the little bits to adhere to the meat.
3. When the machine is at temperature, set the steak(s) in the basket. Leave as much air space between them as possible if you're working with more than one piece of beef. Air-fry undisturbed for 12 minutes, or until lightly brown and crunchy. If the machine is at 360°F, you may need to add 2 minutes to the cooking time.
4. Use kitchen tongs to transfer the steak(s) to a wire rack. Cool for 5 minutes before serving.

Breaded Italian Pork Chops

Servings: 4
Cooking Time: 15 Minutes
Ingredients:
- Olive oil
- 2 eggs, beaten
- ¼ cup whole-wheat bread crumbs
- 1 envelope zesty Italian dressing mix
- 4 thin boneless pork chops, trimmed of excess fat
- Salt
- Freshly ground black pepper

Directions:
1. Spray a fryer basket lightly with olive oil.
2. Place the eggs in a shallow bowl.
3. In a separate shallow bowl, mix together the bread crumbs and Italian dressing mix.
4. Season the pork chops with salt and pepper. Coat the pork chops in the egg, shaking off any excess. Dredge them in the bread crumb mixture.
5. Place the pork chops in the fryer basket in a single layer and spray lightly with olive oil. You may need to cook them in batches.
6. Air fry for 7 minutes. Flip the pork chops over, lightly spray with olive oil, and cook until they reach an internal temperature of at least 145°F, an additional 5 to 8 minutes.

Oregano Pork Tenderloin

Servings: 4
Cooking Time: 25 Minutes
Ingredients:
- 2 cups creamer potatoes, rinsed and dried
- 2 teaspoons olive oil
- 1 1-pound pork tenderloin, diced
- 1 onion, chopped
- 1 red bell pepper, chopped
- 2 garlic cloves, minced
- ½ teaspoon dried oregano
- 2 tablespoons chicken broth

Directions:
1. In a suitable bowl, toss the potatoes and olive oil to coat.
2. Transfer the potatoes to your air fryer basket. Roast for almost 15 minutes.
3. In a medium metal bowl, mix the potatoes, pork, onion, red bell pepper, garlic, and oregano.
4. Drizzle with the chicken broth. Put the bowl in the air fryer basket.
5. Roast for about 10 minutes more, shaking the basket once during cooking, until the pork reaches at least 145 degrees F/ 60 degrees C on a meat thermometer and the potatoes are tender.
6. Serve immediately.

Bacon And Cheese-stuffed Pork Chops

Servings: 4
Cooking Time: 12 Minutes

Ingredients:
- ½ ounce plain pork rinds, finely crushed
- ½ cup shredded sharp Cheddar cheese
- 4 slices cooked sugar-free bacon, crumbled
- 4 boneless pork chops
- ½ teaspoon salt
- ¼ teaspoon ground black pepper

Directions:
1. In a small bowl, mix pork rinds, Cheddar, and bacon.
2. Make a 3" slit in the side of each pork chop and stuff with ¼ pork rind mixture. Sprinkle each side of pork chops with salt and pepper.
3. Place pork chops into ungreased air fryer basket, stuffed side up. Adjust the temperature to 400°F and set the timer for 12 minutes. Pork chops will be browned and have an internal temperature of at least 145°F when done. Serve warm.

Delicious Baby Back Ribs

Servings: 4
Cooking Time: 30 Minutes
Ingredients:
- 1 teaspoon cayenne pepper
- 1 rack baby back ribs, cut into individual pieces
- 1 teaspoon onion powder
- 1 teaspoon garlic powder
- 1 teaspoon pomegranate molasses
- 1 teaspoon dried oregano
- ½ cup barbecue sauce
- Salt and black pepper to taste
- 2 scallions, chopped

Directions:
1. In a bowl, mix up the smoked paprika, cayenne pepper, garlic powder, pomegranate molasses, onion powder, oregano, salt, black pepper and ribs, then toss to coat well.
2. Cover and refrigerate for 30 minutes.
3. Spray the cooking basket of your air fryer with cooking spray.
4. Transfer the marinated ribs to the basket in the air fryer and cook them for 25 minutes at 360 degrees F/ 180 degrees C, flipping halfway through.
5. While cooking the ribs, in a saucepan, sauté the vegetable broth and gravy mix for 2 minutes or until the sauce thickens.
6. When the ribs cooked, drizzle the sautéed sauce, BBQ sauce and scatter scallions on the top, serve and enjoy.

Pretzel-coated Pork Tenderloin

Servings: 4
Cooking Time: 10 Minutes
Ingredients:
- 1 Large egg white(s)
- 2 teaspoons Dijon mustard (gluten-free, if a concern)
- 1½ cups Crushed pretzel crumbs
- 1 pound Pork tenderloin, cut into ¼-pound sections
- Vegetable oil spray

Directions:

1. Preheat the air fryer to 350°F.
2. Set up and fill two shallow soup plates or small pie plates on your counter: one for the egg white(s), whisked with the mustard until foamy; and one for the pretzel crumbs.
3. Dip a section of pork tenderloin in the egg white mixture and turn it to coat well, even on the ends. Let any excess egg white mixture slip back into the rest, then set the pork in the pretzel crumbs. Roll it several times, pressing gently, until the pork is evenly coated, even on the ends. Generously coat the pork section with vegetable oil spray, set it aside, and continue coating and spraying the remaining sections.
4. Set the pork sections in the basket with at least ¼ inch between them. Air-fry undisturbed for 10 minutes, or until an instant-read meat thermometer inserted into the center of one section registers 145°F.
5. Use kitchen tongs to transfer the pieces to a wire rack. Cool for 3 to 5 minutes before serving.

Beef And Broccoli Stir Fry

Servings:4
Cooking Time: 15 Minutes
Ingredients:

- 3 tablespoons dry sherry
- ¼ cup soy sauce
- 4 garlic cloves, minced
- 1 tablespoon sesame oil
- ½ teaspoon red pepper flakes
- 1 pound flank or skirt steak, trimmed and cut into strips
- Olive oil
- ½ pound broccoli florets
- ¼ cup beef broth
- 2 teaspoons cornstarch

Directions:

1. In a small bowl, combine the sherry, soy sauce, garlic, sesame oil, and red pepper flakes to create a marinade.
2. Place the steak and 3 tablespoons of the marinade in a large zip-top plastic bag, seal, and refrigerate for at least 2 hours.
3. Spray a fryer basket lightly with olive oil.
4. Add half the steak to the fryer basket along with half the broccoli florets. Lightly spray with olive oil.
5. Air fry for 8 minutes. Shake the basket to redistribute and cook until cooked through, an additional 4 to 7 minutes. Repeat with the remaining steak and broccoli. Transfer the steak and broccoli to a large bowl.
6. While the steak is cooking, in a small saucepan over medium-high heat, combine the broth and remaining marinade and bring to a boil.
7. In a small bowl combine the cornstarch and 1 tablespoon of water to create a slurry. Add the slurry to the sauce pan and simmer, stirring, until the sauce starts to thicken, a few seconds to 1 minute.
8. Pour the sauce over the cooked steak and broccoli and toss to evenly coat.

Chapter 6: Fish And Seafood Recipes

Tuna Steaks

Servings: 2 Servings
Cooking Time: 30 Minutes
Ingredients:
- 2 skinless yellowfin tuna steaks
- ¼ cup of soy sauce
- ½ teaspoon of rice vinegar
- 2 teaspoons of honey
- 1 teaspoon of sesame or olive oil
- 1 teaspoon of grated ginger
- Lime wedges and avocado-cucumber salsa, for serving

Directions:
1. Mix soy sauce, ginger, honey, vinegar, and oil in a large mixing bowl. Put the tuna steaks in the bowl. Keep covered for 20–30 minutes in the fridge.
2. Preheat your air fryer to 380ºF. Cover the inside of air fryer basket with the perforated parchment paper.
3. Put the marinated tuna steaks in the air fryer basket in a single layer. Cook at 380ºF for 4 minutes. Let it rest for 1–2 minutes before serving.
4. Serve with your favorite salsa and lime wedges. Enjoy your Tuna Steaks!

Easy Marinated Salmon Fillets

Servings:4
Cooking Time: 20 Minutes
Ingredients:
- 1 tablespoon olive oil, plus more for spraying
- ¼ cup soy sauce
- ¼ cup rice wine vinegar
- 1 tablespoon brown sugar
- 1 teaspoon mustard powder
- 1 teaspoon ground ginger
- ½ teaspoon freshly ground black pepper
- ½ teaspoon minced garlic
- 4 (6 ounce) salmon fillets, skin-on

Directions:
1. Spray a fryer basket lightly with olive oil.
2. In a small bowl combine the soy sauce, rice wine vinegar, brown sugar, 1 tablespoon of olive oil, mustard powder, ginger, black pepper, and garlic to make a marinade.
3. Place the fillets in a shallow baking dish and pour the marinade over them. Cover the baking dish and marinate for at least 1 hour in the refrigerator, turning the fillets occasionally to keep them coated in the marinade.
4. Shake off as much marinade as possible from the fillets and place them, skin side down, in the fryer basket in a single layer. You may need to cook the fillets in batches.
5. Air fry for 10 to 15 minutes for medium-rare to medium done salmon or 15 to 20 minutes for well done. The minimum internal temperature should be 145°F at the thickest part of the fillet.

Coriander Cod And Green Beans

Servings: 4
Cooking Time: 15 Minutes
Ingredients:
- 12 oz cod fillet
- ½ cup green beans, trimmed and halved
- 1 tablespoon avocado oil
- 1 teaspoon salt
- 1 teaspoon ground coriander

Directions:
1. Cut the cod fillet on 4 servings and sprinkle every serving with salt and ground coriander. After this, place the fish on 4 foil squares. Top them with green beans and avocado oil and wrap them into parcels. Preheat the air fryer to 400°F. Place the cod parcels in the air fryer and cook them for 15 minutes.

Nacho Chips Crusted Prawns

Servings:2
Cooking Time: 8 Minutes
Ingredients:
- ¾ pound prawns, peeled and deveined
- 1 large egg
- 5 ounces Nacho flavored chips, finely crushed

Directions:
1. In a shallow bowl, beat the egg.
2. In another bowl, place the nacho chips
3. Dip each prawn into the beaten egg and then, coat with the crushed nacho chips.
4. Set the temperature of air fryer to 350°F. Grease an air fryer basket.
5. Arrange prawns into the prepared air fryer basket.
6. Air fry for about 8 minutes.
7. Remove from air fryer and transfer the prawns onto serving plates.
8. Serve hot.

Garlic Tilapia Fillets

Servings: 5
Cooking Time: 10 Minutes
Ingredients:
- 1 tablespoon all-purpose flour
- Sea salt and white pepper, to taste
- 1 teaspoon garlic paste
- 1 tablespoon extra-virgin olive oil
- ½ cup cornmeal
- 5 tilapia fillets, slice into halves

Directions:
1. Prepare a Ziploc bag and mix up the flour, salt, white pepper, garlic paste, olive oil, and cornmeal.
2. Add the fish fillets to the Ziploc bag and coat them well with the spice mixture.
3. Oil the basket of your air fryer with cooking spray and then put the coated fillets in it.
4. Arrange the basket to the air fryer and cook at 400 degrees F/ 205 degrees C for 10 minutes.
5. After 10 minutes, flip the fillets and cook for more 6 minutes.
6. Working in batches is suggested.
7. When done, serve with lemon wedges if desired.
8. Enjoy!

Sesame-glazed Salmon

Servings:4
Cooking Time: 16 Minutes
Ingredients:
- 3 tablespoons soy sauce
- 1 tablespoon rice wine or dry sherry
- 1 tablespoon brown sugar
- 1 tablespoon toasted sesame oil
- 1 teaspoon minced garlic
- ¼ teaspoon minced ginger
- 4 (6 ounce) salmon fillets, skin-on
- Olive oil
- ½ tablespoon sesame seeds

Directions:
1. In a small bowl, mix together the soy sauce, rice wine, brown sugar, toasted sesame oil, garlic, and ginger.
2. Place the salmon in a shallow baking dish and pour the marinade over the fillets. Cover and refrigerate for at least 1 hour, turning the fillets occasionally to coat in the marinade.
3. Spray a fryer basket lightly with olive oil.
4. Shake off as much marinade as possible and place the fillets, skin side down, in the fryer basket in a single layer. Reserve the marinade. You may need to cook them in batches.
5. Air fry for 8 to 10 minutes. Brush the tops of the salmon fillets with the reserved marinade and sprinkle with sesame seeds.
6. Increase the fryer temperature to 400°F and cook for 2 to 5 more minutes for medium, 1 to 3 minutes for medium rare, or 4 to 6 minutes for well done.

Lemon Butter Cod

Servings:4
Cooking Time: 12 Minutes
Ingredients:
- 4 cod fillets
- 2 tablespoons salted butter, melted
- 1 teaspoon Old Bay Seasoning
- ½ medium lemon, cut into 4 slices

Directions:
1. Place cod fillets into an ungreased 6" round nonstick baking dish. Brush tops of fillets with butter and sprinkle with Old Bay Seasoning. Lay 1 lemon slice on each fillet.
2. Cover dish with aluminum foil and place into air fryer basket. Adjust the temperature to 350°F and set the timer for 12 minutes, turning fillets halfway through cooking. Fish will be opaque and have an internal temperature of at least 145°F when done. Serve warm.

Lemon-garlic Tilapia

Servings:4
Cooking Time: 15 Minutes
Ingredients:
- 1 tablespoon lemon juice
- 1 tablespoon olive oil
- 1 teaspoon minced garlic
- ½ teaspoon chili powder
- 4 (5 to 6 ounce) tilapia fillets

Directions:
1. Line a fryer basket with perforated air fryer liners.
2. In a large, shallow bowl, mix together the lemon juice, olive oil, garlic, and chili powder to make a marinade. Place the tilapia fillets in the bowl and coat evenly.
3. Place the fillets in the basket in a single layer, leaving space between each fillet. You may need to cook in more than one batch.
4. Air fry until the fish is cooked and flakes easily with a fork, 10 to 15 minutes.

Crispy Herbed Salmon

Servings:4
Cooking Time: 9 To 12 Minutes
Ingredients:
- 4 (6-ounce) skinless salmon fillets
- 3 tablespoons honey mustard
- ½ teaspoon dried thyme
- ½ teaspoon dried basil
- ¼ cup panko bread crumbs
- ⅓ cup crushed potato chips
- 2 tablespoons olive oil

Directions:
1. Place the salmon on a plate. In a small bowl, combine the mustard, thyme, and basil, and spread evenly over the salmon.
2. In another small bowl, combine the bread crumbs and potato chips and mix well. Drizzle in the olive oil and mix until combined.
3. Place the salmon in the air fryer basket and gently but firmly press the bread crumb mixture onto the top of each fillet.
4. Bake for 9 to 12 minutes or until the salmon reaches at least 145°F on a meat thermometer and the topping is browned and crisp.

Cajun Salmon

Servings:2
Cooking Time: 7 Minutes
Ingredients:
- 2 boneless, skinless salmon fillets
- 2 tablespoons salted butter, softened
- ⅛ teaspoon cayenne pepper
- ½ teaspoon garlic powder
- 1 teaspoon paprika
- ¼ teaspoon ground black pepper

Directions:
1. Brush both sides of each fillet with butter. In a small bowl, mix remaining ingredients and rub into fish on both sides.
2. Place fillets into ungreased air fryer basket. Adjust the temperature to 390°F and set the timer for 7 minutes. Internal temperature will be 145°F when done. Serve warm.

Black Cod With Grapes, Fennel, Pecans And Kale

Servings: 2
Cooking Time: 15 Minutes
Ingredients:
- 2 (6- to 8-ounce) fillets of black cod (or sablefish)
- salt and freshly ground black pepper
- olive oil
- 1 cup grapes, halved
- 1 small bulb fennel, sliced ¼-inch thick
- ½ cup pecans
- 3 cups shredded kale
- 2 teaspoons white balsamic vinegar or white wine vinegar
- 2 tablespoons extra virgin olive oil

Directions:
1. Preheat the air fryer to 400°F.
2. Season the cod fillets with salt and pepper and drizzle, brush or spray a little olive oil on top. Place the fish, presentation side up (skin side down), into the air fryer basket. Air-fry for 10 minutes.
3. When the fish has finished cooking, remove the fillets to a side plate and loosely tent with foil to rest.
4. Toss the grapes, fennel and pecans in a bowl with a drizzle of olive oil and season with salt and pepper. Add the grapes, fennel and pecans to the air fryer basket and air-fry for 5 minutes at 400°F, shaking the basket once during the cooking time.
5. Transfer the grapes, fennel and pecans to a bowl with the kale. Dress the kale with the balsamic vinegar and olive oil, season to taste with salt and pepper and serve along side the cooked fish.

Glazed Salmon With Soy Sauce

Servings: 2
Cooking Time: 14 Minutes
Ingredients:
- 1 teaspoon water
- 2 3½-ounce salmon fillets
- ⅓ cup soy sauce
- ⅓ cup honey
- 3 teaspoons rice wine vinegar

Directions:
1. At 355 degrees F/ 180 degrees C, preheat your air fryer. and grease an air fryer grill pan.
2. Mix all the recipe ingredients in a suitable bowl except salmon.
3. Reserve ½ of the mixture in a suitable bowl and coat the salmon in remaining mixture.
4. Refrigerate, covered for about 2 hours and place the salmon in the air fryer basket.
5. Cook for about 13 minutes, flipping once in between and coat with reserved marinade.
6. Place the leftover salmon marinade in a small pan and cook for about 1 minute.
7. Serve salmon with marinade sauce and enjoy.

Typical Crab Cakes With Lemon Wedges

Servings: 3
Cooking Time: 10 Minutes
Ingredients:
- 1 egg, beaten
- 2 tablespoons milk
- 2 crustless bread slices
- 1 pound lump crabmeat
- 2 tablespoons scallions, chopped
- 1 garlic clove, minced
- 1 teaspoon deli mustard
- 1 teaspoon Sriracha sauce
- Sea salt, to taste
- Ground black pepper, to taste
- 4 lemon wedges, for serving

Directions:
1. Beat the egg and milk until white and frothy, then add the bread in and let it soak for a few minutes.
2. In addition to the lemon wedges, stir in the remaining ingredients.
3. Form 4 equal-size patties, place the patties in the cooking basket of your air fryer and then spray them with a non-stick cooking spray.
4. Arrange the basket to the air fryer and cook the patties at 400 degrees F/ 205 degrees C for 10 minutes, flipping halfway through.
5. Serve warm, garnished with lemon wedges. Bon appétit!

Shrimp Sliders With Avocado

Servings: 4
Cooking Time: 10 Minutes
Ingredients:
- 16 raw jumbo shrimp, peeled, deveined and tails removed (about 1 pound)
- 1 rib celery, finely chopped
- 2 carrots, grated (about ½ cup) 2 teaspoons lemon juice
- 2 teaspoons Dijon mustard
- ¼ cup chopped fresh basil or parsley
- ½ cup breadcrumbs
- ½ teaspoon salt
- freshly ground black pepper
- vegetable or olive oil, in a spray bottle
- 8 slider buns
- mayonnaise
- butter lettuce
- 2 avocados, sliced and peeled

Directions:
1. Put the shrimp into a food processor and pulse it a few times to rough chop the shrimp. Remove three quarters of the shrimp and transfer it to a bowl. Continue to process the remaining shrimp in the food processor until it is a smooth purée. Transfer the purée to the bowl with the chopped shrimp.

2.   Add the celery, carrots, lemon juice, mustard, basil, breadcrumbs, salt and pepper to the bowl and combine well.

3.   Preheat the air fryer to 380°F.

4.   While the air fryer Preheats, shape the shrimp mixture into 8 patties. Spray both sides of the patties with oil and transfer one layer of patties to the air fryer basket. Air-fry for 10 minutes, flipping the patties over halfway through the cooking time.

5.   Prepare the slider rolls by toasting them and spreading a little mayonnaise on both halves. Place a piece of butter lettuce on the bottom bun, top with the shrimp slider and then finish with the avocado slices on top. Pop the top half of the bun on top and enjoy!

Timeless Garlic-lemon Scallops

Servings:2
Cooking Time: 15 Minutes
Ingredients:
- 2 tbsp butter, melted
- 1 garlic clove, minced
- 1 tbsp lemon juice
- 1 lb jumbo sea scallops

Directions:
1.   Preheat air fryer to 400ºF. Whisk butter, garlic, and lemon juice in a bowl. Roll scallops in the mixture to coat all sides. Place scallops in the frying basket and Air Fry for 4 minutes, flipping once. Brush the tops of each scallop with butter mixture and cook for 4 more minutes, flipping once. Serve and enjoy!

Country Shrimp "boil"

Servings:4
Cooking Time: 20 Minutes
Ingredients:
- 2 tablespoons olive oil, plus more for spraying
- 1 pound large shrimp, deveined, tail on
- 1 pound smoked turkey sausage, cut into thick slices
- 2 corn cobs, quartered
- 1 zucchini, cut into bite-sized pieces
- 1 red bell pepper, cut into chunks
- 1 tablespoon Old Bay seasoning

Directions:
1.   Spray the fryer basket lightly with olive oil.

2.   In a large bowl, mix together the shrimp, turkey sausage, corn, zucchini, bell pepper, and Old Bay seasoning, and toss to coat with the spices. Add the 2 tablespoons of olive oil and toss again until evenly coated.

3.   Spread the mixture in the fryer basket in a single layer. You will need to cook in batches.

4.   Air fry until cooked through, 15 to 20 minutes, shaking the basket every 5 minutes for even cooking.

Italian Baked Cod

Servings:4
Cooking Time: 12 Minutes
Ingredients:
- 4 cod fillets

- 2 tablespoons salted butter, melted
- 1 teaspoon Italian seasoning
- ¼ teaspoon salt
- ½ cup low-carb marinara sauce

Directions:
1.   Place cod into an ungreased 6" round nonstick baking dish. Pour butter over cod and sprinkle with Italian seasoning and salt. Top with marinara.

2.   Place dish into air fryer basket. Adjust the temperature to 350°F and set the timer for 12 minutes. Fillets will be lightly browned, easily flake, and have an internal temperature of at least 145°F when done. Serve warm.

Fried Catfish Nuggets

Servings: 4
Cooking Time: 40 Minutes
Ingredients:
- 1 pound catfish fillets, cut into 1-inch chunks
- ½ cup seasoned fish fry breading mix (such as Louisiana Fish Fry)
- Cooking oil

Directions:
1.   Rinse and thoroughly dry the catfish. Pour the seasoned fish fry breading mix into a sealable plastic bag and add the catfish. (You may need to use two bags depending on the size of your nuggets.) Seal the bag and shake to evenly coat the fish with breading.

2.   Spray the air fryer basket with cooking oil.

3.   Transfer the catfish nuggets to the air fryer. Do not overcrowd the basket. You may need to cook the nuggets in two batches. Spray the nuggets with cooking oil. Cook for 10 minutes.

4.   Open the air fryer and shake the basket. Cook for an additional 8 to 10 minutes, or until the fish is crisp.

5.   If necessary, remove the cooked catfish nuggets from the air fryer, then repeat steps 3 and 4 for the remaining fish.

6.   Cool before serving.

Easy Scallops With Lemon Butter

Servings:3
Cooking Time: 4 Minutes
Ingredients:
- 1 tablespoon Olive oil
- 2 teaspoons Minced garlic
- 1 teaspoon Finely grated lemon zest
- ½ teaspoon Red pepper flakes
- ¼ teaspoon Table salt
- 1 pound Sea scallops
- 3 tablespoons Butter, melted
- 1½ tablespoons Lemon juice

Directions:
1.   Preheat the air fryer to 400°F.

2.   Gently stir the olive oil, garlic, lemon zest, red pepper flakes, and salt in a bowl. Add the scallops and stir very gently until they are evenly and well coated.

3. When the machine is at temperature, arrange the scallops in a single layer in the basket. Some may touch. Air-fry undisturbed for 4 minutes, or until the scallops are opaque and firm.

4. While the scallops cook, stir the melted butter and lemon juice in a serving bowl. When the scallops are ready, pour them from the basket into this bowl. Toss well before serving.

Feta & Shrimp Pita

Servings: 4
Cooking Time: 15 Minutes
Ingredients:
- 1 lb peeled shrimp, deveined
- 2 tbsp olive oil
- 1 tsp dried oregano
- ½ tsp dried thyme
- ½ tsp garlic powder
- ¼ tsp shallot powder
- ¼ tsp tarragon powder
- Salt and pepper to taste
- 4 whole-wheat pitas
- 4 oz feta cheese, crumbled
- 1 cup grated lettuce
- 1 tomato, diced
- ¼ cup black olives, sliced
- 1 lemon

Directions:
1. Preheat the oven to 380°F. Mix the shrimp with olive oil, oregano, thyme, garlic powder, shallot powder, tarragon powder salt, and pepper in a bowl. Pour shrimp in a single layer in the frying basket and Bake for 6-8 minutes or until no longer pink and cooked through. Divide the shrimp into warmed pitas with feta, lettuce, tomato, olives, and a squeeze of lemon. Serve and enjoy!

Scallops With Green Vegetables

Servings: 4
Cooking Time:8 To 11 Minutes
Ingredients:
- 1 cup green beans
- 1 cup frozen peas
- 1 cup frozen chopped broccoli
- 2 teaspoons olive oil
- ½ teaspoon dried basil
- ½ teaspoon dried oregano
- 12 ounces sea scallops (see Tip)

Directions:
1. In a large bowl, toss the green beans, peas, and broccoli with the olive oil. Place in the air fryer basket. Air-fry for 4 to 6 minutes, or until the vegetables are crisp-tender.
2. Remove the vegetables from the air fryer basket and sprinkle with the herbs. Set aside.
3. In the air fryer basket, put the scallops and air-fry for 4 to 5 minutes, or until the scallops are firm and reach an internal temperature of just 145°F on a meat thermometer.

4. Toss scallops with the vegetables and serve immediately.

Fish Taco Bowl

Servings:4
Cooking Time: 12 Minutes
Ingredients:
- 2 cups finely shredded cabbage
- ½ cup mayonnaise
- Juice of 1 medium lime, divided
- 4 boneless, skinless tilapia fillets
- 2 teaspoons chili powder
- 1 teaspoon salt
- ½ teaspoon ground black pepper

Directions:
1. In a large bowl, mix cabbage, mayonnaise, and half of lime juice to make a slaw. Cover and refrigerate while the fish cooks.
2. Preheat the air fryer to 400°F.
3. Sprinkle tilapia with chili powder, salt, and pepper. Spritz each side with cooking spray.
4. Place fillets in the air fryer basket and cook 12 minutes, turning halfway through cooking time, until fish is opaque, flakes easily, and reaches an internal temperature of 145°F.
5. Allow fish to cool 5 minutes before chopping into bite-sized pieces. To serve, place ½ cup slaw into each bowl and top with one-fourth of fish. Squeeze remaining lime juice over fish. Serve warm.

Cajun Shrimp With Veggie

Servings: 4
Cooking Time: 20 Minutes
Ingredients:
- 50 small shrimp
- 1 tablespoon Cajun seasoning
- 1 bag of frozen mix vegetables
- 1 tablespoon olive oil

Directions:
1. Line air fryer basket with aluminum foil.
2. Add all the recipe ingredients into the suitable mixing bowl and toss well.
3. Transfer shrimp and vegetable mixture into the air fryer basket and cook at almost 350 degrees F/ 175 degrees C for almost 10 minutes.
4. Toss well and cook for almost 10 minutes more.
5. Serve and enjoy.

Potato-wrapped Salmon Fillets

Servings:3
Cooking Time: 8 Minutes
Ingredients:
- 1 Large 1-pound elongated yellow potato(es), peeled
- 3 6-ounce, 1½-inch-wide, quite thick skinless salmon fillets
- Olive oil spray
- ¼ teaspoon Table salt
- ¼ teaspoon Ground black pepper

Directions:
1. Preheat the air fryer to 400°F.
2. Use a vegetable peeler or mandoline to make long strips from the potato(es). You'll need anywhere from 8 to 12 strips per fillet, depending on the shape of the potato and of the salmon fillet.
3. Drape potato strips over a salmon fillet, overlapping the strips to create an even "crust." Tuck the potato strips under the fillet, overlapping the strips underneath to create as smooth a bottom as you can. Wrap the remaining fillet(s) in the same way.
4. Gently turn the fillets over. Generously coat the bottoms with olive oil spray. Turn them back seam side down and generously coat the tops with the oil spray. Sprinkle the salt and pepper over the wrapped fillets.
5. Use a nonstick-safe spatula to gently transfer the fillets seam side down to the basket. It helps to remove the basket from the machine and set it on your work surface (keeping in mind that the basket's hot). Leave as much air space as possible between the fillets. Air-fry undisturbed for 8 minutes, or until golden brown and crisp.
6. Use a nonstick-safe spatula to gently transfer the fillets to serving plates. Cool for a couple of minutes before serving.

Mediterranean Sea Scallops

Servings: 2
Cooking Time: 20 Minutes
Ingredients:
- 1 tbsp olive oil
- 1 shallot, minced
- 2 tbsp capers
- 2 cloves garlic, minced
- ½ cup heavy cream
- 3 tbsp butter
- 1 tbsp lemon juice
- Salt and pepper to taste
- ¼ tbsp cumin powder
- ¼ tbsp curry powder
- 1 lb jumbo sea scallops
- 2 tbsp chopped parsley
- 1 tbsp chopped cilantro

Directions:
1. Warm the olive oil in a saucepan over medium heat. Add shallot and stir-fry for 2 minutes until translucent. Stir in capers, cumin, curry, garlic, heavy cream, 1 tbsp of butter, lemon juice, salt, and pepper and cook for 2 minutes until rolling a boil. Low the heat and simmer for 3 minutes until the caper sauce thickens. Turn the heat off.
2. Preheat air fryer at 400ºF. In a bowl, add the remaining butter and scallops and toss to coat on all sides. Place scallops in the greased frying basket and Air Fry for 8 minutes, flipping once. Drizzle caper sauce over, scatter with parsley, cilantro and serve.

Teriyaki Salmon

Servings:4
Cooking Time: 27 Minutes
Ingredients:
- ½ cup teriyaki sauce
- ¼ teaspoon salt
- 1 teaspoon ground ginger
- ½ teaspoon garlic powder
- 4 boneless, skinless salmon fillets
- 2 tablespoons toasted sesame seeds

Directions:
1. In a large bowl, whisk teriyaki sauce, salt, ginger, and garlic powder. Add salmon to the bowl, being sure to coat each side with marinade. Cover and let marinate in refrigerator 15 minutes.
2. Preheat the air fryer to 375°F.
3. Spritz fillets with cooking spray and place in the air fryer basket. Cook 12 minutes, turning halfway through cooking time, until glaze has caramelized to a dark brown color, salmon flakes easily, and internal temperature reaches at least 145°F. Sprinkle sesame seeds on salmon and serve warm.

Lemon-pepper Tilapia With Garlic Aioli

Servings: 4
Cooking Time: 15 Minutes
Ingredients:
- For the tilapia
- 4 tilapia fillets (see Prep tip)
- 1 tablespoon extra-virgin olive oil
- 1 teaspoon paprika
- 1 teaspoon garlic powder
- 1 teaspoon dried basil
- Lemon-pepper seasoning (such as McCormick Perfect Pinch Lemon & Pepper Seasoning)
- For the garlic aioli
- 2 garlic cloves, minced
- 1 tablespoon mayonnaise
- 1 teaspoon extra-virgin olive oil
- Juice of ½ lemon
- Salt
- Pepper

Directions:
1. Coat the fish with the olive oil. Season with the paprika, garlic powder, dried basil, and lemon-pepper seasoning.
2. Place the fish in the air fryer. It is okay to stack the fish. Cook for 8 minutes.
3. Open the air fryer and flip the fish. Cook for an additional 7 minutes.
4. In a small bowl, combine the garlic, mayonnaise, olive oil, lemon juice, and salt and pepper to taste. Whisk well to combine.
5. Serve alongside the fish.

Italian Tuna Roast

Servings: 8
Cooking Time: 21 Minutes
Ingredients:
- cooking spray
- 1 tablespoon Italian seasoning
- ⅛ teaspoon ground black pepper
- 1 tablespoon extra-light olive oil
- 1 teaspoon lemon juice
- 1 tuna loin

Directions:
1. Spray baking dish with cooking spray and place in air fryer basket. Preheat air fryer to 390°F.
2. Mix together the Italian seasoning, pepper, oil, and lemon juice.
3. Using a dull table knife or butter knife, pierce top of tuna about every half inch: Insert knife into top of tuna roast and pierce almost all the way to the bottom.
4. Spoon oil mixture into each of the holes and use the knife to push seasonings into the tuna as deeply as possible.
5. Spread any remaining oil mixture on all outer surfaces of tuna.
6. Place tuna roast in baking dish and cook at 390°F for 20 minutes. Check temperature with a meat thermometer. Cook for an additional 1 minutes or until temperature reaches 145°F.
7. Remove basket from fryer and let tuna sit in basket for 10minutes.

Tuna And Fruit Kebabs

Servings: 4
Cooking Time:8 To 12 Minutes
Ingredients:
- 1 pound tuna steaks, cut into 1-inch cubes
- ½ cup canned pineapple chunks, drained, juice reserved
- ½ cup large red grapes
- 1 tablespoon honey
- 2 teaspoons grated fresh ginger
- 1 teaspoon olive oil
- Pinch cayenne pepper

Directions:
1. Thread the tuna, pineapple, and grapes on 8 bamboo (see Tip) or 4 metal skewers that fit in the air fryer.
2. In a small bowl, whisk the honey, 1 tablespoon of reserved pineapple juice, the ginger, olive oil, and cayenne. Brush this mixture over the kebabs. Let them stand for 10 minutes.
3. Grill the kebabs for 8 to 12 minutes, or until the tuna reaches an internal temperature of at least 145°F on a meat thermometer, and the fruit is tender and glazed, brushing once with the remaining sauce. Discard any remaining marinade. Serve immediately.

Garlic-lemon Steamer Clams

Servings:2
Cooking Time: 30 Minutes
Ingredients:
- 25 Manila clams, scrubbed
- 2 tbsp butter, melted
- 1 garlic clove, minced
- 2 lemon wedges

Directions:
1. Add the clams to a large bowl filled with water and let sit for 10 minutes. Drain. Pour more water and let sit for 10 more minutes. Drain. Preheat air fryer to 350ºF. Place clams in the basket and Air Fry for 7 minutes. Discard any clams that don´t open. Remove clams from shells and place them into a large serving dish. Drizzle with melted butter and garlic and squeeze lemon on top. Serve.

Mayonnaise Salmon With Spinach

Servings: 4
Cooking Time: 19 Minutes
Ingredients:
- 25 ounces salmon fillet
- 1 tablespoon green pesto
- 1 cup mayonnaise
- ½ ounce olive oil
- 1-pound fresh spinach
- 2 ounces parmesan cheese, grated
- Black pepper
- Salt

Directions:
1. At 370 degrees F/ 185 degrees C, preheat your air fryer.
2. Grease its air fryer basket with cooking spray.
3. Season salmon fillet with black pepper and salt and place into the air fryer basket.
4. In a suitable bowl, mix together mayonnaise, parmesan cheese, and pesto and spread over the salmon fillet.
5. Cook salmon for 14-16 minutes.
6. Meanwhile, in a pan, sauté spinach with olive oil until spinach is wilted, about 2-3 minutes. Season with black pepper and salt.
7. Transfer spinach in serving plate and top with cooked salmon.
8. Serve and enjoy.

Tuna Patties With Dill Sauce

Servings: 6
Cooking Time: 10 Minutes
Ingredients:
- Two 5-ounce cans albacore tuna, drained
- ½ teaspoon garlic powder
- 2 teaspoons dried dill, divided
- ½ teaspoon black pepper
- ½ teaspoon salt, divided
- ¼ cup minced onion
- 1 large egg
- 7 tablespoons mayonnaise, divided
- ¼ cup panko breadcrumbs
- 1 teaspoon fresh lemon juice
- ¼ teaspoon fresh lemon zest
- 6 pieces butterleaf lettuce
- 1 cup diced tomatoes

Directions:
1. In a large bowl, mix the tuna with the garlic powder, 1 teaspoon of the dried dill, the black pepper, ¼ teaspoon

of the salt, and the onion. Make sure to use the back of a fork to really break up the tuna so there are no large chunks.

2. Mix in the egg and 1 tablespoon of the mayonnaise; then fold in the breadcrumbs so the tuna begins to form a thick batter that holds together.

3. Portion the tuna mixture into 6 equal patties and place on a plate lined with parchment paper in the refrigerator for at least 30 minutes. This will help the patties hold together in the air fryer.

4. When ready to cook, preheat the air fryer to 350°F.

5. Liberally spray the metal trivet that sits inside the air fryer basket with olive oil mist and place the patties onto the trivet.

6. Cook for 5 minutes, flip, and cook another 5 minutes.

7. While the patties are cooking, make the dill sauce by combining the remaining 6 tablespoons of mayonnaise with the remaining 1 teaspoon of dill, the lemon juice, the lemon zest, and the remaining ¼ teaspoon of salt. Set aside.

8. Remove the patties from the air fryer.

9. Place 1 slice of lettuce on a plate and top with the tuna patty and a tomato slice. Repeat to form the remaining servings. Drizzle the dill dressing over the top. Serve immediately.

Potato Chip-crusted Cod

Servings: 2
Cooking Time: 20 Minutes
Ingredients:
- ½ cup crushed potato chips
- 1 tsp chopped tarragon
- 1/8 tsp salt
- 1 tsp cayenne powder
- 1 tbsp Dijon mustard
- ¼ cup buttermilk
- 1 tsp lemon juice
- 1 tbsp butter, melted
- 2 cod fillets

Directions:
1. Preheat air fryer at 350ºF. Mix all ingredients in a bowl. Press potato chip mixture evenly across tops of cod. Place cod fillets in the greased frying basket and Air Fry for 10 minutes until the fish is opaque and flakes easily with a fork. Serve immediately.

Stuffed Shrimp

Servings: 4
Cooking Time: 12 Minutes Per Batch
Ingredients:
- 16 tail-on shrimp, peeled and deveined (last tail section intact)
- ¾ cup crushed panko breadcrumbs
- oil for misting or cooking spray
- Stuffing
- 2 6-ounce cans lump crabmeat
- 2 tablespoons chopped shallots
- 2 tablespoons chopped green onions
- 2 tablespoons chopped celery
- 2 tablespoons chopped green bell pepper
- ½ cup crushed saltine crackers

- 1 teaspoon Old Bay Seasoning
- 1 teaspoon garlic powder
- ¼ teaspoon ground thyme
- 2 teaspoons dried parsley flakes
- 2 teaspoons fresh lemon juice
- 2 teaspoons Worcestershire sauce
- 1 egg, beaten

Directions:
1. Rinse shrimp. Remove tail section (shell) from 4 shrimp, discard, and chop the meat finely.

2. To prepare the remaining 12 shrimp, cut a deep slit down the back side so that the meat lies open flat. Do not cut all the way through.

3. Preheat air fryer to 360°F.

4. Place chopped shrimp in a large bowl with all of the stuffing ingredients and stir to combine.

5. Divide stuffing into 12 portions, about 2 tablespoons each.

6. Place one stuffing portion onto the back of each shrimp and form into a ball or oblong shape. Press firmly so that stuffing sticks together and adheres to shrimp.

7. Gently roll each stuffed shrimp in panko crumbs and mist with oil or cooking spray.

8. Place 6 shrimp in air fryer basket and cook at 360°F for 10minutes. Mist with oil or spray and cook 2 minutes longer or until stuffing cooks through inside and is crispy outside.

9. Repeat step 8 to cook remaining shrimp.

Baked Sardines

Servings: 3
Cooking Time: 40 Minutes
Ingredients:
- 1-pound fresh sardines
- Sea salt, to taste
- Ground black pepper, to taste
- 1 teaspoon Italian seasoning mix
- 2 cloves garlic, minced
- 3 tablespoons olive oil
- ½ lemon, freshly squeezed

Directions:
1. Toss salt, black pepper, Italian seasoning mix and the sardines well.

2. Cook the sardines in your air fryer at 325 degrees F/160 degrees C for 35 to 40 minutes or until skin is crispy.

3. To make the sauce, whisk the remaining ingredients.

4. Serve warm sardines with the sauce on the side. Bon appétit!

Garlic Shrimp With Paprika

Servings: 2
Cooking Time: 8 Minutes
Ingredients:
- 12 ounces shrimp, peeled and deveined
- 1 lemon sliced
- ¼ teaspoon garlic powder
- ¼ teaspoon paprika
- 1 teaspoon lemon pepper
- 1 lemon juice
- 1 tablespoon olive oil

Directions:

1. In a suitable bowl, mix together oil, lemon juice, garlic powder, paprika, and lemon pepper.
2. Add shrimp to the bowl and toss well to coat.
3. Grease its air fryer basket with cooking spray.
4. Transfer shrimp into the air fryer basket and cook at almost 400 degrees F/ 205 degrees C for 8 minutes.
5. Garnish with lemon slices and serve.

Crunchy Clam Strips

Servings:3
Cooking Time: 8 Minutes
Ingredients:
- ½ pound Clam strips, drained
- 1 Large egg, well beaten
- ½ cup All-purpose flour
- ½ cup Yellow cornmeal
- 1½ teaspoons Table salt
- 1½ teaspoons Ground black pepper
- Up to ¾ teaspoon Cayenne
- Vegetable oil spray

Directions:
1. Preheat the air fryer to 400°F.
2. Toss the clam strips and beaten egg in a bowl until the clams are well coated.
3. Mix the flour, cornmeal, salt, pepper, and cayenne in a large zip-closed plastic bag until well combined. Using a flatware fork or small kitchen tongs, lift the clam strips one by one out of the egg, letting any excess egg slip back into the rest. Put the strips in the bag with the flour mixture. Once all the strips are in the bag, seal it and shake gently until the strips are well coated.
4. Use kitchen tongs to pick out the clam strips and lay them on a cutting board (leaving any extra flour mixture in the bag to be discarded). Coat the strips on both sides with vegetable oil spray.
5. When the machine is at temperature, spread the clam strips in the basket in one layer. They may touch in places, but try to leave as much air space as possible around them. Air-fry undisturbed for 8 minutes, or until brown and crunchy.
6. Gently dump the contents of the basket onto a serving platter. Cool for just a minute or two before serving hot.

Salmon

Servings: 4
Cooking Time: 8 Minutes
Ingredients:
- Marinade
- 3 tablespoons low-sodium soy sauce
- 3 tablespoons rice vinegar
- 3 tablespoons ketchup
- 3 tablespoons olive oil
- 3 tablespoons brown sugar
- 1 teaspoon garlic powder
- ½ teaspoon ground ginger
- 4 salmon fillets (½-inch thick, 3 to 4 ounces each)
- cooking spray

Directions:
1. Mix all marinade ingredients until well blended.

2. Place salmon in sealable plastic bag or shallow container with lid. Pour marinade over fish and turn to coat well. Refrigerate for 30minutes.
3. Drain marinade, and spray air fryer basket with cooking spray.
4. Place salmon in basket, skin-side down.
5. Cook at 360°F for 10 minutes, watching closely to avoid overcooking. Salmon is done when just beginning to flake and still very moist.

Healthy Cardamom Salmon

Servings: 2
Cooking Time: 12 Minutes
Ingredients:
- 2 salmon fillets
- 1 tablespoon olive oil
- ¼ teaspoon ground cardamom
- ½ teaspoon paprika
- Salt

Directions:
1. At 350 degrees F/ 175 degrees C, preheat your air fryer.
2. Coat salmon fillets with paprika, cardamom, olive oil, and salt and place into the air fryer basket.
3. Cook salmon for almost 10-12 minutes. Turn halfway through.
4. Serve and enjoy.

Crumbed Fish Fillets With Parmesan Cheese

Servings: 4
Cooking Time: 25 Minutes
Ingredients:
- 2 eggs, beaten
- ½-teaspoon tarragon
- 4 fish fillets, halved
- ½ tablespoon dry white wine
- ⅓ cup Parmesan cheese, grated
- 1 teaspoon seasoned salt
- ⅓-teaspoon mixed peppercorns
- ½-teaspoon fennel seed

Directions:
1. Add the Parmesan cheese, salt, peppercorns, fennel seeds, and tarragon to your food processor; blitz for about 20 seconds.
2. Drizzle dry white wine on the top of these fish fillets.
3. In a shallow dish, dump the egg.
4. Now, coat the fish fillets with the beaten egg on all sides, then coat them with the seasoned cracker mix.
5. Air-fry at 345 degrees F/ 175 degrees C for about 17 minutes. Bon appétit!

Halibut Soy Treat With Rice

Servings: 4
Cooking Time: 12 Minutes
Ingredients:
- 16-ounce Halibut steak
- To make the marinade:
- ⅔ cup soy sauce
- ½ cup cooking vine
- ¼ cup sugar

- 2 tablespoon lime juice
- ¼ cup orange juice
- ¼ teaspoon red pepper flakes, crushed
- ¼ teaspoon ginger ground
- 1 clove garlic (smashed)

Directions:
1. Add the marinade ingredients in a medium-size saucepan.
2. Heat the pan over medium heat for a few minutes. Cool down completely.
3. To marinate, in a zip-lock bag, combine the steak and marinade. Seal and refrigerate for 30-40 minutes.
4. Coat the air-frying basket gently with cooking oil or spray.
5. Place the steak in the basket of your air fryer and cook for 12 minutes at 355 degrees F/ 180 degrees C.
6. When done, serve warm with cooked rice!

Dijon Shrimp Cakes

Servings: 4
Cooking Time: 30 Minutes
Ingredients:
- 1 cup cooked shrimp, minced
- ¾ cup saltine cracker crumbs
- 1 cup lump crabmeat
- 3 green onions, chopped
- 1 egg, beaten
- ¼ cup mayonnaise
- 2 tbsp Dijon mustard
- 1 tbsp lemon juice

Directions:
1. Preheat the air fryer to 375°F. Combine the crabmeat, shrimp, green onions, egg, mayonnaise, mustard, ¼ cup of cracker crumbs, and the lemon juice in a bowl and mix gently. Make 4 patties, sprinkle with the rest of the cracker crumbs on both sides, and spray with cooking oil. Line the frying basket with a round parchment paper with holes poked in it. Coat the paper with cooking spray and lay the patties on it. Bake for 10-14 minutes or until the patties are golden brown. Serve warm.

Creamy Salmon

Servings: 2
Cooking Time: 20 Minutes
Ingredients:
- ¾ lb. salmon, cut into 6 pieces
- ¼ cup yogurt
- 1 tbsp. olive oil
- 1 tbsp. dill, chopped
- 3 tbsp. sour cream
- Salt to taste

Directions:
1. Sprinkle some salt on the salmon.
2. Put the salmon slices in the Air Fryer basket and add in a drizzle of olive oil.
3. Air fry the salmon at 285°F for 10 minutes.
4. In the meantime, combine together the cream, dill, yogurt, and salt.
5. Plate up the salmon and pour the creamy sauce over it. Serve hot.

Very Easy Lime-garlic Shrimps

Servings:1
Cooking Time: 6 Minutes
Ingredients:
- 1 clove of garlic, minced
- 1 cup raw shrimps
- 1 lime, juiced and zested
- Salt and pepper to taste

Directions:
1. In a mixing bowl, combine all Ingredients and give a good stir.
2. Preheat the air fryer to 390°F.
3. Skewer the shrimps onto the metal skewers that come with the double layer rack accessory.
4. Place on the rack and cook for 6 minutes.

Cornmeal Shrimp Po'boy

Servings: 4
Cooking Time: 10 Minutes
Ingredients:
- For the shrimp
- 1 pound shrimp, peeled and deveined (see Prep tip, here)
- 1 egg
- ½ cup flour
- ¾ cup cornmeal
- Salt
- Pepper
- Cooking oil
- For the remoulade
- ½ cup mayonnaise
- 1 teaspoon mustard (I use Dijon)
- 1 teaspoon Worcestershire
- 1 teaspoon minced garlic
- Juice of ½ lemon
- 1 teaspoon Sriracha
- ½ teaspoon Creole seasoning (I use Tony Chachere's brand)
- For the po'boys
- 4 rolls
- 2 cups shredded lettuce
- 8 slices tomato

Directions:
1. Dry the shrimp with paper towels.
2. In a small bowl, beat the egg. In another small bowl, place the flour. Place the cornmeal in a third small bowl, and season with salt and pepper to taste.
3. Spray the air fryer basket with cooking oil.
4. Dip the shrimp in the flour, then the egg, and then the cornmeal.
5. Place the shrimp in the air fryer. Cook for 4 minutes. Open the basket and flip the shrimp. Cook for an additional 4 minutes, or until crisp.
6. Split the rolls and spread them with the remoulade.
7. Let the shrimp cool slightly before assembling the po'boys.
8. Fill each roll with a quarter of the shrimp, ½ cup of shredded lettuce, and 2 slices of tomato. Serve.

King Prawns Al Ajillo

Servings: 4
Cooking Time: 15 Minutes
Ingredients:
- 1 ¼ lb peeled king prawns, deveined
- ½ cup grated Parmesan
- 1 tbsp olive oil
- 1 tbsp lemon juice
- ½ tsp garlic powder
- 2 garlic cloves, minced

Directions:
1. Preheat the air fryer to 350°F. In a large bowl, add the prawns and sprinkle with olive oil, lemon juice, and garlic powder. Toss in the minced garlic and Parmesan, then toss to coat. Put the prawns in the frying basket and Air Fry for 10-15 minutes or until the prawns cook through. Shake the basket once while cooking. Serve immediately.

Honey Pecan Shrimp

Servings: 4
Cooking Time: 10 Minutes
Ingredients:
- ¼ cup cornstarch
- ¾ teaspoon sea salt, divided
- ¼ teaspoon pepper
- 2 egg whites
- ⅔ cup finely chopped pecans
- 1 pound raw, peeled, and deveined shrimp
- ¼ cup honey
- 2 tablespoons mayonnaise

Directions:
1. In a small bowl, whisk together the cornstarch, ½ teaspoon of the salt, and the pepper.
2. In a second bowl, whisk together the egg whites until soft and foamy. (They don't need to be whipped to peaks or even soft peaks, just frothy.)
3. In a third bowl, mix together the pecans and the remaining ¼ teaspoon of sea salt.
4. Pat the shrimp dry with paper towels. Working in small batches, dip the shrimp into the cornstarch, then into the egg whites, and then into the pecans until all the shrimp are coated with pecans.
5. Preheat the air fryer to 330°F.
6. Place the coated shrimp inside the air fryer basket and spray with cooking spray. Cook for 5 minutes, toss the shrimp, and cook another 5 minutes.
7. Meanwhile, place the honey in a microwave-safe bowl and microwave for 30 seconds. Whisk in the mayonnaise until smooth and creamy. Pour the honey sauce into a serving bowl. Add the cooked shrimp to the serving bowl while hot and toss to coat. Serve immediately.

Herbed And Garlic Salmon Fillets

Servings: 3
Cooking Time: 12 Minutes
Ingredients:
- 1 pound salmon fillets
- Sea salt, to taste
- Ground black pepper, to taste
- 1 tablespoon olive oil
- 1 sprig thyme
- 2 sprigs rosemary
- 2 cloves garlic, minced
- 1 lemon, sliced

Directions:
1. Season the salmon fillets that have been patted dry with salt and pepper.
2. Drizzle the salmon fillets with olive oil and place them in the cooking basket of your air fryer.
3. Cook the salmon fillets at 380 degrees F/ 195 degrees C for 12 minutes.
4. After 7 minutes of cooking time, turn them over, top with thyme, rosemary and garlic and continue to cook them for 5 minutes more.
5. Serve topped with lemon slices and enjoy!

Easy Lobster Tail With Salted Butetr

Servings:4
Cooking Time: 6 Minutes
Ingredients:
- 2 tablespoons melted butter
- 4 lobster tails
- Salt and pepper to taste

Directions:
1. Preheat the air fryer to 390°F.
2. Place the grill pan accessory.
3. Cut the lobster through the tail section using a pair of kitchen scissors.
4. Brush the lobster tails with melted butter and season with salt and pepper to taste.
5. Place on the grill pan and cook for 6 minutes.

Aromatic Ahi Tuna Steaks

Servings: 4
Cooking Time: 15 Minutes
Ingredients:
- 1 tsp garlic powder
- ½ tsp salt
- ¼ tsp dried thyme
- ¼ tsp dried oregano
- ¼ tsp cayenne pepper
- 4 ahi tuna steaks
- 2 tbsp olive oil
- 1 lemon, cut into wedges

Directions:
1. Preheat air fryer to 380°F. Stir together the garlic powder, salt, thyme, cayenne pepper and oregano in a bowl to combine. Coat the tuna steaks with olive oil. Season both sides of each steak with the seasoning mix. Put the steaks in the frying basket. Air Fry for 5 minutes, then flip and cook for an additional 3-4 minutes. Serve warm with lemon wedges on the side.

Chapter 7: Poultry Recipes

Spicy Coconut Chicken Wings

Servings: 4
Cooking Time: 20 Minutes
Ingredients:

- For the coconut chicken
- 16 chicken drumettes (party wings)
- ¼ cup full-fat coconut milk
- 1 tablespoon Sriracha
- 1 teaspoon onion powder
- 1 teaspoon garlic powder
- Salt
- Pepper
- ⅓ cup shredded unsweetened coconut
- ½ cup all-purpose flour
- Cooking oil
- For the mango salsa
- 1 cup mango sliced into ½ inch chunks
- ¼ cup cilantro, chopped
- ½ cup red onion, chopped
- 2 garlic cloves, minced
- Juice of ½ lime

Directions:
1. Place the drumettes in a sealable plastic bag.
2. In a small bowl, combine the coconut milk and Sriracha. Whisk until fully combined.
3. Drizzle the drumettes with the spicy coconut milk mixture. Season the drumettes with the onion powder, garlic powder, and salt and pepper to taste.
4. Seal the bag. Shake it thoroughly to combine the seasonings and coat the chicken. Marinate for at least 30 minutes, preferably overnight, in the refrigerator.
5. When the drumettes are almost done marinating, combine the shredded coconut and flour in a large bowl. Stir.
6. Spray the air fryer basket with cooking oil.
7. Dip the drumettes in the coconut and flour mixture. Place the drumettes in the air fryer. It is okay to stack them on top of each other. Spray the drumettes with cooking oil, being sure to cover the bottom layer. Cook for 5 minutes.
8. Remove the basket and shake it to ensure all of the pieces will cook fully.
9. Return the basket to the air fryer and continue to cook the chicken. Repeat shaking every 5 minutes until a total of 20 minutes has passed.
10. Cool before serving.

Spiced Turkey Tenderloin

Servings:4
Cooking Time: 30 Minutes
Ingredients:

- ½ teaspoon paprika
- ½ teaspoon garlic powder
- ½ teaspoon salt
- ½ teaspoon freshly ground black pepper
- Pinch cayenne pepper
- 1½ pounds (680 g) turkey breast tenderloin
- Olive oil spray

Directions:
1. Preheat the air fryer to 370ºF (188ºC). Spray the air fryer basket lightly with olive oil spray.
2. In a small bowl, combine the paprika, garlic powder, salt, black pepper, and cayenne pepper. Rub the mixture all over the turkey.
3. Place the turkey in the air fryer basket and lightly spray with olive oil spray.
4. Air fry for 15 minutes. Flip the turkey over and lightly spray with olive oil spray. Air fry until the internal temperature reaches at least 170ºF (77ºC) for an additional 10 to 15 minutes.
5. Let the turkey rest for 10 minutes before slicing and serving.

Ginger Lemon Chicken

Servings: 4
Cooking Time: 24 Minutes
Ingredients:

- 2 tablespoons spring onions, minced
- 1 tablespoon ginger, grated
- 4 garlic cloves, minced
- 2 tablespoons coconut aminos
- 8 chicken drumsticks
- ½ cup chicken stock
- Black pepper and salt to the taste
- 1 teaspoon olive oil
- ¼ cup cilantro, chopped
- 1 tablespoon lemon juice

Directions:
1. Heat up a suitable pan with the oil over medium-high heat, add the chicken drumsticks, brown the chicken drumsticks for 2 minutes per side and transfer to a pan that fits the air fryer.
2. Add all the other ingredients, toss everything, put the pan in the air fryer and cook at almost 370 degrees F/ 185 degrees C for 20 minutes.
3. Divide the chicken and lemon sauce between plates and serve.

Chicken Drumettes With Mustard

Servings: 3
Cooking Time: 12 Minutes
Ingredients:

- ¼ cup soy sauce
- 1 teaspoon brown mustard
- 1 teaspoon garlic paste
- 2 tablespoons tomato paste
- 2 tablespoons sesame oil
- 1 tablespoon brown sugar
- 2 tablespoons rice vinegar
- 1 pound chicken drumettes

Directions:
1. Add all the ingredients in a resealable bag and let it marinate for 2 hours.
2. Transfer the chicken drumettes to the air fryer basket and reserve the rest mixture.

3. Cook in your air fryer at 400 degrees F/ 205 degrees C for 12 minutes. Shake the basket once or twice to cook evenly.
4. Meanwhile, in a small saucepan, boil the reserved marinade and reduce heat to low to simmer until the sauce thickens.
5. Pour the sauce over the chicken drumettes.
6. Serve immediately.

Sticky Drumsticks

Servings: 4
Cooking Time: 45 Minutes
Ingredients:
- 1 lb chicken drumsticks
- 1 tbsp chicken seasoning
- 1 tsp dried chili flakes
- Salt and pepper to taste
- ¼ cup honey
- 1 cup barbecue sauce

Directions:
1. Preheat air fryer to 390°F. Season drumsticks with chicken seasoning, chili flakes, salt, and pepper. Place one batch of drumsticks in the greased frying basket and Air Fry for 18-20 minutes, flipping once until golden.
2. While the chicken is cooking, combine honey and barbecue sauce in a small bowl. Remove the drumsticks to a serving dish. Drizzle honey-barbecue sauce over and serve.

Homemade Chicken Sliders

Servings: 3
Cooking Time: 30 Minutes
Ingredients:
- ½ cup all-purpose flour
- 1 teaspoon garlic salt
- ½ teaspoon black pepper
- 1 teaspoon celery seeds
- ½ teaspoon mustard seeds
- ½ teaspoon dried basil
- 1 egg
- 2 chicken breasts, cut in thirds
- 6 small-sized dinner rolls

Directions:
1. In mixing bowl, thoroughly combine the flour and seasonings.
2. In a separate shallow bowl, beat the egg until frothy.
3. Dredge the cleaned chicken through the flour mixture, then into egg; afterwards, roll them over the flour mixture again.
4. Spritz the chicken pieces with a cooking spray on all sides. Transfer them to the cooking basket.
5. Cook in the preheated Air Fryer at 380 degrees F/ 195 degrees C for 15 minutes; flip them and continue cooking for 10 to 12 minutes.
6. Test for doneness and adjust the seasonings.
7. Serve immediately on dinner rolls.

Juicy Turkey Breast

Servings: 10 Servings
Cooking Time: 1 Hour
Ingredients:
- 3–4 pounds of bone-in turkey breast
- ½ tablespoon of poultry seasonings
- 1 teaspoon of dried thyme
- 1 teaspoon of ground sage
- 2 tablespoons of olive oil
- Pinch of salt or black pepper, to taste

Directions:
1. Preheat your air fryer to 350ºF.
2. Grease both sides of the turkey breast with olive oil. Spread seasonings over both sides and rub them into it.
3. Put the turkey breast in the air fryer basket skin-side down. Cook at 350ºF for 25 minutes. Flip it and cook for additional 25–30 minutes. If the turkey is not 165ºF internally, cook for additional 10–15 minutes.
4. Let it rest for 10 minutes before slicing. Serve warm and enjoy your Juicy Turkey Breast!

Mouthwatering Chicken Wings

Servings: 4
Cooking Time: 40 Minutes
Ingredients:
- 2 pounds' chicken wings
- ⅛ teaspoon paprika
- 2 teaspoons seasoned salt
- ½ cup coconut flour
- ¼ teaspoon garlic powder
- ¼ teaspoon chili powder

Directions:
1. At 370 degrees F/ 185 degrees C, preheat your air fryer.
2. In a suitable bowl, add all the recipe ingredients except chicken wings and mix well.
3. Add chicken wings into the bowl coat well.
4. Grease its air fryer basket with cooking spray.
5. Add chicken wings into the air fryer basket.
6. Cook for 35-40 minutes. Shake halfway through.
7. Serve and enjoy.

Bacon-wrapped Chicken

Servings: 6
Cooking Time: 20 Minutes
Ingredients:
- 1 chicken breast, cut into 6 pieces
- 6 rashers back bacon
- 1 tbsp. soft cheese

Directions:
1. Put the bacon rashers on a flat surface and cover one side with the soft cheese.
2. Lay the chicken pieces on each bacon rasher. Wrap the bacon around the chicken and use a toothpick stick to hold each one in place. Put them in Air Fryer basket.
3. Air fry at 350°F for 15 minutes.

Farmhouse Chicken Rolls

Servings: 4
Cooking Time: 14 Minutes
Ingredients:
- 4 slices smoked bacon, chopped
- 4 slices Monterey-Jack cheese, sliced
- 1 ½ pounds chicken fillets
- 1 celery stick, chopped
- 1 small sized onion, chopped
- 1 teaspoon hot sauce
- Sea salt, to taste
- Ground black pepper, to season
- 1 lemon, cut into slices

Directions:
1. Before cooking, heat your air fryer to 380 degrees F/ 195 degrees C.
2. On the chicken fillets, add 1 bacon slice and 1 cheese slice for each.
3. Then add onion and celery between the fillets.
4. Drizzle hot sauce on the top and add salt and black pepper to season as you like. Then roll them up and tie the rolls with kitchen twine.
5. Roast in your air fryer for 8 minutes. Flip and cook the chicken rolls for 5 to 6 minutes or more.
6. Serve the rolls with lemon slices. Enjoy!

Mushroom & Turkey Bread Pizza

Servings: 4
Cooking Time: 35 Minutes
Ingredients:
- 10 cooked turkey sausages, sliced
- 1 cup shredded mozzarella cheese
- 1 cup shredded Cheddar cheese
- 1 French loaf bread
- 2 tbsp butter, softened
- 1 tsp garlic powder
- 1 1/3 cups marinara sauce
- 1 tsp Italian seasoning
- 2 scallions, chopped
- 1 cup mushrooms, sliced

Directions:
1. Preheat the air fryer to 370°F. Cut the bread in half crosswise, then split each half horizontally. Combine butter and garlic powder, then spread on the cut sides of the bread. Bake the halves in the fryer for 3-5 minutes or until the leaves start to brown. Set the toasted bread on a work surface and spread marinara sauce over the top. Sprinkle the Italian seasoning, then top with sausages, scallions, mushrooms, and cheeses. Set the pizzas in the air fryer and Bake for 8-12 minutes or until the cheese is melted and starting to brown. Serve hot.

Crispy Chicken Nuggets With Turnip

Servings: 3
Cooking Time: 32 Minutes
Ingredients:
- 1 egg
- ½ teaspoon cayenne pepper
- ⅓ cup panko crumbs
- ¼ teaspoon Romano cheese, grated
- 2 teaspoons canola oil
- 1 pound chicken breast, cut into slices
- 1 medium-sized turnip, trimmed and sliced
- ½ teaspoon garlic powder
- Sea salt, to taste
- Ground black pepper, to taste

Directions:
1. Whisk the egg together with the cayenne pepper until frothy in a bowl.
2. Mix the cheese together with the panko crumbs in another shallow until well combined.
3. Dredge the chicken slices firstly in the egg mixture, then in the panko mixture until coat well.
4. Then using 1 teaspoon of canola oil brush the slices.
5. To season, add salt and pepper.
6. Before cooking, heat your air fryer to 380 degrees F/ 195 degrees C.
7. Cook the chicken slices in the air fryer for 12 minutes. Shake the basket halfway through cooking.
8. When done, the internal temperature of their thickest part should read 165 degrees F/ 75 degrees C.
9. Remove from the air fryer and reserve. Keep warm.
10. With the remaining canola oil, drizzle over the turnip slices.
11. To season, add salt, pepper, and garlic powder.
12. Cook the slices in your air fryer at 370 degrees F/ 185 degrees C for about 20 minutes.
13. Serve the parsnip slices with chicken nuggets. Enjoy!

Piri-piri Chicken Thighs

Servings:4
Cooking Time: 25 Minutes
Ingredients:
- ¼ cup piri-piri sauce
- 1 tablespoon freshly squeezed lemon juice
- 2 tablespoons brown sugar, divided
- 2 cloves garlic, minced
- 1 tablespoon extra-virgin olive oil
- 4 bone-in, skin-on chicken thighs, each weighing approximately 7 to 8 ounces (198 to 227 g)
- ½ teaspoon cornstarch

Directions:
1. To make the marinade, whisk together the piri-piri sauce, lemon juice, 1 tablespoon of brown sugar, and the garlic in a small bowl. While whisking, slowly pour in the oil in a steady stream and continue to whisk until emulsified. Using a skewer, poke holes in the chicken thighs and place them in a small glass dish. Pour the marinade over the chicken and turn the thighs to coat them with the sauce. Cover the dish and refrigerate for at least 15 minutes and up to 1 hour.
2. Preheat the air fryer to 375ºF (191ºC). Remove the chicken thighs from the dish, reserving the marinade, and place them skin-side down in the air fryer basket. Air fry until the internal temperature reaches 165ºF (74ºC), 15 to 20 minutes.

3. Meanwhile, whisk the remaining brown sugar and the cornstarch into the marinade and microwave it on high power for 1 minute until it is bubbling and thickened to a glaze.
4. Once the chicken is cooked, turn the thighs over and brush them with the glaze. Air fry for a few additional minutes until the glaze browns and begins to char in spots.
5. Remove the chicken to a platter and serve with additional piri-piri sauce, if desired.

Shishito Pepper Rubbed Wings
Servings:6
Cooking Time: 30 Minutes
Ingredients:
- 1 ½ cups shishito peppers, pureed
- 2 tablespoons sesame oil
- 3 pounds chicken wings
- Salt and pepper to taste
Directions:
1. Place all Ingredients in a Ziploc bowl and allow to marinate for at least 2 hours in the fridge.
2. Preheat the air fryer to 390°F.
3. Place the grill pan accessory in the air fryer.
4. Grill for at least 30 minutes flipping the chicken every 5 minutes and basting with the remaining sauce.

Turkey Breast With Shallot Sauce
Servings: 4
Cooking Time: 28 Minutes
Ingredients:
- 1 big turkey breast, skinless, boneless and cubed
- 1 tablespoon olive oil
- ¼ teaspoon sweet paprika
- Black pepper and salt to the taste
- 1 cup chicken stock
- 3 tablespoons butter, melted
- 4 shallots, chopped
Directions:
1. Heat up a pan that fits the air fryer with the olive oil and the butter over medium high heat, add the turkey cubes, and brown for 3 minutes on each side.
2. Add the shallots, stir and sauté for 5 minutes more.
3. Add the paprika, stock, black pepper and salt, toss, put the pan in the air fryer and cook at almost 370 degrees F/ 185 degrees C for 20 minutes.
4. Divide into bowls and serve.

Garlic Soy Chicken Thighs
Servings:2
Cooking Time: 30 Minutes
Ingredients:
- 2 tablespoons chicken stock
- 2 tablespoons reduced-sodium soy sauce
- 1½ tablespoons sugar
- 4 garlic cloves, smashed and peeled
- 2 large scallions, cut into 2- to 3-inch batons, plus more, thinly sliced, for garnish

- 2 bone-in, skin-on chicken thighs (7 to 8 ounces / 198 to 227 g each)
Directions:
1. Preheat the air fryer to 375ºF (191ºC).
2. In a metal cake pan, combine the chicken stock, soy sauce, and sugar and stir until the sugar dissolves. Add the garlic cloves, scallions, and chicken thighs, turning the thighs to coat them in the marinade, then resting them skin-side up. Place the pan in the air fryer and bake, flipping the thighs every 5 minutes after the first 10 minutes, until the chicken is cooked through and the marinade is reduced to a sticky glaze over the chicken, about 30 minutes.
3. Remove the pan from the air fryer and serve the chicken thighs warm, with any remaining glaze spooned over top and sprinkled with more sliced scallions.

Chicken Strips
Servings: 4
Cooking Time: 8 Minutes
Ingredients:
- 1 pound chicken tenders
- Marinade
- ¼ cup olive oil
- 2 tablespoons water
- 2 tablespoons honey
- 2 tablespoons white vinegar
- ½ teaspoon salt
- ½ teaspoon crushed red pepper
- 1 teaspoon garlic powder
- 1 teaspoon onion powder
- ½ teaspoon paprika
Directions:
1. Combine all marinade ingredients and mix well.
2. Add chicken and stir to coat. Cover tightly and let marinate in refrigerator for 30minutes.
3. Remove tenders from marinade and place them in a single layer in the air fryer basket.
4. Cook at 390°F for 3minutes. Turn tenders over and cook for 5 minutes longer or until chicken is done and juices run clear.
5. Repeat step 4 to cook remaining tenders.

Yellow Curry Chicken Thighs With Peanuts
Servings:6
Cooking Time: 20 Minutes
Ingredients:
- ½ cup unsweetened full-fat coconut milk
- 2 tablespoons yellow curry paste
- 1 tablespoon minced fresh ginger
- 1 tablespoon minced garlic
- 1 teaspoon kosher salt
- 1 pound (454 g) boneless, skinless chicken thighs, halved crosswise
- 2 tablespoons chopped peanuts
Directions:

1. In a large bowl, stir together the coconut milk, curry paste, ginger, garlic, and salt until well blended. Add the chicken; toss well to coat. Marinate at room temperature for 30 minutes, or cover and refrigerate for up to 24 hours.
2. Preheat the air fryer to 375ºF (191ºC).
3. Place the chicken (along with marinade) in a baking pan. Place the pan in the air fryer basket. Bake for 20 minutes, turning the chicken halfway through the cooking time. Use a meat thermometer to ensure the chicken has reached an internal temperature of 165ºF (74ºC).
4. Sprinkle the chicken with the chopped peanuts and serve.

Crunchy Chicken Bites

Servings: 3
Cooking Time: 10 Minutes
Ingredients:
- 1 pound chicken tenders
- ¼ cup all-purpose flour
- ½ teaspoon onion powder
- ½ teaspoon garlic powder
- ½ teaspoon cayenne pepper
- Sea salt, to taste
- Ground black pepper, to taste
- ½ cup breadcrumbs
- 1 egg
- 1 tablespoon olive oil

Directions:
1. Using kitchen towels, pat the chicken dry and cut the chicken into bites.
2. Mix the onion powder, cayenne pepper, garlic powder, black pepper, and salt in a shallow bowl.
3. Dip the chicken bites in the mixture and rub to coat the bites well.
4. Add the breadcrumbs into a separate bowl.
5. Then beat the egg in a third bowl.
6. Dip the chicken firstly in the whisked egg, and then dredge in the breadcrumbs pressing to coat well.
7. Brush olive oil over the chicken fingers.
8. Cook the chicken bites in the air fryer at 360 degrees F/ 180 degrees C for 8 to 10 minutes. Halfway through cooking, turn the chicken fingers over to cook evenly.
9. As you desired, serve the chicken fingers with your favorite dipping sauce.

Turkey Hoisin Burgers

Servings:4
Cooking Time: 20 Minutes
Ingredients:
- 1 pound (454 g) lean ground turkey
- ¼ cup whole-wheat bread crumbs
- ¼ cup hoisin sauce
- 2 tablespoons soy sauce
- 4 whole-wheat buns
- Olive oil spray

Directions:

1. In a large bowl, mix together the turkey, bread crumbs, hoisin sauce, and soy sauce.
2. Form the mixture into 4 equal patties. Cover with plastic wrap and refrigerate the patties for 30 minutes.
3. Preheat the air fryer to 370ºF (188ºC). Spray the air fryer basket lightly with olive oil spray.
4. Place the patties in the air fryer basket in a single layer. Spray the patties lightly with olive oil spray.
5. Air fry for 10 minutes. Flip the patties over, lightly spray with olive oil spray, and air fry for an additional 5 to 10 minutes, until golden brown.
6. Place the patties on buns and top with your choice of low-calorie burger toppings like sliced tomatoes, onions, and cabbage slaw. Serve immediately.

Mayonnaise Taco Chicken

Servings: 3
Cooking Time: 20 Minutes
Ingredients:
- 1 pound chicken legs, skinless, boneless
- ½ cup mayonnaise
- ½ cup milk
- ⅓ cup all-purpose flour
- Sea salt, to season
- Ground black pepper, to season
- ½ teaspoon cayenne pepper
- ⅓ cup tortilla chips, crushed
- 1 teaspoon Taco seasoning blend
- ½ teaspoon dried Mexican oregano

Directions:
1. Before cooking, heat your air fryer to 385 degrees F/ 195 degrees C.
2. Pat the chicken legs dry and set aside.
3. Combine milk, flour, black pepper, cayenne pepper, salt, and mayonnaise together in a mixing bowl.
4. Mix taco seasoning blend, Mexican oregano, and the crushed tortilla chip in another shallow bowl.
5. Dredge the chicken legs with the mayonnaise mixture. Coat the tortilla chip mixture over the chicken legs. Shake off any excess crumbs.
6. Cook for 20 minutes. Flip halfway through cooking.
7. Serve and enjoy!

Yummy Shredded Chicken

Servings: 2
Cooking Time: 15 Minutes
Ingredients:
- 2 large chicken breasts
- ¼ tsp Pepper
- 1 tsp garlic puree
- 1 tsp mustard
- Salt

Directions:
1. Add all ingredients to the bowl and toss well.
2. Transfer chicken into the air fryer basket and cook at 360ºF for 15 minutes.
3. Remove chicken from air fryer and shred using a fork.
4. Serve and enjoy.

Sweet-and-sour Chicken

Servings: 6
Cooking Time: 10 Minutes
Ingredients:
- 1 cup pineapple juice
- 1 cup plus 3 tablespoons cornstarch, divided
- ¼ cup sugar
- ¼ cup ketchup
- ¼ cup apple cider vinegar
- 2 tablespoons soy sauce or tamari
- 1 teaspoon garlic powder, divided
- ¼ cup flour
- 1 tablespoon sesame seeds
- ½ teaspoon salt
- ¼ teaspoon ground black pepper
- 2 large eggs
- 2 pounds chicken breasts, cut into 1-inch cubes
- 1 red bell pepper, cut into 1-inch pieces
- 1 carrot, sliced into ¼-inch-thick rounds

Directions:
1. In a medium saucepan, whisk together the pineapple juice, 3 tablespoons of the cornstarch, the sugar, the ketchup, the apple cider vinegar, the soy sauce or tamari, and ½ teaspoon of the garlic powder. Cook over medium-low heat, whisking occasionally as the sauce thickens, about 6 minutes. Stir and set aside while preparing the chicken.
2. Preheat the air fryer to 370°F.
3. In a medium bowl, place the remaining 1 cup of cornstarch, the flour, the sesame seeds, the salt, the remaining ½ teaspoon of garlic powder, and the pepper.
4. In a second medium bowl, whisk the eggs.
5. Working in batches, place the cubed chicken in the cornstarch mixture to lightly coat; then dip it into the egg mixture, and return it to the cornstarch mixture. Shake off the excess and place the coated chicken in the air fryer basket. Spray with cooking spray and cook for 5 minutes, shake the basket, and spray with more cooking spray. Cook an additional 3 to 5 minutes, or until completely cooked and golden brown.
6. On the last batch of chicken, add the bell pepper and carrot to the basket and cook with the chicken.
7. Place the cooked chicken and vegetables into a serving bowl and toss with the sweet-and-sour sauce to serve.

Southern Fried Chicken

Servings: 2
Cooking Time: 30 Minutes
Ingredients:
- 2 x 6-oz. boneless skinless chicken breasts
- 2 tbsp. hot sauce
- ½ tsp. onion powder
- 1 tbsp. chili powder
- 2 oz. pork rinds, finely ground

Directions:

1. Lengthwise cut the chicken breasts in half and rub in the hot sauce. Combine the onion powder with the chili powder, then rub into the chicken. Leave to marinate for at least a half hour.
2. Use the ground pork rinds to coat the chicken breasts in the ground pork rinds, covering them thoroughly. Place the chicken in your air fryer.
3. Set the fryer at 350 degrees F/ 175 degrees C and cook the chicken for 13 minutes. Flip the chicken and then cook the other side for another 13 minutes or until golden.
4. Test the chicken with a meat thermometer. When fully cooked, it should reach 165 degrees F/ 75 degrees C. Serve hot, with the sides of your choice.

Family Chicken Fingers

Servings: 4
Cooking Time: 30 Minutes
Ingredients:
- 1 lb chicken breast fingers
- 1 tbsp chicken seasoning
- ½ tsp mustard powder
- Salt and pepper to taste
- 2 eggs
- 1 cup bread crumbs

Directions:
1. Preheat air fryer to 400°F. Add the chicken fingers to a large bowl along with chicken seasoning, mustard, salt, and pepper; mix well. Set up two small bowls. In one bowl, beat the eggs. In the second bowl, add the bread crumbs. Dip the chicken in the egg, then dredge in breadcrumbs. Place the nuggets in the air fryer. Lightly spray with cooking oil, then Air Fry for 8 minutes, shaking the basket once until crispy and cooked through. Serve warm.

Thai Cornish Game Hens

Servings:4
Cooking Time: 20 Minutes
Ingredients:
- 1 cup chopped fresh cilantro leaves and stems
- ¼ cup fish sauce
- 1 tablespoon soy sauce
- 1 serrano chile, seeded and chopped
- 8 garlic cloves, smashed
- 2 tablespoons sugar
- 2 tablespoons lemongrass paste
- 2 teaspoons black pepper
- 2 teaspoons ground coriander
- 1 teaspoon kosher salt
- 1 teaspoon ground turmeric
- 2 Cornish game hens, giblets removed, split in half lengthwise

Directions:
1. In a blender, combine the cilantro, fish sauce, soy sauce, serrano, garlic, sugar, lemongrass, black pepper, coriander, salt, and turmeric. Blend until smooth.

2. Place the game hen halves in a large bowl. Pour the cilantro mixture over the hen halves and toss to coat. Marinate at room temperature for 30 minutes, or cover and refrigerate for up to 24 hours.

3. Preheat the air fryer to 400°F (204°C).

4. Arrange the hen halves in a single layer in the air fryer basket. Roast for 20 minutes. Use a meat thermometer to ensure the game hens have reached an internal temperature of 165°F (74°C). Serve warm.

Harissa Chicken Wings

Servings: 4
Cooking Time: 25 Minutes
Ingredients:
- 8 whole chicken wings
- 1 tsp garlic powder
- ¼ tsp dried oregano
- 1 tbsp harissa seasoning

Directions:
1. Preheat air fryer to 400°F. Season the wings with garlic, harissa seasoning, and oregano. Place them in the greased frying basket and spray with cooking oil spray. Air Fry for 10 minutes, shake the basket, and cook for another 5-7 minutes until golden and crispy. Serve warm.

Creole Chicken Drumettes

Servings:4
Cooking Time: 50 Minutes
Ingredients:
- 1 lb chicken drumettes
- ½ cup flour
- ½ cup heavy cream
- ½ cup sour cream
- ½ cup bread crumbs
- 1 tbsp Creole seasoning
- 2 tbsp melted butter

Directions:
1. Preheat air fryer to 370°F. Combine chicken drumettes and flour in a bowl. Shake away excess flour and set aside. Mix the heavy cream and sour cream in a bowl. In another bowl, combine bread crumbs and Creole seasoning. Dip floured drumettes in cream mixture, then dredge them in crumbs. Place the chicken drumettes in the greased frying basket and Air Fry for 20 minutes, tossing once and brushing with melted butter. Let rest for a few minutes on a plate and serve.

Spicy Pork Rind Fried Chicken

Servings:4
Cooking Time: 20 Minutes
Ingredients:
- ¼ cup buffalo sauce
- 4 boneless, skinless chicken breasts
- ½ teaspoon paprika
- ½ teaspoon garlic powder
- ¼ teaspoon ground black pepper
- 2 ounces plain pork rinds, finely crushed

Directions:

1. Pour buffalo sauce into a large sealable bowl or bag. Add chicken and toss to coat. Place sealed bowl or bag into refrigerator and let marinate at least 30 minutes up to overnight.

2. Remove chicken from marinade but do not shake excess sauce off chicken. Sprinkle both sides of thighs with paprika, garlic powder, and pepper.

3. Place pork rinds into a large bowl and press each chicken breast into pork rinds to coat evenly on both sides.

4. Place chicken into ungreased air fryer basket. Adjust the temperature to 400°F and set the timer for 20 minutes, turning chicken halfway through cooking. Chicken will be golden and have an internal temperature of at least 165°F when done. Serve warm.

Honey Lemon Thyme Glazed Cornish Hen

Servings: 2
Cooking Time: 20 Minutes
Ingredients:
- 1 (2-pound) Cornish game hen, split in half
- olive oil
- salt and freshly ground black pepper
- ¼ teaspoon dried thyme
- ¼ cup honey
- 1 tablespoon lemon zest
- juice of 1 lemon
- 1½ teaspoons chopped fresh thyme leaves
- ½ teaspoon soy sauce
- freshly ground black pepper

Directions:
1. Split the game hen in half by cutting down each side of the backbone and then cutting through the breast. Brush or spray both halves of the game hen with the olive oil and then season with the salt, pepper and dried thyme.

2. Preheat the air fryer to 390°F.

3. Place the game hen, skin side down, into the air fryer and air-fry for 5 minutes. Turn the hen halves over and air-fry for 10 minutes.

4. While the hen is cooking, combine the honey, lemon zest and juice, fresh thyme, soy sauce and pepper in a small bowl.

5. When the air fryer timer rings, brush the honey glaze onto the game hen and continue to air-fry for another 3 to 5 minutes, just until the hen is nicely glazed, browned and has an internal temperature of 165°F.

6. Let the hen rest for 5 minutes and serve warm.

Simple Chicken Burgers

Servings: 4
Cooking Time: 11 Minutes
Ingredients:
- 1 ¼ pounds chicken white meat, ground
- ½ white onion, finely chopped
- 1 teaspoon fresh garlic, finely chopped
- Sea salt, to taste

- Ground black pepper, to taste
- 1 teaspoon paprika
- ½ cup cornmeal
- 1 ½ cups breadcrumbs
- 4 burger buns
- 4 lettuce leaves
- 2 small pickles, sliced
- 2 tablespoons ketchup
- 1 teaspoon yellow mustard

Directions:
1. In a mixing dish, combine thoroughly the onion, salt, black pepper, garlic, and chicken. Then make 4 equal patties from the mixture.
2. Mix cornmeal, breadcrumbs, and paprika in a shallow bowl.
3. Dredge the patties in the breadcrumb mixture. Press the patties to coat the both sides.
4. Using a non-stick cooking spray, spritz an air fryer basket.
5. Place the coated patties inside the air fryer basket.
6. Cook the patties in your air fryer at 370 degrees F/ 185 degrees C for 11 minutes or until it reaches the doneness as you desired.
7. When cooked, remove from the air fryer and place on burger buns. Serve with toppings. Enjoy!
8. Place your burgers on burger buns and serve with toppings. Bon appétit!

Baked Chicken Nachos

Servings:4
Cooking Time: 7 Minutes
Ingredients:
- 50 tortilla chips
- 2 cups shredded cooked chicken breast, divided
- 2 cups shredded Mexican-blend cheese, divided
- ½ cup sliced pickled jalapeño peppers, divided
- ½ cup diced red onion, divided

Directions:
1. Preheat the air fryer to 300°F.
2. Use foil to make a bowl shape that fits the shape of the air fryer basket. Place half tortilla chips in the bottom of foil bowl, then top with 1 cup chicken, 1 cup cheese, ¼ cup jalapeños, and ¼ cup onion. Repeat with remaining chips and toppings.
3. Place foil bowl in the air fryer basket and cook 7 minutes until cheese is melted and toppings heated through. Serve warm.

Moroccan-style Chicken Strips

Servings: 4
Cooking Time: 30 Minutes
Ingredients:
- 4 chicken breasts, cut into strips
- 2 tsp olive oil
- 2 tbsp cornstarch
- 3 garlic cloves, minced
- ½ cup chicken broth
- ¼ cup lemon juice

- 1 tbsp honey
- ½ tsp ras el hanout
- 1 cup cooked couscous

Directions:
1. Preheat air fryer to 400°F. Mix the chicken and olive oil in a bowl, then add the cornstarch. Stir to coat. Add the garlic and transfer to a baking pan. Put the pan in the fryer. Bake for 10 minutes. Stir at least once during cooking.
2. When done, pour in the chicken broth, lemon juice, honey, and ras el hanout. Bake for an additional 6-9 minutes or until the sauce is thick and the chicken cooked through with no pink showing. Serve with couscous.

Chipotle Chicken Drumsticks

Servings: 4
Cooking Time: 40 Minutes
Ingredients:
- 1 can chipotle chilies packed in adobe sauce
- 2 tbsp grated Mexican cheese
- 6 chicken drumsticks
- 1 egg, beaten
- ½ cup bread crumbs
- 1 tbsp corn flakes
- Salt and pepper to taste

Directions:
1. Preheat air fryer to 350°F. Place the chilies in the sauce in your blender and pulse until a fine paste is formed. Transfer to a bowl and add the beaten egg. Combine thoroughly. Mix the breadcrumbs, Mexican cheese, corn flakes, salt, and pepper in a separate bowl, and set aside.
2. Coat the chicken drumsticks with the crumb mixture, then dip into the bowl with wet ingredients, then dip again into the dry ingredients. Arrange the chicken drumsticks on the greased frying basket in a single flat layer. Air Fry for 14-16 minutes, turning each chicken drumstick over once. Serve warm.

Honey Turkey Tenderloin

Servings: 4
Cooking Time: 55 Minutes
Ingredients:
- 1 tablespoon honey
- ¼ cup vermouth
- 2 tablespoons lemon juice
- 1 teaspoon marjoram
- 1 teaspoon oregano, dried
- 1 turkey tenderloin, quartered
- 1 tablespoon sesame oil
- Sea salt flakes as needed
- ¾ teaspoon smoked paprika
- 1 teaspoon crushed sage leaves, dried
- ½ teaspoon ground pepper

Directions:
1. To marinate, combine honey, vermouth, lemon juice, marjoram, and oregano together in a zip-lock bag.

2. Seal and marinate at room temperature for 3 hours.
3. On a flat kitchen surface, plug your air fryer and turn it on.
4. Before cooking, heat your air fryer to 355 degrees F/ 180 degrees C for 4 to 5 minutes.
5. Gently coat the air fryer basket with cooking oil or spray.
6. Place the turkey tenderloin inside the air fryer basket.
7. Cook in your air fryer for 50 to 55 minutes.
8. When cooked, remove from the air fryer and serve warm.

Indian Chicken Tandoori

Servings: 2
Cooking Time: 35 Minutes
Ingredients:
- 2 chicken breasts, cubed
- ½ cup hung curd
- 1 tsp turmeric powder
- 1 tsp red chili powder
- 1 tsp chaat masala powder
- Pinch of salt

Directions:
1. Preheat air fryer to 350°F. Mix the hung curd, turmeric, red chili powder, chaat masala powder, and salt in a mixing bowl. Stir until the mixture is free of lumps. Coat the chicken with the mixture, cover, and refrigerate for 30 minutes to marinate. Place the marinated chicken chunks in a baking pan and drizzle with the remaining marinade. Bake for 25 minutes until the chicken is juicy and spiced. Serve warm.

Quick Chicken For Filling

Servings: 2
Cooking Time: 8 Minutes
Ingredients:
- 1 pound chicken tenders, skinless and boneless
- ½ teaspoon ground cumin
- ½ teaspoon garlic powder
- cooking spray

Directions:
1. Sprinkle raw chicken tenders with seasonings.
2. Spray air fryer basket lightly with cooking spray to prevent sticking.
3. Place chicken in air fryer basket in single layer.
4. Cook at 390°F for 4minutes, turn chicken strips over, and cook for an additional 4minutes.
5. Test for doneness. Thick tenders may require an additional minute or two.

Poblano Bake

Servings: 4
Cooking Time: 11 Minutes Per Batch
Ingredients:
- 2 large poblano peppers (approx. 5½ inches long excluding stem)
- ¾ pound ground turkey, raw
- ¾ cup cooked brown rice
- 1 teaspoon chile powder

- ½ teaspoon ground cumin
- ½ teaspoon garlic powder
- 4 ounces sharp Cheddar cheese, grated
- 1 8-ounce jar salsa, warmed

Directions:
1. Slice each pepper in half lengthwise so that you have four wide, flat pepper halves.
2. Remove seeds and membrane and discard. Rinse inside and out.
3. In a large bowl, combine turkey, rice, chile powder, cumin, and garlic powder. Mix well.
4. Divide turkey filling into 4 portions and stuff one into each of the 4 pepper halves. Press lightly to pack down.
5. Place 2 pepper halves in air fryer basket and cook at 390°F for 10minutes or until turkey is well done.
6. Top each pepper half with ¼ of the grated cheese. Cook 1 more minute or just until cheese melts.
7. Repeat steps 5 and 6 to cook remaining pepper halves.
8. To serve, place each pepper half on a plate and top with ¼ cup warm salsa.

Crisp Chicken Wings

Servings:4
Cooking Time: 20 Minutes
Ingredients:
- 1 pound (454 g) chicken wings
- 3 tablespoons vegetable oil
- ½ cup all-purpose flour
- ½ teaspoon smoked paprika
- ½ teaspoon garlic powder
- ½ teaspoon kosher salt
- 1½ teaspoons freshly cracked black pepper

Directions:
1. Preheat the air fryer to 400ºF (204ºC).
2. Place the chicken wings in a large bowl. Drizzle the vegetable oil over wings and toss to coat.
3. In a separate bowl, whisk together the flour, paprika, garlic powder, salt, and pepper until combined.
4. Dredge the wings in the flour mixture one at a time, coating them well, and place in the air fryer basket. Air fry for 20 minutes, turning the wings halfway through the cooking time, until the breading is browned and crunchy.
5. Serve hot.

Berry-glazed Turkey Breast

Servings: 4
Cooking Time: 1 Hour 25 Minutes
Ingredients:
- 1 bone-in, skin-on turkey breast
- 1 tbsp olive oil
- Salt and pepper to taste
- 1 cup raspberries
- 1cup chopped strawberries
- 2 tbsp balsamic vinegar
- 2 tbsp butter, melted

- 1 tbsp honey mustard
- 1 tsp dried rosemary

Directions:

1. Preheat the air fryer to 350°F. Lay the turkey breast skin-side up in the frying basket, brush with the oil, and sprinkle with salt and pepper. Bake for 55-65 minutes, flipping twice. Meanwhile, mix the berries, vinegar, melted butter, rosemary and honey mustard in a blender and blend until smooth. Turn the turkey skin-side up inside the fryer and brush with half of the berry mix. Bake for 5 more minutes. Put the remaining berry mix in a small saucepan and simmer for 3-4 minutes while the turkey cooks. When the turkey is done, let it stand for 10 minutes, then carve. Serve with the remaining glaze.

Garlic Chicken Breast

Servings: 3
Cooking Time: 17 Minutes
Ingredients:

- 1-pound chicken breast, skinless, boneless
- 1 teaspoon garlic powder
- 1 teaspoon dried thyme
- 1 teaspoon salt
- ½ teaspoon black pepper
- ½ teaspoon cayenne pepper
- 2 teaspoons sunflower oil

Directions:

1. Sprinkle the chicken breast with garlic powder, dried thyme, salt, black pepper, and cayenne pepper.
2. Then gently brush the chicken with sunflower oil and put it in the air fryer.
3. Cook the chicken breast for almost 17 minutes at 385 degrees F/ 195 degrees C.
4. Slice the cooked chicken into servings.

Buttermilk Paprika Chicken

Servings:4
Cooking Time: 17 To 23 Minutes
Ingredients:

- 4 (5-ounce / 142-g) low-sodium boneless, skinless chicken breasts, pounded to about ½ inch thick
- ½ cup buttermilk
- ½ cup all-purpose flour
- 2 tablespoons cornstarch
- 1 teaspoon dried thyme
- 1 teaspoon ground paprika
- 1 egg white
- 1 tablespoon olive oil

Directions:

1. Preheat the air fryer to 390°F (199°C).
2. In a shallow bowl, mix the chicken and buttermilk. Let stand for 10 minutes.
3. Meanwhile, in another shallow bowl, mix the flour, cornstarch, thyme, and paprika.
4. In a small bowl, whisk the egg white and olive oil. Quickly stir this egg mixture into the flour mixture so the dry ingredients are evenly moistened.

5. Remove the chicken from the buttermilk and shake off any excess liquid. Dip each piece of chicken into the flour mixture to coat.
6. Air fry the chicken in the air fryer basket for 17 to 23 minutes, or until the chicken reaches an internal temperature of 165ºF (74ºC) on a meat thermometer. Serve immediately.

Crusted Chicken Tenders

Servings: 3
Cooking Time: 10 Minutes
Ingredients:

- 1 pound chicken tenders
- Sea salt and black pepper, to taste
- ½ teaspoon shallot powder
- ½ teaspoon porcini powder
- ½ teaspoon dried rosemary
- ⅓ cup tortilla chips, crushed

Directions:

1. Before cooking, heat your air fryer to 360 degrees F/ 180 degrees C.
2. Rub salt, shallot powder, dried rosemary, pepper, tortilla chips, and porcini powder over the chicken tenders.
3. Using a nonstick cooking spray, spritz the air fryer basket.
4. Transfer the chicken tenders inside the air fryer basket.
5. Cook the coated chicken in your air fryer for 10 minutes. Flip halfway through cooking.
6. Serve warm with your favorite dipping sauce.

Maewoon Chicken Legs

Servings: 4
Cooking Time: 30 Minutes + Chilling Time
Ingredients:

- 4 scallions, sliced, whites and greens separated
- ¼ cup tamari
- 2 tbsp sesame oil
- 1 tsp sesame seeds
- ¼ cup honey
- 2 tbsp gochujang
- 2 tbsp ketchup
- 4 cloves garlic, minced
- ½ tsp ground ginger
- Salt and pepper to taste
- 1 tbsp parsley
- 1 ½ lb chicken legs

Directions:

1. Whisk all ingredients, except chicken and scallion greens, in a bowl. Reserve ¼ cup of marinade. Toss chicken legs in the remaining marinade and chill for 30 minutes.
2. Preheat air fryer at 400°F. Place chicken legs in the greased frying basket and Air Fry for 10 minutes. Turn chicken. Cook for 8 more minutes. Let sit in a serving dish for 5 minutes. Coat the cooked chicken with the reserved marinade and scatter with scallion greens, sesame seeds and parsley to serve.

Southern-style Chicken Legs

Servings: 6
Cooking Time: 20 Minutes
Ingredients:
- 2 cups buttermilk
- 1 tablespoon hot sauce
- 12 chicken legs
- ½ teaspoon salt
- ½ teaspoon pepper
- 1 teaspoon paprika
- ½ teaspoon onion powder
- 1 teaspoon garlic powder
- 1 cup all-purpose flour

Directions:
1. In an airtight container, place the buttermilk, hot sauce, and chicken legs and refrigerate for 4 to 8 hours.
2. In a medium bowl, whisk together the salt, pepper, paprika, onion powder, garlic powder, and flour. Drain the chicken legs from the buttermilk and dip the chicken legs into the flour mixture, stirring to coat well.
3. Preheat the air fryer to 390°F.
4. Place the chicken legs in the air fryer basket and spray with cooking spray. Cook for 10 minutes, turn the chicken legs over, and cook for another 8 to 10 minutes. Check for an internal temperature of 165°F.

Indian-style Chicken With Raita

Servings: 2
Cooking Time: 12 Minutes
Ingredients:
- 2 chicken fillets
- Sea salt and ground black pepper, to taste
- 2 teaspoons garam masala
- 1 teaspoon ground turmeric
- ½ cup plain yogurt
- 1 English cucumber, shredded and drained
- 1 tablespoon fresh cilantro, coarsely chopped
- ½ red onion, chopped
- A pinch of grated nutmeg
- A pinch of ground cinnamon

Directions:
1. Before cooking, heat your air fryer to 380 degrees F/ 195 degrees C.
2. Rub pepper, garam masala, ground turmeric, and salt over the chicken fillets until well coated.
3. Cook in your air fryer for 12 minutes. Flip once or twice halfway through cooking.
4. To make additional raita, mix all the rest of the ingredients in a mixing bowl.
5. Serve the chicken with raita sauce.

Hot Chicken Skin

Servings: 4
Cooking Time: 30 Minutes
Ingredients:
- ½ teaspoon chili paste
- 8 oz chicken skin
- 1 teaspoon sesame oil
- ½ teaspoon chili powder
- ½ teaspoon salt

Directions:
1. In the shallow bowl mix up chili paste, sesame oil, chili powder, and salt. Then brush the chicken skin with chili mixture well and leave for 10 minutes to marinate. Meanwhile, preheat the air fryer to 365°F. Put the marinated chicken skin in the air fryer and cook it for 20 minutes. When the time is finished, flip the chicken skin on another side and cook it for 10 minutes more or until the chicken skin is crunchy.

Lemon Whole Chicken

Servings: 2
Cooking Time: 28 Minutes
Ingredients:
- 1-pound whole chicken
- 1 lemon, juiced
- 1 teaspoon lemon zest
- 1 tablespoon soy sauce
- 1 ½ tablespoon honey

Directions:
1. Place all of the recipe ingredients in a suitable bowl and combine well. Refrigerate for 1 hour.
2. Put the marinated and seasoned chicken in the air fryer basket.
3. Air fry at 320 degrees F/ 160 degrees C for almost 18 minutes.
4. Raise the air fryer's heat to 350 degrees F/ 175 degrees C and cook for another 10 minutes or until chicken has turned light brown.
5. Serve.

Chicken And Veggies Salad

Servings: 2
Cooking Time: 12 Minutes
Ingredients:
- ½ pound chicken breasts, boneless and skinless
- 1 cup grape tomatoes, halved
- 1 Serrano pepper, deveined and chopped
- 2 bell peppers, deveined and chopped
- 2 tablespoons olives, pitted and sliced
- 1 cucumber, sliced
- 1 red onion, sliced
- 1 cup arugula
- 1 cup baby spinach
- ¼ cup mayonnaise
- 2 tablespoons Greek-style yogurt
- 1 teaspoon lime juice
- ¼ teaspoon oregano
- ¼ teaspoon basil
- ¼ teaspoon red pepper flakes, crushed
- Sea salt, to taste
- Ground black pepper, to taste

Directions:
1. Before cooking, heat your air fryer to 380 degrees F/ 195 degrees C.

2. Using a nonstick cooking oil, spray the chicken breasts.

3. Transfer the chicken breasts inside the air fryer basket.

4. Cook in your air fryer for 12 minutes.

5. When the cooking time is up, cool for a while and cut into strips.

6. In a salad bowl, add the chicken strips and the remaining ingredients. Then place in your refrigerator.

7. When ready, serve and enjoy!

Chicken Fillets With Lemon Pepper & Cheddar Cheese

Servings: 2
Cooking Time: 14 Minutes
Ingredients:
- 1 lemon pepper
- ¼ cup Cheddar cheese, shredded
- 8 oz. chicken fillets
- ½ teaspoon dried cilantro
- 1 teaspoon coconut oil, melted
- ¼ teaspoon smoked paprika

Directions:
1. Cut the lemon pepper into halves and remove the seeds.

2. Then cut the chicken fillet into 2 fillets.

3. Make the horizontal cuts in every chicken fillet.

4. Then sprinkle the chicken fillets with smoked paprika and dried cilantro. After this, fill them with lemon pepper halves and Cheddar cheese.

5. At 385 degrees F/ 195 degrees C, preheat your air fryer.

6. Put the chicken fillets in the preheated Air Fryer and sprinkle with melted coconut oil. Cook the chicken for 14 minutes.

7. Carefully transfer the chicken fillets in the serving plates.

8. Serve.

Chapter 8: Vegetable Side Dishes Recipes

Roasted Garlic

Servings: 20
Cooking Time: 40 Minutes
Ingredients:
- 20 Peeled medium garlic cloves
- 2 tablespoons, plus more Olive oil

Directions:
1. Preheat the air fryer to 400°F.
2. Set a 10-inch sheet of aluminum foil on your work surface for a small batch, a 14-inch sheet for a medium batch, or a 16-inch sheet for a large batch. Put the garlic cloves in its center in one layer without bunching the cloves together. Drizzle the small batch with 1 tablespoon oil, the medium batch with 2 tablespoons, or the large one with 3 tablespoons. Fold up the sides and seal the foil into a packet.
3. When the machine is at temperature, put the packet in the basket. Air-fry for 40 minutes, or until very fragrant. The cloves inside should be golden and soft.
4. Transfer the packet to a cutting board. Cool for 5 minutes, then open and use the cloves hot. Or cool them to room temperature, set them in a small container or jar, pour in enough olive oil to cover them, seal or cover the container, and refrigerate for up to 2 weeks.

Awesome Chicken Taquitos

Servings: 4
Cooking Time: 12 Minutes
Ingredients:
- 1 cup shredded mozzarella cheese
- ¼ cup salsa
- ¼ cup Greek yogurt
- Salt and black pepper
- 8 flour tortillas

Directions:
1. In a suitable bowl, mix chicken, cheese, salsa, sour cream, salt, and black pepper.
2. Spray 1 side of the tortilla with cooking spray.
3. Lay 2 tablespoon of the chicken mixture at the center of the non-oiled side the tortillas.
4. Roll tightly around the mixture. Arrange taquitos on your air fryer basket.
5. Cook for almost 12 minutes at 380 degrees F/ 195 degrees C.
6. Serve.

Flaky Biscuits

Servings:8
Cooking Time: 15 Minutes Per Batch
Ingredients:
- ¼ cup salted butter
- 2 cups self-rising flour
- ¼ teaspoon salt
- ⅔ cup whole milk

Directions:
1. Preheat the air fryer to 320°F. Cut parchment paper to fit the air fryer basket.
2. Place butter in the freezer 10 minutes. In a large bowl, mix flour and salt.

3. Grate butter into bowl and use a wooden spoon to evenly distribute. Add milk and stir until a soft dough forms.
4. Turn dough onto a lightly floured surface. Gently press and flatten dough until mostly smooth and uniform. Gently roll into an 8" × 10" rectangle. Use a sharp knife dusted in flour to cut dough into eight squares.
5. Place biscuits on parchment paper in the air fryer basket, working in batches as necessary, and cook 15 minutes until golden brown on the top and edges and feel firm to the touch. Let cool 5 minutes before serving.

Spiced Okra

Servings: 2
Cooking Time: 20 Minutes
Ingredients:
- ½ pound okra, ends trimmed and sliced
- 1 teaspoon olive oil
- ½ teaspoon mango powder
- ½ teaspoon chili powder
- ½ teaspoon ground coriander
- ½ teaspoon ground cumin
- ⅛ teaspoon black pepper
- ¼ teaspoon salt

Directions:
1. At 350 degrees F/ 175 degrees C, preheat your air fryer.
2. Add all the recipe ingredients into the suitable bowl and toss well.
3. Grease its air fryer basket with cooking spray.
4. Transfer okra mixture into the air fryer basket and cook for almost 10 minutes. Shake basket halfway through.
5. Toss okra well and cook for 2 minutes more.
6. Serve and enjoy.

Parmesan Zucchini Gratin

Servings: 2
Cooking Time: 15 Minutes
Ingredients:
- 5 ounces parmesan cheese, shredded
- 1 tablespoon coconut flour
- 1 tablespoon dried parsley
- 2 zucchinis
- 1 teaspoon butter, melted

Directions:
1. In a bowl, add the coconut flour and parmesan cheese together.
2. To season, add parsley.
3. Cut the zucchinis lengthwise in half and slice the halves into four slices.
4. Before cooking, heat your air fryer to 400 degrees F/ 205 degrees C.
5. Then coat the zucchinis with the melted butter and dip in the parmesan-flour mixture to thoroughly coat the zucchini slices.
6. Cook in your air fryer for 13 minutes.

Garlic Sautéed Artichokes

Servings: 4
Cooking Time: 15 Minutes
Ingredients:
- 10 ounces artichoke hearts, halved
- 3 garlic cloves
- 2 cups baby spinach
- ¼ cup veggie stock
- 2 teaspoons lime juice
- Black pepper and salt to the taste

Directions:
1. In a suitable pan that fits your air fryer, mix all the recipe ingredients, toss, introduce in the fryer and cook at almost 370 degrees F/ 185 degrees C for almost 15 minutes.
2. Divide the mixture between plates and serve as a side dish.

Lemon Tempeh

Servings: 4
Cooking Time: 12 Minutes
Ingredients:
- 1 teaspoon lemon juice
- 1 tablespoon sunflower oil
- ¼ teaspoon ground coriander
- 6 oz tempeh, chopped

Directions:
1. Sprinkle the tempeh with lemon juice, sunflower oil, and ground coriander. Massage the tempeh gently with the help of the fingertips. After this, preheat the air fryer to 325°F. Put the tempeh in the air fryer and cook it for 12 minutes. Flip the tempeh every 2 minutes during cooking.

Herbed Mushroom Pilau

Servings: 4
Cooking Time: 25 Minutes
Ingredients:
- 1 ½ cups cauliflower rice
- 3 cups vegetable broth
- 2 tbsps. olive oil
- 1 lb. fresh porcini mushrooms, sliced
- 2 tablespoons. olive oil
- 2 garlic cloves
- 1 onion, chopped
- ¼ cup dry vermouth
- 1 tsp. dried thyme
- ½ tsp. dried tarragon
- 1 tsp. sweet Hungarian paprika

Directions:
1. Lightly grease a suitable baking dish.
2. Mix all the ingredients in the dish until well combined.
3. Before cooking, heat your air fryer to 370 degrees F/ 185 degrees C.
4. Place the baking dish in your air fryer. Cook for 20 minutes.
5. Check periodically to make sure it is evenly cooked.

6. Serve your meal in bowls. Enjoy!

Turmeric Cauliflower Patties

Servings: 2
Cooking Time: 10 Minutes
Ingredients:
- ¼ cup cauliflower, shredded
- 1 egg yolk
- ½ teaspoon ground turmeric
- ¼ teaspoon onion powder
- ¼ teaspoon salt
- 2 ounces Cheddar cheese, shredded
- ¼ teaspoon baking powder
- 1 teaspoon heavy cream
- 1 tablespoon coconut flakes
- Cooking spray

Directions:
1. Squeeze the shredded cauliflower and put it in the bowl.
2. Add egg yolk, ground turmeric, baking powder, onion powder, heavy cream, salt, and coconut flakes.
3. Then melt Cheddar cheese and add it in the cauliflower mixture.
4. Stir the ingredients until you get the smooth mass.
5. After this, make the medium size cauliflower patties.
6. At 365 degrees F/ 185 degrees C, preheat your air fryer.
7. Grease its air fryer basket with cooking spray and put the patties inside.
8. Cook them for almost 5 minutes from each side.
9. Serve warm.

Balsamic Greens And Green Beans Medley

Servings: 4
Cooking Time: 12 Minutes
Ingredients:
- 1 bunch mustard greens, trimmed
- 1-pound green beans, halved
- 2 tablespoons olive oil
- ¼ cup keto tomato sauce
- 3 garlic cloves, minced
- Black pepper and salt to the taste
- 1 tablespoon balsamic vinegar

Directions:
1. In a suitable pan that fits your air fryer, mix the mustard greens with the rest of the ingredients, toss, put the pan in the air fryer and cook them together in your air fryer for 12 minutes at almost 350 degrees F/ 175 degrees C.
2. Divide everything between plates and serve.

Cayenne Chicken Wing Dip

Servings: 4
Cooking Time: 20 Minutes
Ingredients:
- 1 teaspoon cayenne pepper
- Salt to taste

- 2 tablespoon grapeseed oil
- 2 teaspoon chili flakes
- 1 cup heavy cream
- 3 ounces gorgonzola cheese, crumbled
- ½ lemon, juiced
- ½ teaspoon garlic powder

Directions:

1. At 380 degrees F/ 195 degrees C, preheat your air fryer.
2. Coat the chicken with cayenne pepper, salt, and oil.
3. Place in the basket and cook for 20 minutes. In a suitable bowl, mix heavy cream, gorgonzola cheese, lemon juice, and garlic powder.
4. Serve with chicken wings.

Rutabaga Fries

Servings: 4
Cooking Time: 20 Minutes
Ingredients:

- 15 ounces rutabaga, cut into fries
- 4 tablespoons olive oil
- ½ teaspoon chili powder
- A pinch of salt and black pepper

Directions:

1. Mix the rutabaga, olive oil, chili powder, salt, and black pepper in a bowl.
2. Transfer into your air fryer basket.
3. Cook the seasoned rutabaga in your air fryer at 400 degrees F/ 205 degrees C for 20 minutes.
4. Serve on plates as a side dish.

Spinach And Cheese-stuffed Mushrooms

Servings:4
Cooking Time: 10 Minutes
Ingredients:

- Olive oil
- 4 ounces reduced-fat cream cheese, softened
- ¾ cup shredded Italian blend cheese
- ¼ cup whole-wheat bread crumbs
- 1 egg
- ¼ teaspoon salt
- ¼ teaspoon freshly ground black pepper
- 1 cup fresh baby spinach, chopped
- 20 large mushrooms, stems removed

Directions:

1. Spray a fryer basket lightly with olive oil.
2. In a medium bowl, use an electric mixer to combine the cream cheese, Italian blend cheese, bread crumbs, egg, salt, and pepper.
3. Add the spinach and stir with a spoon to combine.
4. Spoon the mixture into each mushroom, pressing the mixture into the mushroom and leaving a little bit popping out of the top.
5. Place the stuffed mushrooms in a single layer in the fryer basket. Spray lightly with olive oil. You may need to cook these in more than one batch.

6. Air fry until the mushrooms have started to brown lightly and the cheese is lightly brown on top, 7 to 10 minutes.

Truffle Vegetable Croquettes

Servings: 4
Cooking Time: 40 Minutes
Ingredients:

- 2 cooked potatoes, mashed
- 1 cooked carrot, mashed
- 1 tbsp onion, minced
- 2 eggs, beaten
- 2 tbsp melted butter
- 1 tbsp truffle oil
- ½ tbsp flour
- Salt and pepper to taste

Directions:

1. Preheat air fryer to 350°F. Sift the flour, salt, and pepper in a bowl and stir to combine. Add the potatoes, carrot, onion, butter, and truffle oil to a separate bowl and mix well. Shape the potato mixture into small bite-sized patties. Dip the potato patties into the beaten eggs, coating thoroughly, then roll in the flour mixture to cover all sides. Arrange the croquettes in the greased frying basket and Air Fry for 14-16 minutes. Halfway through cooking, shake the basket. The croquettes should be crispy and golden. Serve hot and enjoy!

Grits Casserole

Servings: 4
Cooking Time: 30 Minutes
Ingredients:

- 10 fresh asparagus spears, cut into 1-inch pieces
- 2 cups cooked grits, cooled to room temperature
- 1 egg, beaten
- 2 teaspoons Worcestershire sauce
- ½ teaspoon garlic powder
- ¼ teaspoon salt
- 2 slices provolone cheese (about 1½ ounces)
- oil for misting or cooking spray

Directions:

1. Mist asparagus spears with oil and cook at 390°F for 5minutes, until crisp-tender.
2. In a medium bowl, mix together the grits, egg, Worcestershire, garlic powder, and salt.
3. Spoon half of grits mixture into air fryer baking pan and top with asparagus.
4. Tear cheese slices into pieces and layer evenly on top of asparagus.
5. Top with remaining grits.
6. Bake at 360°F for 25 minutes. The casserole will rise a little as it cooks. When done, the top will have browned lightly with just a hint of crispiness.

Roasted Garlic And Thyme Tomatoes

Servings: 2
Cooking Time: 15 Minutes
Ingredients:

- 4 Roma tomatoes
- 1 tablespoon olive oil

- salt and freshly ground black pepper
- 1 clove garlic, minced
- ½ teaspoon dried thyme

Directions:
1. Preheat the air fryer to 390°F.
2. Cut the tomatoes in half and scoop out the seeds and any pithy parts with your fingers. Place the tomatoes in a bowl and toss with the olive oil, salt, pepper, garlic and thyme.
3. Transfer the tomatoes to the air fryer, cut side up. Air-fry for 15 minutes. The edges should just start to brown. Let the tomatoes cool to an edible temperature for a few minutes and then use in pastas, on top of crostini, or as an accompaniment to any poultry, meat or fish.

Spicy Bean Stuffed Potatoes

Servings: 4
Cooking Time: 60 Minutes
Ingredients:
- 1 lb russet potatoes, scrubbed and perforated with a fork
- 1 can diced green chilies, including juice
- 1/3 cup grated Mexican cheese blend
- 1 green bell pepper, diced
- 1 yellow bell pepper, diced
- ¼ cup torn iceberg lettuce
- 2 tsp olive oil
- 2 tbsp sour cream
- ½ tsp chili powder
- 2-3 jalapeños, sliced
- 1 red bell pepper, chopped
- Salt and pepper to taste
- 1/3 cup canned black beans
- 4 grape tomatoes, sliced
- ¼ cup chopped parsley

Directions:
1. Preheat air fryer at 400°F. Brush olive oil over potatoes. Place them in the frying basket and Bake for 45 minutes, turning at 30 minutes mark. Let cool on a cutting board for 10 minutes until cool enough to handle. Slice each potato lengthwise and scoop out all but a ¼" layer of potato to form 4 boats.
2. Mash potato flesh, sour cream, green chilies, cheese, chili powder, jalapeños, green, yellow, and red peppers, salt, and pepper in a bowl until smooth. Fold in black beans. Divide between potato skin boats. Place potato boats in the frying basket and Bake for 2 minutes. Remove them to a serving plate. Top each boat with lettuce, tomatoes, and parsley. Sprinkle tops with salt and serve.

Garlic Cauliflower & Broccoli

Servings: 6
Cooking Time: 12 Minutes
Ingredients:
- 3 cups cauliflower florets
- 3 cups broccoli florets
- ¼ teaspoon paprika
- ½ teaspoon garlic powder

- 2 tablespoons olive oil
- ⅛ teaspoon black pepper
- ¼ teaspoon salt

Directions:
1. At 400 degrees F/ 205 degrees C, preheat your Air fryer.
2. Add broccoli in microwave-safe bowl and microwave for 3 minutes. Drain well.
3. Add broccoli in a suitable mixing bowl. Add remaining ingredients and toss well.
4. Transfer broccoli and cauliflower mixture into the air fryer basket and cook for 12 minutes.
5. Toss halfway through.
6. Serve and enjoy.

Radishes And Green Onions Mix

Servings: 4
Cooking Time: 15 Minutes
Ingredients:
- 20 radishes, halved
- 1 tablespoon olive oil
- 3 green onions, chopped
- Black pepper and salt to the taste
- 3 teaspoons black sesame seeds
- 2 tablespoons olive oil

Directions:
1. In a suitable bowl, mix all the recipe ingredients and toss well.
2. Put the radishes in your air fryer basket, Cook at almost 400 degrees F/ 205 degrees C for almost 15 minutes.
3. Serve.

Black Bean And Tomato Chili

Servings:6
Cooking Time: 23 Minutes
Ingredients:
- 1 tablespoon olive oil
- 1 medium onion, diced
- 3 garlic cloves, minced
- 1 cup vegetable broth
- 3 cans black beans, drained and rinsed
- 2 cans diced tomatoes
- 2 chipotle peppers, chopped
- 2 teaspoons cumin
- 2 teaspoons chili powder
- 1 teaspoon dried oregano
- ½ teaspoon salt

Directions:
1. Over a medium heat, fry the garlic and onions in the olive oil for 3 minutes.
2. Add the remaining ingredients, stirring constantly and scraping the bottom to prevent sticking.
3. Preheat the air fryer to 400°F (204°C).
4. Take a dish and place the mixture inside. Put a sheet of aluminum foil on top.
5. Transfer to the air fryer and bake for 20 minutes.
6. When ready, plate up and serve immediately.

Caraway Seed Pretzel Sticks

Servings: 4
Cooking Time: 30 Minutes
Ingredients:
- ½ pizza dough
- 1 tsp baking soda
- 2 tbsp caraway seeds
- 1 cup of hot water
- Cooking spray

Directions:
1. Preheat air fryer to 400°F. Roll out the dough, on parchment paper, into a rectangle, then cut it into 8 strips. Whisk the baking soda and 1 cup of hot water until well dissolved in a bowl. Submerge each strip, shake off any excess, and stretch another 1 to 2 inches. Scatter with caraway seeds and let rise for 10 minutes in the frying basket. Grease with cooking spray and Air Fry for 8 minutes until golden brown, turning once. Serve.

Sesame Taj Tofu

Servings:4
Cooking Time: 25 Minutes
Ingredients:
- 1 block firm tofu, pressed and cut into 1-inch thick cubes
- 2 tablespoons soy sauce
- 2 teaspoons toasted sesame seeds
- 1 teaspoon rice vinegar
- 1 tablespoon cornstarch

Directions:
1. Preheat the air fryer to 400ºF (204ºC).
2. Add the tofu, soy sauce, sesame seeds, and rice vinegar in a bowl together and mix well to coat the tofu cubes. Then cover the tofu in cornstarch and put it in the air fryer basket.
3. Air fry for 25 minutes, giving the basket a shake at five-minute intervals to ensure the tofu cooks evenly.
4. Serve immediately.

Spicy Fried Green Beans

Servings: 2
Cooking Time: 8 Minutes
Ingredients:
- 12 ounces green beans, trimmed
- 2 small dried hot red chili peppers (like árbol)
- ¼ cup panko breadcrumbs
- 1 tablespoon olive oil
- ½ teaspoon salt
- ⅛ teaspoon crushed red pepper flakes
- 2 scallions, thinly sliced

Directions:
1. Preheat the air fryer to 400°F.
2. Toss the green beans, chili peppers and panko breadcrumbs with the olive oil, salt and crushed red pepper flakes.
3. Air-fry for 8 minutes, shaking the basket once during the cooking process. The crumbs will fall into the bottom drawer – don't worry.

4. Transfer the green beans to a serving dish, sprinkle the scallions and the toasted crumbs from the air fryer drawer on top and serve. The dried peppers are not to be eaten, but they do look nice with the green beans. You can leave them in, or take them out as you please.

Black Bean Burgers

Servings:4
Cooking Time: 10 Minutes
Ingredients:
- 1 can black beans, drained and rinsed
- ½ cup diced yellow onion
- 1 medium red bell pepper, seeded and diced
- 1 large egg
- ½ cup plain bread crumbs
- ½ teaspoon salt
- ¼ teaspoon ground black pepper

Directions:
1. Preheat the air fryer to 370°F.
2. In a large bowl, add black beans and use a paper towel to pat dry and remove as much excess moisture as possible. Use a fork to mash until beans are mostly broken down.
3. Mix in onion, bell pepper, egg, bread crumbs, salt, and black pepper. Fold until well combined.
4. Separate mixture into four portions, then form each into a patty about ½" thick. Spritz both sides of each patty with cooking spray.
5. Place in the air fryer basket and cook 10 minutes, turning halfway through cooking time, until burgers are firm and hold together. Serve warm.

Loaded Sweet Potatoes

Servings: 4
Cooking Time: 40 Minutes
Ingredients:
- 4 sweet potatoes
- 2 tablespoons butter
- 2 tablespoons honey
- 1 teaspoon cinnamon
- ½ teaspoon vanilla extract

Directions:
1. Using a fork, poke three holes in the top of each sweet potato.
2. Place the sweet potatoes in the air fryer. Cook for 40 minutes.
3. Meanwhile, in a small, microwave-safe bowl, melt the butter and honey together in the microwave for 15 to 20 seconds.
4. Remove the bowl from the microwave. Add the cinnamon and vanilla extract to the butter and honey mixture, and stir.
5. Remove the cooked sweet potatoes from the air fryer and allow them to cool for 5 minutes.
6. Cut open each sweet potato. Drizzle the butter mixture over each, and serve.

Spinach Salad With Mustard

Servings: 4
Cooking Time: 10 Minutes
Ingredients:
- 1 pound baby spinach
- Salt and black pepper to the taste
- 1 tablespoon mustard
- Cooking spray
- ¼ cup apple cider vinegar
- 1 tablespoon chives, chopped

Directions:
1. Spray a suitable baking pan with cooking spray.
2. In the pan, combine the baby spinach, salt, black pepper, mustard, apple cider vinegar, and the chopped chives together.
3. Cook in your air fryer at 350 degrees F/ 175 degrees C for 10 minutes.
4. Serve on plates as a side dish.

Bean-mushroom Casserole

Servings: 6
Cooking Time: 15 Minutes
Ingredients:
- 2 cups mushrooms, sliced
- 1 teaspoon onion powder
- ½ teaspoon ground sage
- ½ tablespoon garlic powder
- 1 fresh lemon juice
- 1 ½ pounds green beans, trimmed
- ¼ teaspoon black pepper
- ½ teaspoon salt

Directions:
1. In a suitable mixing bowl, toss together green beans, onion powder, sage, garlic powder, lemon juice, mushrooms, black pepper, and salt.
2. Grease its air fryer basket with cooking spray.
3. Transfer green bean mixture into the air fryer basket.
4. Cook for almost 10-12 minutes at 400 degrees F/ 205 degrees C. Shake after every 3 minutes.
5. Serve and enjoy.

Buttery Stuffed Tomatoes

Servings: 6
Cooking Time: 15 Minutes
Ingredients:
- 3 8-ounce round tomatoes
- ½ cup plus 1 tablespoon Plain panko bread crumbs (gluten-free, if a concern)
- 3 tablespoons (about ½ ounce) Finely grated Parmesan cheese
- 3 tablespoons Butter, melted and cooled
- 4 teaspoons Stemmed and chopped fresh parsley leaves
- 1 teaspoon Minced garlic
- ¼ teaspoon Table salt
- Up to ¼ teaspoon Red pepper flakes
- Olive oil spray

Directions:

1. Preheat the air fryer to 375°F .
2. Cut the tomatoes in half through their "equators" (that is, not through the stem ends). One at a time, gently squeeze the tomato halves over a trash can, using a clean finger to gently force out the seeds and most of the juice inside, working carefully so that the tomato doesn't lose its round shape or get crushed.
3. Stir the bread crumbs, cheese, butter, parsley, garlic, salt, and red pepper flakes in a bowl until the bread crumbs are moistened and the parsley is uniform throughout the mixture. Pile this mixture into the spaces left in the tomato halves. Press gently to compact the filling. Coat the tops of the tomatoes with olive oil spray.
4. Place the tomatoes cut side up in the basket. They may touch each other. Air-fry for 15 minutes, or until the filling is lightly browned and crunchy.
5. Use nonstick-safe spatula and kitchen tongs for balance to gently transfer the stuffed tomatoes to a platter or a cutting board. Cool for a couple of minutes before serving.

Carrot Chips

Servings:4
Cooking Time: 10 Minutes
Ingredients:
- 1 tablespoon olive oil plus more for spraying
- 4 to 5 medium carrots, trimmed
- 1 teaspoon seasoned salt

Directions:
1. Spray a fryer basket lightly with olive oil.
2. Using a mandolin slicer set to the smallest setting or a sharp knife, cut the carrots into very thin slices.
3. In a medium bowl, toss the carrot slices with 1 tablespoon of olive oil and the seasoned salt.
4. Put half the carrots the fryer basket. Do not overcrowd the basket.
5. Air fry for 5 minutes. Shake the basket and cook until crispy, 3 to 5 additional minutes. The longer you cook the carrot slices, the crispier they will become. Watch closely because smaller slices could burn.
6. Repeat with the remaining carrots.

Glazed Carrots

Servings: 4
Cooking Time: 10 Minutes
Ingredients:
- 2 teaspoons honey
- 1 teaspoon orange juice
- ½ teaspoon grated orange rind
- ⅛ teaspoon ginger
- 1 pound baby carrots
- 2 teaspoons olive oil
- ¼ teaspoon salt

Directions:
1. Combine honey, orange juice, grated rind, and ginger in a small bowl and set aside.
2. Toss the carrots, oil, and salt together to coat well and pour them into the air fryer basket.

3. Cook at 390°F for 5minutes. Shake basket to stir a little and cook for 4 minutes more, until carrots are barely tender.
4. Pour carrots into air fryer baking pan.
5. Stir the honey mixture to combine well, pour glaze over carrots, and stir to coat.
6. Cook at 360°F for 1 minute or just until heated through.

Buttered Brussels Sprouts

Servings: 4
Cooking Time: 30 Minutes
Ingredients:
- ¼ cup grated Parmesan
- 2 tbsp butter, melted
- 1 lb Brussels sprouts
- Salt and pepper to taste

Directions:
1. Preheat air fryer to 330°F. Trim the bottoms of the sprouts and remove any discolored leaves. Place the sprouts in a medium bowl along with butter, salt and pepper. Toss to coat, then place them in the frying basket. Roast for 20 minutes, shaking the basket twice. When done, the sprouts should be crisp with golden-brown color. Plate the sprouts in a serving dish and toss with Parmesan cheese.

Homemade Potato Puffs

Servings: 4
Cooking Time: 15 Minutes
Ingredients:
- 1¾ cups Water
- 4 tablespoons (¼ cup/½ stick) Butter
- 2 cups plus 2 tablespoons Instant mashed potato flakes
- 1½ teaspoons Table salt
- ¾ teaspoon Ground black pepper
- ¼ teaspoon Mild paprika
- ¼ teaspoon Dried thyme
- 1¼ cups Seasoned Italian-style dried bread crumbs (gluten-free, if a concern)
- Olive oil spray

Directions:
1. Heat the water with the butter in a medium saucepan set over medium-low heat just until the butter melts. Do not bring to a boil.
2. Remove the saucepan from the heat and stir in the potato flakes, salt, pepper, paprika, and thyme until smooth. Set aside to cool for 5 minutes.
3. Preheat the air fryer to 400°F. Spread the bread crumbs on a dinner plate.
4. Scrape up 2 tablespoons of the potato flake mixture and form it into a small, oblong puff, like a little cylinder about 1½ inches long. Gently roll the puff in the bread crumbs until coated on all sides. Set it aside and continue making more, about 12 for the small batch, 18 for the medium batch, or 24 for the large.

5. Coat the potato cylinders with olive oil spray on all sides, then arrange them in the basket in one layer with some air space between them. Air-fry undisturbed for 15 minutes, or until crisp and brown.
6. Gently dump the contents of the basket onto a wire rack. Cool for 5 minutes before serving.

Blistered Tomatoes

Servings: 20
Cooking Time: 15 Minutes
Ingredients:
- 1½ pounds Cherry or grape tomatoes
- Olive oil spray
- 1½ teaspoons Balsamic vinegar
- ¼ teaspoon Table salt
- ¼ teaspoon Ground black pepper

Directions:
1. Put the basket in a drawer-style air fryer, or a baking tray in the lower third of a toaster oven–style air fryer. Place a 6-inch round cake pan in the basket or on the tray for a small batch, a 7-inch round cake pan for a medium batch, or an 8-inch round cake pan for a large one. Heat the air fryer to 400°F with the pan in the basket. When the machine is at temperature, keep heating the pan for 5 minutes more.
2. Place the tomatoes in a large bowl, coat them with the olive oil spray, toss gently, then spritz a couple of times more, tossing after each spritz, until the tomatoes are glistening.
3. Pour the tomatoes into the cake pan and air-fry undisturbed for 10 minutes, or until they split and begin to brown.
4. Use kitchen tongs and a nonstick-safe spatula, or silicone baking mitts, to remove the cake pan from the basket. Toss the hot tomatoes with the vinegar, salt, and pepper. Cool in the pan for a few minutes before serving.

Potato And Broccoli With Tofu Scramble

Servings:3
Cooking Time: 30 Minutes
Ingredients:
- 2½ cups chopped red potato
- 2 tablespoons olive oil, divided
- 1 block tofu, chopped finely
- 2 tablespoons tamari
- 1 teaspoon turmeric powder
- ½ teaspoon onion powder
- ½ teaspoon garlic powder
- ½ cup chopped onion
- 4 cups broccoli florets

Directions:
1. Preheat the air fryer to 400ºF (204ºC).
2. Toss together the potatoes and 1 tablespoon of the olive oil.
3. Air fry the potatoes in a baking dish for 15 minutes, shaking once during the cooking time to ensure they fry evenly.

4. Combine the tofu, the remaining 1 tablespoon of the olive oil, turmeric, onion powder, tamari, and garlic powder together, stirring in the onions, followed by the broccoli.

5. Top the potatoes with the tofu mixture and air fry for an additional 15 minutes. Serve warm.

Mediterranean Roasted Vegetables

Servings: 4
Cooking Time: 30 Minutes
Ingredients:
- 1 red bell pepper, cut into chunks
- 1 cup sliced mushrooms
- 1 cup green beans, diced
- 1 zucchini, sliced
- 1/3 cup diced red onion
- 3 garlic cloves, sliced
- 2 tbsp olive oil
- 1 tsp rosemary
- ½ tsp flaked sea salt

Directions:
1. Preheat air fryer to 350°F. Add the bell pepper, mushrooms, green beans, red onion, zucchini, rosemary, and garlic to a bowl and mix, then spritz with olive oil. Stir until well-coated. Put the veggies in the frying basket and Air Fry for 14-18 minutes. The veggies should be soft and crispy. Serve sprinkled with flaked sea salt.

Fried Cauliflowerwith Parmesan Lemon Dressing

Servings: 2
Cooking Time: 12 Minutes
Ingredients:
- 4 cups cauliflower florets (about half a large head)
- 1 tablespoon olive oil
- salt and freshly ground black pepper
- 1 teaspoon finely chopped lemon zest
- 1 tablespoon fresh lemon juice (about half a lemon)
- ¼ cup grated Parmigiano-Reggiano cheese
- 4 tablespoons extra virgin olive oil
- ¼ teaspoon salt
- lots of freshly ground black pepper
- 1 tablespoon chopped fresh parsley

Directions:
1. Preheat the air fryer to 400°F.
2. Toss the cauliflower florets with the olive oil, salt and freshly ground black pepper. Air-fry for 12 minutes, shaking the basket a couple of times during the cooking process.
3. While the cauliflower is frying, make the dressing. Combine the lemon zest, lemon juice, Parmigiano-Reggiano cheese and olive oil in a small bowl. Season with salt and lots of freshly ground black pepper. Stir in the parsley.
4. Turn the fried cauliflower out onto a serving platter and drizzle the dressing over the top.

Potatoes With Zucchinis

Servings:4
Cooking Time: 45 Minutes
Ingredients:
- 2 potatoes, peeled and cubed
- 4 carrots, cut into chunks
- 1 head broccoli, cut into florets
- 4 zucchinis, sliced thickly
- Salt and ground black pepper, to taste
- ¼ cup olive oil
- 1 tablespoon dry onion powder

Directions:
1. Preheat the air fryer to 400ºF (204ºC).
2. In a baking dish, add all the ingredients and combine well.
3. Bake for 45 minutes in the air fryer, ensuring the vegetables are soft and the sides have browned before serving.

Roasted Bell Peppers

Servings: 3
Cooking Time: 8 Minutes
Ingredients:
- 3 ½ cups bell peppers, cut into chunks
- Black pepper
- Salt

Directions:
1. Grease its air fryer basket with cooking spray.
2. Add bell peppers into the air fryer basket and cook at almost 360 degrees F/ 180 degrees C for 8 minutes.
3. Season bell peppers with black pepper and salt.
4. Serve and enjoy.

Spicy Fries

Servings:4
Cooking Time: 20 Minutes
Ingredients:
- 2 tsp olive oil
- 2 tsp cayenne pepper
- 1 tsp paprika
- Salt and black pepper

Directions:
1. Place the fries into a bowl and sprinkle with oil, cayenne, paprika, salt, and black pepper. Toss and place them in the fryer. Cook for 7 minutes at 360ºF, until golden and crispy. Give it a toss after 7-8 minutes and continue cooking for another 8 minutes. Serve.

Breaded Artichoke Hearts

Servings: 2
Cooking Time: 25 Minutes
Ingredients:
- 1 can artichoke hearts in water, drained
- 1 egg
- ¼ cup bread crumbs
- ¼ tsp salt
- ¼ tsp hot paprika
- ½ lemon

- ¼ cup garlic aioli

Directions:
1. Preheat air fryer to 380°F. Whisk together the egg and 1 tbsp of water in a bowl until frothy. Mix together the bread crumbs, salt, and hot paprika in a separate bowl. Dip the artichoke hearts into the egg mixture, then coat in the bread crumb mixture. Put the artichoke hearts in a single layer in the frying basket. Air Fry for 15 minutes.
2. Remove the artichokes from the air fryer, and squeeze fresh lemon juice over the top. Serve with garlic aioli.

Cauliflower Bake With Basil Pesto
Servings: 6
Cooking Time: 20 Minutes
Ingredients:
- 1 cup heavy whipping cream
- 2 tablespoons basil pesto
- Salt and black pepper to the taste
- Juice of ½ lemon
- 1 pound cauliflower, florets separated
- 4 ounces cherry tomatoes, halved
- 3 tablespoons ghee, melted
- 7 ounces cheddar cheese, grated

Directions:
1. Drizzle a suitable baking pan with ghee.
2. Gently toss together the lemon juice, pesto, cream, and the cauliflower in the pan.
3. Add the tomatoes and cover the top with cheese.
4. Cook in your air fryer at 380 degrees F/ 195 degrees C for 20 minutes.
5. Serve on plates as a side dish.

Latkes
Servings: 12
Cooking Time: 13 Minutes
Ingredients:
- 1 russet potato
- ¼ onion
- 2 eggs, lightly beaten
- ⅓ cup flour*
- ½ teaspoon baking powder
- 1 teaspoon salt
- freshly ground black pepper
- canola or vegetable oil, in a spray bottle
- chopped chives, for garnish
- apple sauce
- sour cream

Directions:
1. Shred the potato and onion with a coarse box grater or a food processor with the shredding blade. Place the shredded vegetables into a colander or mesh strainer and squeeze or press down firmly to remove the excess water.
2. Transfer the onion and potato to a large bowl and add the eggs, flour, baking powder, salt and black pepper. Mix to combine and then shape the mixture into patties, about ¼-cup of mixture each. Brush or spray both sides of the latkes with oil.
3. Preheat the air fryer to 400°F.

4. Air-fry the latkes in batches. Transfer one layer of the latkes to the air fryer basket and air-fry at 400°F for 12 to 13 minutes, flipping them over halfway through the cooking time. Transfer the finished latkes to a platter and cover with aluminum foil, or place them in a warm oven to keep warm.
5. Garnish the latkes with chopped chives and serve with sour cream and applesauce.

Parmesan Asparagus
Servings: 2
Cooking Time: 5 Minutes
Ingredients:
- 1 bunch asparagus, stems trimmed
- 1 teaspoon olive oil
- salt and freshly ground black pepper
- ¼ cup coarsely grated Parmesan cheese
- ½ lemon

Directions:
1. Preheat the air fryer to 400°F.
2. Toss the asparagus with the oil and season with salt and freshly ground black pepper.
3. Transfer the asparagus to the air fryer basket and air-fry at 400°F for 5 minutes, shaking the basket to turn the asparagus once or twice during the cooking process.
4. When the asparagus is cooked to your liking, sprinkle the asparagus generously with the Parmesan cheese and close the air fryer drawer again. Let the asparagus sit for 1 minute in the turned-off air fryer. Then, remove the asparagus, transfer it to a serving dish and finish with a grind of black pepper and a squeeze of lemon juice.

Super Veg Rolls
Servings:6
Cooking Time: 10 Minutes
Ingredients:
- 2 potatoes, mashed
- ¼ cup peas
- ¼ cup mashed carrots
- 1 small cabbage, sliced
- ¼ cups beans
- 2 tablespoons sweetcorn
- 1 small onion, chopped
- ½ cup bread crumbs
- 1 packet spring roll sheets
- ½ cup cornstarch slurry

Directions:
1. Preheat the air fryer to 390ºF (199ºC).
2. Boil all the vegetables in water over a low heat. Rinse and allow to dry.
3. Unroll the spring roll sheets and spoon equal amounts of vegetable onto the center of each one. Fold into spring rolls and coat each one with the slurry and bread crumbs.
4. Air fry the rolls in the preheated air fryer for 10 minutes.
5. Serve warm.

Cheesy Potato Skins

Servings: 6
Cooking Time: 54 Minutes
Ingredients:
- 3 6- to 8-ounce small russet potatoes
- 3 Thick-cut bacon strips, halved widthwise (gluten-free, if a concern)
- ¾ teaspoon Mild paprika
- ¼ teaspoon Garlic powder
- ¼ teaspoon Table salt
- ¼ teaspoon Ground black pepper
- ½ cup plus 1 tablespoon (a little over 2 ounces) Shredded Cheddar cheese
- 3 tablespoons Thinly sliced trimmed chives
- 6 tablespoons (a little over 1 ounce) Finely grated Parmesan cheese

Directions:
1. Preheat the air fryer to 375°F .
2. Prick each potato in four places with a fork (not four places in a line but four places all around the potato). Set the potatoes in the basket with as much air space between them as possible. Air-fry undisturbed for 45 minutes, or until the potatoes are tender when pricked with a fork.
3. Use kitchen tongs to gently transfer the potatoes to a wire rack. Cool for 15 minutes. Maintain the machine's temperature.
4. Lay the bacon strip halves in the basket in one layer. They may touch but should not overlap. Air-fry undisturbed for 5 minutes, until crisp. Use those same tongs to transfer the bacon pieces to the wire rack. If there's a great deal of rendered bacon fat in the basket's bottom or on a tray under the basket attachment, pour this into a bowl, cool, and discard. Don't throw it down the drain!
5. Cut the potatoes in half lengthwise (not just slit them open but actually cut in half). Use a flatware spoon to scoop the hot, soft middles into a bowl, leaving ½ inch of potato all around the inside of the spud next to the skin. Sprinkle the inside of the potato "shells" evenly with paprika, garlic powder, salt, and pepper.
6. Chop the bacon pieces into small bits. Sprinkle these along with the Cheddar and chives evenly inside the potato shells. Crumble 2 to 3 tablespoons of the soft potato insides over the filling mixture. Divide the grated Parmesan evenly over the tops of the potatoes.
7. Set the stuffed potatoes in the basket with as much air space between them as possible. Air-fry undisturbed for 4 minutes, until the cheese melts and lightly browns.
8. Use kitchen tongs to gently transfer the stuffed potato halves to a wire rack. Cool for 5 minutes before serving.

Roasted Butternut Squash With Cranberries

Servings: 6
Cooking Time: 35 Minutes
Ingredients:
- 4 cups butternut squash, diced
- ¼ cup dried cranberries
- 3 garlic cloves, minced
- 1 tablespoon soy sauce
- 1 tablespoon balsamic vinegar
- 1 tablespoon olive oil
- 8 ounces mushrooms, quartered
- 1 cup green onions, sliced

Directions:
1. In a suitable mixing bowl, mix together squash, mushrooms, and green onion and set aside.
2. In a suitable bowl, whisk together oil, garlic, vinegar, and soy sauce.
3. Pour oil mixture over squash and toss to coat.
4. Grease its air fryer basket with cooking spray.
5. Add squash mixture into the air fryer basket and cook for 30-35 minutes at 400 degrees F/ 205 degrees C. Shake after every 5 minutes.
6. Toss with cranberries and serve hot.

Flavorful Radish Salad

Servings: 4
Cooking Time: 30 Minutes
Ingredients:
- 1 ½ pounds radishes, trimmed and halved
- 2 tablespoons olive oil
- Pepper and salt, as needed
- For the Salad:
- 1 teaspoon olive oil
- 1 tablespoon balsamic vinegar
- ½ pound mozzarella, sliced
- 1 teaspoon honey
- Pepper and salt, as needed

Directions:
1. Mix thoroughly the salt, black pepper, oil, and the radishes in medium sized bowl.
2. On a flat kitchen surface, plug your air fryer and turn it on.
3. Before cooking, heat your air fryer to 350 degrees F/ 175 degrees C for 4 to 5 minutes.
4. Place the mixture onto the air fryer basket.
5. Cook in your air fryer for 3 minutes.
6. In another medium sized bowl, mix thoroughly the cheese and fried radish.
7. Mix the remaining ingredients in a small bowl. Drizzle over the salad to serve.

Tasty Cauliflower Croquettes

Servings: 4
Cooking Time: 20 Minutes
Ingredients:
- 1 pound cauliflower florets
- 2 eggs
- 1 tablespoon olive oil
- 2 tablespoons scallions, chopped
- 1 garlic clove, minced
- 1 cup Colby cheese, shredded
- ½ cup parmesan cheese, grated

- Salt and black pepper, to taste
- ¼ teaspoon dried dill weed
- 1 teaspoon paprika

Directions:

1. Bring the salted water in a pot and blanch the cauliflower florets until al dente, for about 3 to 4 minutes. Drain well and pulse in a food processor.
2. Add the remaining ingredients; mix to combine well. Shape the cauliflower mixture into bite-sized tots.
3. At 375 degrees F/ 190 degrees C, heat your air fryer in advance.
4. Grease its air fryer basket with cooking spray.
5. Cook the cauliflower croquettes in the preheated air fryer for almost 16 minutes, shaking halfway through the cooking time. Serve with your favorite sauce for dipping. Serve!

Honey-roasted Parsnips

Servings: 3
Cooking Time: 23 Minutes
Ingredients:

- 1½ pounds Medium parsnips, peeled
- Olive oil spray
- 1 tablespoon Honey
- 1½ teaspoons Water
- ¼ teaspoon Table salt

Directions:

1. Preheat the air fryer to 350°F .
2. If the thick end of a parsnip is more than ½ inch in diameter, cut the parsnip just below where it swells to its large end, then slice the large section in half lengthwise. If the parsnips are larger than the basket, trim off the thin end so the parsnips will fit. Generously coat the parsnips on all sides with olive oil spray.
3. When the machine is at temperature, set the parsnips in the basket with as much air space between them as possible. Air-fry undisturbed for 20 minutes.
4. Whisk the honey, water, and salt in a small bowl until smooth. Brush this mixture over the parsnips. Air-fry undisturbed for 3 minutes more, or until the glaze is lightly browned.
5. Use kitchen tongs to transfer the parsnips to a wire rack or a serving platter. Cool for a couple of minutes before serving.

Sweet Potato Puffs

Servings: 18
Cooking Time: 35 Minutes
Ingredients:

- 3 8- to 10-ounce sweet potatoes
- 1 cup Seasoned Italian-style dried bread crumbs
- 3 tablespoons All-purpose flour
- 3 tablespoons Instant mashed potato flakes
- ¾ teaspoon Onion powder
- ¾ teaspoon Table salt
- Olive oil spray

Directions:

1. Preheat the air fryer to 350°F .
2. Prick the sweet potatoes in four or five different places with the tines of a flatware fork.
3. When the machine is at temperature, set the sweet potatoes in the basket with as much air space between them as possible. Air-fry undisturbed for 20 minutes.
4. Use kitchen tongs to transfer the sweet potatoes to a wire rack. Cool for 10 to 15 minutes. Meanwhile, increase the machine's temperature to 400°F. Spread the bread crumbs on a dinner plate.
5. Peel the sweet potatoes. Shred them through the large holes of a box grater into a large bowl. Stir in the flour, potato flakes, onion powder, and salt until well combined.
6. Scoop up 2 tablespoons of the sweet potato mixture. Form it into a small puff, a cylinder about like a Tater Tot. Set this cylinder in the bread crumbs. Gently roll it around to coat on all sides, even the ends. Set aside on a cutting board and continue making more puffs: 11 more for a small batch, 17 more for a medium batch, or 23 more for a large batch.
7. Generously coat the puffs with olive oil spray on all sides. Set the puffs in the basket with as much air space between them as possible. They should not be touching, but even a fraction of an inch will work well. Air-fry undisturbed for 15 minutes, or until lightly browned and crunchy.
8. Gently turn the contents of the basket out onto a wire rack. Cool the puffs for a couple of minutes before serving.

Chapter 9: Vegetarians Recipes

Tortilla Pizza Margherita

Servings: 1
Cooking Time: 15 Minutes
Ingredients:
- 1 flour tortilla
- ¼ cup tomato sauce
- 1/3 cup grated mozzarella
- 3 basil leaves

Directions:
1. Preheat air fryer to 350°F. Put the tortilla in the greased basket and pour the sauce in the center. Spread across the whole tortilla. Sprinkle with cheese and Bake for 8-10 minutes or until crisp. Remove carefully and top with basil leaves. Serve hot.

Spicy Celery Sticks

Servings: 4
Cooking Time: 20 Minutes
Ingredients:
- 1 pound celery, cut into matchsticks
- 2 tablespoons peanut oil
- 1 jalapeño, seeded and minced
- 1/4 teaspoon dill
- 1/2 teaspoon basil
- Salt and white pepper to taste

Directions:
1. Start by preheating your Air Fryer to 380°F.
2. Toss all ingredients together and place them in the Air Fryer basket.
3. Cook for 15 minutes, shaking the basket halfway through the cooking time. Transfer to a serving platter and enjoy!

Spicy Bean Patties

Servings: 4
Cooking Time: 20 Minutes
Ingredients:
- 1 cup canned black beans
- 1 bread slice, torn
- 2 tbsp spicy brown mustard
- 1 tbsp chili powder
- 1 egg white
- 2 tbsp grated carrots
- ¼ diced green bell pepper
- 1-2 jalapeño peppers, diced
- ¼ tsp ground cumin
- ¼ tsp smoked paprika
- 2 tbsp cream cheese
- 1 tbsp olive oil

Directions:
1. Preheat air fryer at 350°F. Using a fork, mash beans until smooth. Stir in the remaining ingredients, except olive oil. Form mixture into 4 patties. Place bean patties in the greased frying basket and Air Fry for 6 minutes, turning once, and brush with olive oil. Serve immediately.

Basil Tomatoes

Servings:2
Cooking Time:10 Minutes
Ingredients:
- 2 tomatoes, halved
- 1 tablespoon fresh basil, chopped
- Olive oil cooking spray
- Salt and black pepper, as required

Directions:
1. Preheat the Air fryer to 320°F and grease an Air fryer basket.
2. Spray the tomato halves evenly with olive oil cooking spray and season with salt, black pepper and basil.
3. Arrange the tomato halves into the Air fryer basket, cut sides up.
4. Cook for about 10 minutes and dish out onto serving plates.

Spaghetti Squash And Kale Fritters With Pomodoro Sauce

Servings: 3
Cooking Time: 45 Minutes
Ingredients:
- 1½-pound spaghetti squash (about half a large or a whole small squash)
- olive oil
- ½ onion, diced
- ½ red bell pepper, diced
- 2 cloves garlic, minced
- 4 cups coarsely chopped kale
- salt and freshly ground black pepper
- 1 egg
- ⅓ cup breadcrumbs, divided*
- ⅓ cup grated Parmesan cheese
- ½ teaspoon dried rubbed sage
- pinch nutmeg
- Pomodoro Sauce:
- 2 tablespoons olive oil
- ½ onion, chopped
- 1 to 2 cloves garlic, minced
- 1 (28-ounce) can peeled tomatoes
- ¼ cup red wine
- 1 teaspoon Italian seasoning
- 2 tablespoons chopped fresh basil, plus more for garnish
- salt and freshly ground black pepper
- ½ teaspoon sugar (optional)

Directions:
1. Preheat the air fryer to 370°F.
2. Cut the spaghetti squash in half lengthwise and remove the seeds. Rub the inside of the squash with olive oil and season with salt and pepper. Place the squash, cut side up, into the air fryer basket and air-fry for 30 minutes, flipping the squash over halfway through the cooking process.

3. While the squash is cooking, Preheat a large sauté pan over medium heat on the stovetop. Add a little olive oil and sauté the onions for 3 minutes, until they start to soften. Add the red pepper and garlic and continue to sauté for an additional 4 minutes. Add the kale and season with salt and pepper. Cook for 2 more minutes, or until the kale is soft. Transfer the mixture to a large bowl and let it cool.

4. While the squash continues to cook, make the Pomodoro sauce. Preheat the large sauté pan again over medium heat on the stovetop. Add the olive oil and sauté the onion and garlic for 2 to 3 minutes, until the onion begins to soften. Crush the canned tomatoes with your hands and add them to the pan along with the red wine and Italian seasoning and simmer for 20 minutes. Add the basil and season to taste with salt, pepper and sugar (if using).

5. When the spaghetti squash has finished cooking, use a fork to scrape the inside flesh of the squash onto a sheet pan. Spread the squash out and let it cool.

6. Once cool, add the spaghetti squash to the kale mixture, along with the egg, breadcrumbs, Parmesan cheese, sage, nutmeg, salt and freshly ground black pepper. Stir to combine well and then divide the mixture into 6 thick portions. You can shape the portions into patties, but I prefer to keep them a little random and unique in shape. Spray or brush the fritters with olive oil.

7. Preheat the air fryer to 370°F.

8. Brush the air fryer basket with a little olive oil and transfer the fritters to the basket. Air-fry the squash and kale fritters at 370°F for 15 minutes, flipping them over halfway through the cooking process.

9. Serve the fritters warm with the Pomodoro sauce spooned over the top or pooled on your plate. Garnish with the fresh basil leaves.

Mushroom-rice Stuffed Bell Peppers

Servings: 4
Cooking Time: 30 Minutes
Ingredients:
- 4 red bell peppers, tops sliced
- 1 ½ cups cooked rice
- ¼ cup chopped leeks
- ¼ cup sliced mushrooms
- ¾ cup tomato sauce
- Salt and pepper to taste
- ¾ cup shredded mozzarella
- 2 tbsp parsley, chopped

Directions:
1. Fill a large pot of water and heat on high until it boils. Remove seeds and membranes from the peppers. Carefully place peppers into the boiling water for 5 minutes. Remove and set aside to cool. Mix together rice, leeks, mushrooms, tomato sauce, parsley, salt, and pepper in a large bowl. Stuff each pepper with the rice mixture. Top with mozzarella.

2. Preheat air fryer to 350°F. Arrange the peppers on the greased frying basket and Bake for 10 minutes. Serve.

Green Bean Sautée

Servings: 4
Cooking Time: 25 Minutes
Ingredients:
- 1 ½ lb green beans, trimmed
- 1 tbsp olive oil
- ½ tsp garlic powder
- Salt and pepper to taste
- 4 garlic cloves, thinly sliced
- 1 tbsp fresh basil, chopped

Directions:
1. Preheat the air fryer to 375°F. Toss the beans with the olive oil, garlic powder, salt, and pepper in a bowl, then add to the frying basket. Air Fry for 6 minutes, shaking the basket halfway through the cooking time. Add garlic to the air fryer and cook for 3-6 minutes or until the green beans are tender and the garlic slices start to brown. Sprinkle with basil and serve warm.

Vegan French Toast

Servings: 4
Cooking Time: 15 Minutes
Ingredients:
- 1 ripe banana, mashed
- ¼ cup protein powder
- ½ cup milk
- 2 tbsp ground flaxseed
- 4 bread slices
- 2 tbsp agave syrup

Directions:
1. Preheat air fryer to 370°F. Combine the banana, protein powder, milk, and flaxseed in a shallow bowl and mix well Dip bread slices into the mixture. Place the slices on a lightly greased pan in a single layer and pour any of the remaining mixture evenly over the bread. Air Fry for 10 minutes, or until golden brown and crispy, flipping once. Serve warm topped with agave syrup.

Cheddar-bean Flautas

Servings: 4
Cooking Time: 15 Minutes
Ingredients:
- 8 corn tortillas
- 1 can refried beans
- 1 cup shredded cheddar
- 1 cup guacamole

Directions:
1. Preheat air fryer to 390°F. Wet the tortillas with water. Spray the frying basket with oil and stack the tortillas inside. Air Fry for 1 minute. Remove to a flat surface, laying them out individually. Scoop an equal amount of beans in a line down the center of each tortilla. Top with cheddar cheese. Roll the tortilla sides over the filling and put seam-side down in the greased frying basket. Air Fry for 7 minutes or until the tortillas are golden and crispy. Serve immediately topped with guacamole.

Black Bean Stuffed Potato Boats

Servings: 4
Cooking Time: 55 Minutes
Ingredients:
- 4 russets potatoes
- 1 cup chipotle mayonnaise
- 1 cup canned black beans
- 2 tomatoes, chopped
- 1 scallion, chopped
- 1/3 cup chopped cilantro
- 1 poblano chile, minced
- 1 avocado, diced

Directions:
1. Preheat air fryer to 390°F. Clean the potatoes, poke with a fork, and spray with oil. Put in the air fryer and Bake for 30 minutes or until softened.
2. Heat the beans in a pan over medium heat. Put the potatoes on a plate and cut them across the top. Open them with a fork so you can stuff them. Top each potato with chipotle mayonnaise, beans, tomatoes, scallions, cilantro, poblano chile, and avocado. Serve immediately.

Vegetarian Paella

Servings: 3
Cooking Time: 50 Minutes
Ingredients:
- ½ cup chopped artichoke hearts
- ½ sliced red bell peppers
- 4 mushrooms, thinly sliced
- ½ cup canned diced tomatoes
- ½ cup canned chickpeas
- 3 tbsp hot sauce
- 2 tbsp lemon juice
- 1 tbsp allspice
- 1 cup rice

Directions:
1. Preheat air fryer to 400°F. Combine the artichokes, peppers, mushrooms, tomatoes and their juices, chickpeas, hot sauce, lemon juice, and allspice in a baking pan. Roast for 10 minutes. Pour in rice and 2 cups of boiling water, cover with aluminum foil, and Roast for 22 minutes. Discard the foil and Roast for 3 minutes until the top is crisp. Let cool slightly before stirring. Serve.

Avocado Rolls

Servings:5
Cooking Time: 15 Minutes
Ingredients:
- 10 egg roll wrappers
- 1 tomato, diced
- ¼ tsp pepper
- ½ tsp salt

Directions:
1. Place all filling ingredients in a bowl; mash with a fork until somewhat smooth. There should be chunks left. Divide the feeling between the egg wrappers. Wet your finger and brush along the edges, so the wrappers can seal well. Roll and seal the wrappers.
2. Arrange them on a baking sheet lined dish, and place in the air fryer. Cook at 350°F for 5 minutes. Serve with sweet chili dipping and enjoy.

Caprese Eggplant Stacks

Servings:4
Cooking Time: 8 Minutes
Ingredients:
- 1 medium eggplant, cut into 4 (½") slices
- ½ teaspoon salt
- ¼ teaspoon ground black pepper
- 4 (¼") slices tomato
- 2 ounces fresh mozzarella cheese, cut into 4 slices
- 1 tablespoon olive oil
- ¼ cup fresh basil, sliced

Directions:
1. Preheat the air fryer to 320°F.
2. In a 6" round pan, place eggplant slices. Sprinkle with salt and pepper. Top each with a tomato slice, then a mozzarella slice, and drizzle with oil.
3. Place in the air fryer basket and cook 8 minutes until eggplant is tender and cheese is melted. Garnish with fresh basil to serve.

Tex-mex Stuffed Sweet Potatoes

Servings: 2
Cooking Time: 40 Minutes
Ingredients:
- 2 medium sweet potatoes
- 1 can black beans
- 2 scallions, finely sliced
- 1 tbsp hot sauce
- 1 tsp taco seasoning
- 2 tbsp lime juice
- ¼ cup Ranch dressing

Directions:
1. Preheat air fryer to 400°F. Add in sweet potatoes and Roast for 30 minutes. Toss the beans, scallions, hot sauce, taco seasoning, and lime juice. Set aside. Once the potatoes are ready, cut them lengthwise, 2/3 through. Spoon 1/4 of the bean mixture into each half and drizzle Ranch dressing before serving.

Balsamic Caprese Hasselback

Servings:4
Cooking Time: 15 Minutes
Ingredients:
- 4 tomatoes
- 12 fresh basil leaves
- 1 ball fresh mozzarella
- Salt and pepper to taste
- 1 tbsp olive oil
- 2 tsp balsamic vinegar
- 1 tbsp basil, torn

Directions:

1. Preheat air fryer to 325ºF. Remove the bottoms from the tomatoes to create a flat surface. Make 4 even slices on each tomato, 3/4 of the way down. Slice the mozzarella and the cut into 12 pieces. Stuff 1 basil leaf and a piece of mozzarella into each slice. Sprinkle with salt and pepper. Place the stuffed tomatoes in the frying basket and Air Fry for 3 minutes. Transfer to a large serving plate. Drizzle with olive oil and balsamic vinegar and scatter the basil over. Serve and enjoy!

Egg Rolls

Servings: 4
Cooking Time: 8 Minutes
Ingredients:
- 1 clove garlic, minced
- 1 teaspoon sesame oil
- 1 teaspoon olive oil
- ½ cup chopped celery
- ½ cup grated carrots
- 2 green onions, chopped
- 2 ounces mushrooms, chopped
- 2 cups shredded Napa cabbage
- 1 teaspoon low-sodium soy sauce
- 1 teaspoon cornstarch
- salt
- 1 egg
- 1 tablespoon water
- 4 egg roll wraps
- olive oil for misting or cooking spray

Directions:
1. In a large skillet, sauté garlic in sesame and olive oils over medium heat for 1 minute.
2. Add celery, carrots, onions, and mushrooms to skillet. Cook 1 minute, stirring.
3. Stir in cabbage, cover, and cook for 1 minute or just until cabbage slightly wilts.
4. In a small bowl, mix soy sauce and cornstarch. Stir into vegetables to thicken. Remove from heat. Salt to taste if needed.
5. Beat together egg and water in a small bowl.
6. Divide filling into 4 portions and roll up in egg roll wraps. Brush all over with egg wash to seal.
7. Mist egg rolls very lightly with olive oil or cooking spray and place in air fryer basket.
8. Cook at 390°F for 4minutes. Turn over and cook 4 more minutes, until golden brown and crispy.

Cottage And Mayonnaise Stuffed Peppers

Servings: 2
Cooking Time: 20 Minutes
Ingredients:
- 1 red bell pepper, top and seeds removed
- 1 yellow bell pepper, top and seeds removed
- Salt and pepper, to taste
- 1 cup Cottage cheese
- 4 tablespoons mayonnaise
- 2 pickles, chopped

Directions:
1. Arrange the peppers in the lightly greased cooking basket. Cook in the preheated Air Fryer at 400°F for 15 minutes, turning them over halfway through the cooking time.
2. Season with salt and pepper.
3. Then, in a mixing bowl, combine the cream cheese with the mayonnaise and chopped pickles. Stuff the pepper with the cream cheese mixture and serve. Enjoy!

Crispy Wings With Lemony Old Bay Spice

Servings:4
Cooking Time: 25 Minutes
Ingredients:
- ½ cup butter
- ¾ cup almond flour
- 1 tablespoon old bay spices
- 1 teaspoon lemon juice, freshly squeezed
- 3 pounds chicken wings
- Salt and pepper to taste

Directions:
1. Preheat the air fryer for 5 minutes.
2. In a mixing bowl, combine all ingredients except for the butter.
3. Place in the air fryer basket.
4. Cook for 25 minutes at 350°F.
5. Halfway through the cooking time, shake the fryer basket for even cooking.
6. Once cooked, drizzle with melted butter.

Basil Green Beans

Servings: 4
Cooking Time: 15 Minutes
Ingredients:
- 1 ½ lb green beans, trimmed
- 1 tbsp olive oil
- 1 tbsp fresh basil, chopped
- Garlic salt to taste

Directions:
1. Preheat air fryer to 400°F. Coat the green beans with olive oil in a large bowl. Combine with fresh basil powder and garlic salt. Put the beans in the frying basket and Air Fry for 7-9 minutes, shaking once until the beans begin to brown. Serve warm and enjoy!

Caprese-style Sandwiches

Servings: 2
Cooking Time: 20 Minutes
Ingredients:
- 2 tbsp balsamic vinegar
- 4 sandwich bread slices
- 2 oz mozzarella shreds
- 3 tbsp pesto sauce
- 2 tomatoes, sliced
- 8 basil leaves
- 8 baby spinach leaves
- 2 tbsp olive oil

Directions:
1. Preheat air fryer at 350ºF. Drizzle balsamic vinegar on the bottom of bread slices and smear with pesto sauce. Then, layer mozzarella cheese, tomatoes, baby spinach leaves and basil leaves on top. Add top bread slices. Rub the outside top and bottom of each sandwich with olive oil. Place them in the frying basket and Bake for 5 minutes, flipping once. Serve right away.

Roasted Vegetable Pita Pizza

Servings: 4
Cooking Time: 20 Minutes
Ingredients:
- 1 medium red bell pepper, seeded and cut into quarters
- 1 teaspoon extra-virgin olive oil
- ⅛ teaspoon black pepper
- ⅛ teaspoon salt
- Two 6-inch whole-grain pita breads
- 6 tablespoons pesto sauce
- ¼ small red onion, thinly sliced
- ½ cup shredded part-skim mozzarella cheese

Directions:
1. Preheat the air fryer to 400°F.
2. In a small bowl, toss the bell peppers with the olive oil, pepper, and salt.
3. Place the bell peppers in the air fryer and cook for 15 minutes, shaking every 5 minutes to prevent burning.
4. Remove the peppers and set aside. Turn the air fryer temperature down to 350°F.
5. Lay the pita bread on a flat surface. Cover each with half the pesto sauce; then top with even portions of the red bell peppers and onions. Sprinkle cheese over the top. Spray the air fryer basket with olive oil mist.
6. Carefully lift the pita bread into the air fryer basket with a spatula.
7. Cook for 5 to 8 minutes, or until the outer edges begin to brown and the cheese is melted.
8. Serve warm with desired sides.

Zucchini Topped With Coconut Cream 'n Bacon

Servings:3
Cooking Time: 20 Minutes
Ingredients:
- 1 tablespoon lemon juice
- 3 slices bacon, fried and crumbled
- 3 tablespoons olive oil
- 3 zucchini squashes
- 4 tablespoons coconut cream
- Salt and pepper to taste

Directions:
1. Preheat the air fryer for 5 minutes.
2. Line up chopsticks on both sides of the zucchini and slice thinly until you hit the stick. Brush the zucchinis with olive oil. Set aside.
3. Place the zucchini in the air fryer. Bake for 20 minutes at 350°F.

4. Meanwhile, combine the coconut cream and lemon juice in a mixing bowl. Season with salt and pepper to taste.
5. Once the zucchini is cooked, scoop the coconut cream mixture and drizzle on top.
6. Sprinkle with bacon bits.

Lemony Green Beans

Servings:3
Cooking Time:12 Minutes
Ingredients:
- 1 pound green beans, trimmed and halved
- 1 teaspoon butter, melted
- 1 tablespoon fresh lemon juice
- ¼ teaspoon garlic powder

Directions:
1. Preheat the Air fryer to 400°F and grease an Air fryer basket.
2. Mix all the ingredients in a bowl and toss to coat well.
3. Arrange the green beans into the Air fryer basket and cook for about 12 minutes.
4. Dish out in a serving plate and serve hot.

Caribbean-style Fried Plantains

Servings: 2
Cooking Time: 20 Minutes
Ingredients:
- 2 plantains, peeled and cut into slices
- 2 tablespoons avocado oil
- 2 teaspoons Caribbean Sorrel Rum Spice Mix

Directions:
1. Toss the plantains with the avocado oil and spice mix.
2. Cook in the preheated Air Fryer at 400°F for 10 minutes, shaking the cooking basket halfway through the cooking time.
3. Adjust the seasonings to taste and enjoy!

Tofu & Spinach Lasagna

Servings: 4
Cooking Time: 30 Minutes
Ingredients:
- 8 oz cooked lasagne noodles
- 1 tbsp olive oil
- 2 cups crumbled tofu
- 2 cups fresh spinach
- 2 tbsp cornstarch
- 1 tsp onion powder
- Salt and pepper to taste
- 2 garlic cloves, minced
- 2 cups marinara sauce
- ½ cup shredded mozzarella

Directions:
1. Warm the olive oil in a large pan over medium heat. Add the tofu and spinach and stir-fry for a minute. Add the cornstarch, onion powder, salt, pepper, and garlic. Stir until the spinach wilts. Remove from heat.

2. Preheat air fryer to 390°F. Pour a thin layer of pasta sauce in a baking pan. Layer 2-3 lasagne noodles on top of the marinara sauce. Top with a little more sauce and some of the tofu mix. Add another 2-3 noodles on top, then another layer of sauce, then another layer of tofu. Finish with a layer of noodles and a final layer of sauce. Sprinkle with mozzarella cheese on top. Place the pan in the air fryer and Bake for 15 minutes or until the noodle edges are browned and the cheese is melted. Cut and serve.

Chive Potato Pierogi

Servings: 4
Cooking Time: 55 Minutes
Ingredients:
- 2 boiled potatoes, mashed
- Salt and pepper to taste
- 1 tsp cumin powder
- 2 tbsp sour cream
- ¼ cup grated Parmesan
- 2 tbsp chopped chives
- 1 tbsp chopped parsley
- 1 ¼ cups flour
- ¼ tsp garlic powder
- ¾ cup Greek yogurt
- 1 egg

Directions:
1. Combine the mashed potatoes along with sour cream, cumin, parsley, chives, pepper, and salt and stir until slightly chunky. Mix the flour, salt, and garlic powder in a large bowl. Stir in yogurt until it comes together as a sticky dough. Knead in the bowl for about 2-3 minutes to make it smooth. Whisk the egg and 1 teaspoon of water in a small bowl. Roll out the dough on a lightly floured work surface to ¼-inch thickness. Cut out 12 circles with a cookie cutter.
2. Preheat air fryer to 350°F. Divide the potato mixture and Parmesan cheese between the dough circles. Brush the edges of them with the egg wash and fold the dough over the filling into half-moon shapes. Crimp the edges with a fork to seal. Arrange the on the greased frying basket and Air Fry for 8-10 minutes, turning the pierogies once, until the outside is golden. Serve warm.

Authentic Mexican Esquites

Servings: 4
Cooking Time: 25 Minutes
Ingredients:
- 4 ears of corn, husk and silk removed
- 1 tbsp ground coriander
- 1 tbsp smoked paprika
- 1 tsp sea salt
- 1 tsp garlic powder
- 1 tsp onion powder
- 1 tsp dried lime peel
- 1 tsp cayenne pepper
- 3 tbsp mayonnaise
- 3 tbsp grated Cotija cheese
- 1 tbsp butter, melted

- 1 tsp epazote seasoning
Directions:
1. Preheat the air fryer to 400°F. Combine the coriander, paprika, salt, garlic powder, onion powder, lime peel, epazote and cayenne pepper in a small bowl and mix well. Pour into a small glass jar. Put the corn in the greased frying basket and Bake for 6-8 minutes or until the corn is crispy but tender. Make sure to rearrange the ears halfway through cooking.
2. While the corn is frying, combine the mayonnaise, cheese, and melted butter in a small bowl. Spread the mixture over the cooked corn, return to the fryer, and Bake for 3-5 minutes more or until the corn has brown spots. Remove from the fryer and sprinkle each cob with about ½ tsp of the spice mix.

Zucchini Fritters

Servings:4
Cooking Time: 12 Minutes
Ingredients:
- 1½ medium zucchini, trimmed and grated
- ½ teaspoon salt, divided
- 1 large egg, whisked
- ¼ teaspoon garlic powder
- ¼ cup grated Parmesan cheese

Directions:
1. Place grated zucchini on a kitchen towel and sprinkle with ¼ teaspoon salt. Wrap in towel and let sit 30 minutes, then wring out as much excess moisture as possible.
2. Place zucchini into a large bowl and mix with egg, remaining salt, garlic powder, and Parmesan. Cut a piece of parchment to fit air fryer basket. Divide mixture into four mounds, about ⅓ cup each, and press out into 4" rounds on ungreased parchment.
3. Place parchment with rounds into air fryer basket. Adjust the temperature to 400°F and set the timer for 12 minutes, turning fritters halfway through cooking. Fritters will be crispy on the edges and tender but firm in the center when done. Serve warm.

Curried Eggplant

Servings:2
Cooking Time:10 Minutes
Ingredients:
- 1 large eggplant, cut into ½-inch thick slices
- 1 garlic clove, minced
- ½ fresh red chili, chopped
- 1 tablespoon vegetable oil
- ¼ teaspoon curry powder
- Salt, to taste

Directions:
1. Preheat the Air fryer to 300°F and grease an Air fryer basket.
2. Mix all the ingredients in a bowl and toss to coat well.
3. Arrange the eggplant slices in the Air fryer basket and cook for about 10 minutes, tossing once in between.
4. Dish out onto serving plates and serve hot.

Roasted Vegetable Lasagna

Servings: 6
Cooking Time: 55 Minutes
Ingredients:

- 1 zucchini, sliced
- 1 yellow squash, sliced
- 8 ounces mushrooms, sliced
- 1 red bell pepper, cut into 2-inch strips
- 1 tablespoon olive oil
- 2 cups ricotta cheese
- 2 cups grated mozzarella cheese, divided
- 1 egg
- 1 teaspoon salt
- freshly ground black pepper
- ¼ cup shredded carrots
- ½ cup chopped fresh spinach
- 8 lasagna noodles, cooked
- Béchamel Sauce:
- 3 tablespoons butter
- 3 tablespoons flour
- 2½ cups milk
- ½ cup grated Parmesan cheese
- ½ teaspoon salt
- freshly ground black pepper
- pinch of ground nutmeg

Directions:

1. Preheat the air fryer to 400°F.
2. Toss the zucchini, yellow squash, mushrooms and red pepper in a large bowl with the olive oil and season with salt and pepper. Air-fry for 10 minutes, shaking the basket once or twice while the vegetables cook.
3. While the vegetables are cooking, make the béchamel sauce and cheese filling. Melt the butter in a medium saucepan over medium-high heat on the stovetop. Add the flour and whisk, cooking for a couple of minutes. Add the milk and whisk vigorously until smooth. Bring the mixture to a boil and simmer until the sauce thickens. Stir in the Parmesan cheese and season with the salt, pepper and nutmeg. Set the sauce aside.
4. Combine the ricotta cheese, 1¼ cups of the mozzarella cheese, egg, salt and pepper in a large bowl and stir until combined. Fold in the carrots and spinach.
5. When the vegetables have finished cooking, build the lasagna. Use a baking dish that is 6 inches in diameter and 4 inches high. Cover the bottom of the baking dish with a little béchamel sauce. Top with two lasagna noodles, cut to fit the dish and overlapping each other a little. Spoon a third of the ricotta cheese mixture and then a third of the roasted veggies on top of the noodles. Pour ½ cup of béchamel sauce on top and then repeat these layers two more times: noodles – cheese mixture – vegetables – béchamel sauce. Sprinkle the remaining mozzarella cheese over the top. Cover the dish with aluminum foil, tenting it loosely so the aluminum doesn't touch the cheese.
6. Lower the dish into the air fryer basket using an aluminum foil sling (fold a piece of aluminum foil into a strip about 2-inches wide by 24-inches long). Fold the ends of the aluminum foil over the top of the dish before returning the basket to the air fryer. Air-fry for 45 minutes, removing the foil for the last 2 minutes, to slightly brown the cheese on top.
7. Let the lasagna rest for at least 20 minutes to set up a little before slicing into it and serving.

Pesto Vegetable Skewers

Servings:8
Cooking Time: 8 Minutes
Ingredients:

- 1 medium zucchini, trimmed and cut into ½" slices
- ½ medium yellow onion, peeled and cut into 1" squares
- 1 medium red bell pepper, seeded and cut into 1" squares
- 16 whole cremini mushrooms
- ⅓ cup basil pesto
- ½ teaspoon salt
- ¼ teaspoon ground black pepper

Directions:

1. Divide zucchini slices, onion, and bell pepper into eight even portions. Place on 6" skewers for a total of eight kebabs. Add 2 mushrooms to each skewer and brush kebabs generously with pesto.
2. Sprinkle each kebab with salt and black pepper on all sides, then place into ungreased air fryer basket. Adjust the temperature to 375°F and set the timer for 8 minutes, turning kebabs halfway through cooking. Vegetables will be browned at the edges and tender-crisp when done. Serve warm.

Curried Potato, Cauliflower And Pea Turnovers

Servings: 4
Cooking Time: 40 Minutes
Ingredients:

- Dough:
- 2 cups all-purpose flour
- ½ teaspoon baking powder
- 1 teaspoon salt
- freshly ground black pepper
- ¼ teaspoon dried thyme
- ¼ cup canola oil
- ½ to ⅔ cup water
- Turnover Filling:
- 1 tablespoon canola or vegetable oil
- 1 onion, finely chopped
- 1 clove garlic, minced
- 1 tablespoon grated fresh ginger
- ½ teaspoon cumin seeds
- ½ teaspoon fennel seeds
- 1 teaspoon curry powder
- 2 russet potatoes, diced
- 2 cups cauliflower florets
- ½ cup frozen peas

- 2 tablespoons chopped fresh cilantro
- salt and freshly ground black pepper
- 2 tablespoons butter, melted
- mango chutney, for serving

Directions:

1. Start by making the dough. Combine the flour, baking powder, salt, pepper and dried thyme in a mixing bowl or the bowl of a stand mixer. Drizzle in the canola oil and pinch it together with your fingers to turn the flour into a crumby mixture. Stir in the water (enough to bring the dough together). Knead the dough for 5 minutes or so until it is smooth. Add a little more water or flour as needed. Let the dough rest while you make the turnover filling.

2. Preheat a large skillet on the stovetop over medium-high heat. Add the oil and sauté the onion until it starts to become tender – about 4 minutes. Add the garlic and ginger and continue to cook for another minute. Add the dried spices and toss everything to coat. Add the potatoes and cauliflower to the skillet and pour in 1½ cups of water. Simmer everything together for 20 to 25 minutes, or until the potatoes are soft and most of the water has evaporated. If the water has evaporated and the vegetables still need more time, just add a little water and continue to simmer until everything is tender. Stir well, crushing the potatoes and cauliflower a little as you do so. Stir in the peas and cilantro, season to taste with salt and freshly ground black pepper and set aside to cool.

3. Divide the dough into 4 balls. Roll the dough balls out into ¼-inch thick circles. Divide the cooled potato filling between the dough circles, placing a mound of the filling on one side of each piece of dough, leaving an empty border around the edge of the dough. Brush the edges of the dough with a little water and fold one edge of circle over the filling to meet the other edge of the circle, creating a half moon. Pinch the edges together with your fingers and then press the edge with the tines of a fork to decorate and seal.

4. Preheat the air fryer to 380°F.

5. Spray or brush the air fryer basket with oil. Brush the turnovers with the melted butter and place 2 turnovers into the air fryer basket. Air-fry for 15 minutes. Flip the turnovers over and air-fry for another 5 minutes. Repeat with the remaining 2 turnovers.

6. These will be very hot when they come out of the air fryer. Let them cool for at least 20 minutes before serving warm with mango chutney.

Roasted Cauliflower

Servings: 2
Cooking Time: 20 Minutes
Ingredients:

- medium head cauliflower
- 2 tbsp. salted butter, melted
- 1 medium lemon
- 1 tsp. dried parsley

- ½ tsp. garlic powder

Directions:

1. Having removed the leaves from the cauliflower head, brush it with the melted butter. Grate the rind of the lemon over it and then drizzle some juice. Finally add the parsley and garlic powder on top.

2. Transfer the cauliflower to the basket of the fryer.

3. Cook for fifteen minutes at 350°F, checking regularly to ensure it doesn't overcook. The cauliflower is ready when it is hot and fork tender.

4. Take care when removing it from the fryer, cut up and serve.

Crunchy Rice Paper Samosas

Servings: 2
Cooking Time: 20 Minutes
Ingredients:

- 1 boiled potato, mashed
- ¼ cup green peas
- 1 tsp garam masala powder
- ½ tsp ginger garlic paste
- ½ tsp cayenne pepper
- ½ tsp turmeric powder
- Salt and pepper to taste
- 3 rice paper wrappers

Directions:

1. Preheat air fryer to 350°F. Place the mashed potatoes in a bowl. Add the peas, garam masala powder, ginger garlic paste, cayenne pepper, turmeric powder, salt, and pepper and stir until ingredients are evenly blended.

2. Lay the rice paper wrappers out on a lightly floured surface. Divide the potato mixture between the wrappers and fold the top edges over to seal. Transfer the samosas to the greased frying basket and Air Fry for 12 minutes, flipping once until the samosas are crispy and flaky. Remove and leave to cool for 5 minutes. Serve and enjoy!

Smoky Sweet Potato Fries

Servings: 4
Cooking Time: 25 Minutes
Ingredients:

- 2 large sweet potatoes, peeled and sliced
- 1 tbsp olive oil
- Salt and pepper to taste
- ¼ tsp garlic powder
- ¼ tsp smoked paprika
- 1 tbsp pumpkin pie spice
- 1 tbsp chopped parsley

Directions:

1. Preheat air fryer to 375°F. Toss sweet potato slices, olive oil, salt, pepper, garlic powder, pumpkin pie spice and paprika in a large bowl. Arrange the potatoes in a single layer in the frying basket. Air Fry for 5 minutes, then shake the basket. Air Fry for another 5 minutes and shake the basket again. Air Fry for 2-5 minutes until crispy. Serve sprinkled with parsley and enjoy.

Chapter 10: Desserts And Sweets Recipes

Gingerbread

Servings: 6
Cooking Time: 20 Minutes
Ingredients:
- cooking spray
- 1 cup flour
- 2 tablespoons sugar
- ¾ teaspoon ground ginger
- ¼ teaspoon cinnamon
- 1 teaspoon baking powder
- ½ teaspoon baking soda
- ⅛ teaspoon salt
- 1 egg
- ¼ cup molasses
- ½ cup buttermilk
- 2 tablespoons oil
- 1 teaspoon pure vanilla extract

Directions:
1. Preheat air fryer to 330°F.
2. Spray 6 x 6-inch baking dish lightly with cooking spray.
3. In a medium bowl, mix together all the dry ingredients.
4. In a separate bowl, beat the egg. Add molasses, buttermilk, oil, and vanilla and stir until well mixed.
5. Pour liquid mixture into dry ingredients and stir until well blended.
6. Pour batter into baking dish and cook at 330°F for 20minutes or until toothpick inserted in center of loaf comes out clean.

Vanilla Cheesecake

Servings:6
Cooking Time: 10 Minutes
Ingredients:
- 2 eggs
- 16 ounces cream cheese, softened
- 2 tablespoons sour cream
- ½ teaspoon fresh lemon juice
- 1 teaspoon vanilla
- ¾ cup erythritol

Directions:
1. Before cooking, heat your air fryer to 350 degrees F/ 175 degrees C.
2. In a large bowl, mix the whisked eggs, vanilla, lemon juice, and sweetener together and use a hand mixer to beat until smooth.
3. Then beat in cream cheese and sour cream until fluffy.
4. Divide the batter into 2 4-inch springform pan that fits in your air fryer.
5. Cook in your air fryer at 350 degrees F/ 175 degrees C for 8 to 10 minutes.
6. When cooked, remove from the air fryer and set it aside to cool completely.
7. Transfer in the fridge to reserve.
8. Serve and enjoy!

Apple-cinnamon Hand Pies

Servings:8
Cooking Time: 20 Minutes
Ingredients:
- 2 apples, cored and diced
- ¼ cup honey
- 1 teaspoon cinnamon
- 1 teaspoon vanilla extract
- ⅛ teaspoon nutmeg
- 2 teaspoons cornstarch
- 1 teaspoon water
- 4 frozen piecrusts, thawed if frozen hard
- Cooking oil

Directions:
1. Place a saucepan over medium-high heat. Add the apples, honey, cinnamon, vanilla, and nutmeg. Stir and cook for 2 to 3 minutes, until the apples are soft.
2. In a small bowl, mix the cornstarch and water. Add to the pan and stir. Cook for 30 seconds.
3. Cut each piecrust into two 4-inch circles. You should have 8 circles of crust total.
4. Lay the piecrusts on a flat work surface. Mound ⅓ cup of apple filling on the center of each.
5. Fold each piecrust over so that the top layer of crust is about an inch short of the bottom layer. (The edges should not meet.)
6. Using your fingers, tap along the edges of the top layer to seal. Use the back of a fork to press lines into the edges.
7. Place the hand pies in the air fryer. I do not recommend stacking the hand pies. They will stick together if stacked. You may need to prepare them in two batches. Cook for 10 minutes.
8. Allow the hand pies to cool fully before removing from the air fryer.

Air-fried Strawberry Hand Tarts

Servings: 9
Cooking Time: 9 Minutes
Ingredients:
- ½ cup butter, softened
- ½ cup sugar
- 2 eggs
- 1 teaspoon vanilla extract
- 2 tablespoons lemon zest
- 2½ cups all-purpose flour
- 1 teaspoon baking powder
- ¼ teaspoon salt
- 1¼ cups strawberry jam, divided
- 1 egg white, beaten
- 1 cup powdered sugar
- 2 teaspoons milk

Directions:
1. Combine the butter and sugar in a bowl and beat with an electric mixer until the mixture is light and fluffy. Add the eggs one at a time. Add the vanilla extract and lemon zest and mix well. In a separate bowl, combine the

flour, baking powder and salt. Add the dry ingredients to the wet ingredients, mixing just until the dough comes together. Transfer the dough to a floured surface and knead by hand for 10 minutes. Cover with a clean kitchen towel and let the dough rest for 30 minutes. (Alternatively, dough can be mixed and kneaded in a stand mixer.)

2. Divide the dough in half and roll each half out into a ¼-inch thick rectangle that measures 12-inches x 9-inches. Cut each rectangle of dough into nine 4-inch x 3-inch rectangles (a pizza cutter is very helpful for this task). You should have 18 rectangles. Spread two teaspoons of strawberry jam in the center of nine of the rectangles leaving a ¼-inch border around the edges. Brush the egg white around the edges of each rectangle and top with the remaining nine rectangles of dough. Press the back of a fork around the edges to seal the tarts shut. Brush the top of the tarts with the beaten egg white and pierce the dough three or four times down the center of the tart with a fork.

3. Preheat the air fryer to 350°F.

4. Air-fry the tarts in batches at 350°F for 6 minutes. Flip the tarts over and air-fry for an additional 3 minutes.

5. While the tarts are air-frying, make the icing. Combine the powdered sugar, ¼ cup strawberry preserves and milk in a bowl, whisking until the icing is smooth. Spread the icing over the top of each tart, leaving an empty border around the edges. Decorate with sprinkles if desired.

Baked Caramelized Peaches

Servings: 6
Cooking Time: 25 Minutes
Ingredients:
- 3 pitted peaches, halved
- 2 tbsp brown sugar
- 1 cup heavy cream
- 1 tsp vanilla extract
- ¼ tsp ground cinnamon
- 1 cup fresh blueberries

Directions:
1. Preheat air fryer to 380°F. Lay the peaches in the frying basket with the cut side up, then top them with brown sugar. Bake for 7-11 minutes, allowing the peaches to brown around the edges. In a mixing bowl, whisk heavy cream, vanilla, and cinnamon until stiff peaks form. Fold the peaches into a plate. Spoon the cream mixture into the peach cups, top with blueberries, and serve.

Cheese Muffins With Cinnamon

Servings: 10
Cooking Time: 16 Minutes
Ingredients:
- 2 eggs
- ½ cup erythritol
- 8 ounces cream cheese
- 1 teaspoon ground cinnamon
- ½ tsp vanilla

Directions:
1. Before cooking, heat your air fryer to 325 degrees F/ 160 degrees C.
2. Mix together vanilla, erythritol, eggs, and cream cheese until smooth.
3. Divide the batter into the silicone muffin molds. Top the muffins with cinnamon.
4. In the air fryer basket, transfer the muffin molds.
5. Cook in your air fryer for 16 minutes.
6. Serve and enjoy!

Rich Blueberry Biscuit Shortcakes

Servings: 4
Cooking Time: 35 Minutes
Ingredients:
- 1 lb blueberries, halved
- ¼ cup granulated sugar
- 1 tsp orange zest
- 1 cup heavy cream
- 1 tbsp orange juice
- 2 tbsp powdered sugar
- ¼ tsp cinnamon
- ¼ tsp nutmeg
- 2 cups flour
- 1 egg yolk
- 1 tbsp baking powder
- ½ tsp baking soda
- ½ tsp cornstarch
- ½ tsp salt
- ½ tsp vanilla extract
- ½ tsp honey
- 4 tbsp cold butter, cubed
- 1 ¼ cups buttermilk

Directions:
1. Combine blueberries, granulated sugar, and orange zest in a bowl. Let chill the topping covered in the fridge until ready to use. Beat heavy cream, orange juice, egg yolk, vanilla extract and powdered sugar in a metal bowl until peaks form. Let chill the whipped cream covered in the fridge until ready to use.
2. Preheat air fryer at 350ºF. Combine flour, cinnamon, nutmeg, baking powder, baking soda, cornstarch, honey, butter cubes, and buttermilk in a bowl until a sticky dough forms. Flour your hands and form dough into 8 balls. Place them on a lightly greased pizza pan. Place pizza pan in the frying basket and Air Fry for 8 minutes. Transfer biscuits to serving plates and cut them in half. Spread blueberry mixture to each biscuit bottom and place tops of biscuits. Garnish with whipped cream and serve.

Carrot-oat Cake Muffins

Servings: 4
Cooking Time: 20 Minutes
Ingredients:
- 3 tbsp butter, softened
- ¼ cup brown sugar
- 1 tbsp maple syrup

- 1 egg white
- ½ tsp vanilla extract
- 1/3 cup finely grated carrots
- ½ cup oatmeal
- 1/3 cup flour
- ½ tsp baking soda
- ¼ cup raisins

Directions:
1. Preheat air fryer to 350°F. Mix the butter, brown sugar, and maple syrup until smooth, then toss in the egg white, vanilla, and carrots. Whisk well and add the oatmeal, flour, baking soda, and raisins. Divide the mixture between muffin cups. Bake in the fryer for 8-10 minutes.

Simple Blueberry Muffins

Servings: 5
Cooking Time: 14 Minutes
Ingredients:
- 1 egg
- 1 teaspoon baking powder
- 3 tablespoons butter, melted
- ¾ cup blueberries
- ⅔ cup almond flour
- 2 tablespoons erythritol
- ⅓ cup unsweetened almond milk

Directions:
1. Spray silicone muffins molds with cooking spray and set aside.
2. Add all the recipe ingredients into the bowl and mix until well combined.
3. Pour batter into the prepared molds and place into the air fryer basket.
4. Cook at almost 320 degrees F/ 160 degrees C for 14 minutes.
5. Serve and enjoy.

Cinnamon And Pecan Pie

Servings:4
Cooking Time: 25 Minutes
Ingredients:
- 1 pie dough
- ½ teaspoons cinnamon
- ¾ teaspoon vanilla extract
- 2 eggs
- ¾ cup maple syrup
- ⅛ teaspoon nutmeg
- 3 tablespoons melted butter, divided
- 2 tablespoons sugar
- ½ cup chopped pecans

Directions:
1. Preheat the air fryer to 370ºF (188ºC).
2. In a small bowl, coat the pecans in 1 tablespoon of melted butter.
3. Transfer the pecans to the air fryer and air fry for about 10 minutes.
4. Put the pie dough in a greased pie pan and add the pecans on top.

5. In a bowl, mix the rest of the ingredients. Pour this over the pecans.
6. Put the pan in the air fryer and bake for 25 minutes.
7. Serve immediately.

Fiesta Pastries

Servings:8
Cooking Time:20 Minutes
Ingredients:
- ½ of apple, peeled, cored and chopped
- 1 teaspoon fresh orange zest, grated finely
- 7.05-ounce prepared frozen puff pastry, cut into 16 squares
- ½ tablespoon white sugar
- ½ teaspoon ground cinnamon

Directions:
1. Preheat the Air fryer to 390°F and grease an Air fryer basket.
2. Mix all ingredients in a bowl except puff pastry.
3. Arrange about 1 teaspoon of this mixture in the center of each square.
4. Fold each square into a triangle and slightly press the edges with a fork.
5. Arrange the pastries in the Air fryer basket and cook for about 10 minutes.
6. Dish out and serve immediately.

Chocolate Cake

Servings: 8
Cooking Time: 20 Minutes
Ingredients:
- ½ cup sugar
- ¼ cup flour, plus 3 tablespoons
- 3 tablespoons cocoa
- ½ teaspoon baking powder
- ½ teaspoon baking soda
- ¼ teaspoon salt
- 1 egg
- 2 tablespoons oil
- ½ cup milk
- ½ teaspoon vanilla extract

Directions:
1. Preheat air fryer to 330°F.
2. Grease and flour a 6 x 6-inch baking pan.
3. In a medium bowl, stir together the sugar, flour, cocoa, baking powder, baking soda, and salt.
4. Add all other ingredients and beat with a wire whisk until smooth.
5. Pour batter into prepared pan and bake at 330°F for 20 minutes, until toothpick inserted in center comes out clean or with crumbs clinging to it.

Glazed Cherry Turnovers

Servings: 8
Cooking Time: 14 Minutes
Ingredients:
- 2 sheets frozen puff pastry, thawed
- 1 (21-ounce) can premium cherry pie filling

- 2 teaspoons ground cinnamon
- 1 egg, beaten
- 1 cup sliced almonds
- 1 cup powdered sugar
- 2 tablespoons milk

Directions:

1. Roll a sheet of puff pastry out into a square that is approximately 10-inches by 10-inches. Cut this large square into quarters.

2. Mix the cherry pie filling and cinnamon together in a bowl. Spoon ¼ cup of the cherry filling into the center of each puff pastry square. Brush the perimeter of the pastry square with the egg wash. Fold one corner of the puff pastry over the cherry pie filling towards the opposite corner, forming a triangle. Seal the two edges of the pastry together with the tip of a fork, making a design with the tines. Brush the top of the turnovers with the egg wash and sprinkle sliced almonds over each one. Repeat these steps with the second sheet of puff pastry. You should have eight turnovers at the end.

3. Preheat the air fryer to 370°F.

4. Air-fry two turnovers at a time for 14 minutes, carefully turning them over halfway through the cooking time.

5. While the turnovers are cooking, make the glaze by whisking the powdered sugar and milk together in a small bowl until smooth. Let the glaze sit for a minute so the sugar can absorb the milk. If the consistency is still too thick to drizzle, add a little more milk, a drop at a time, and stir until smooth.

6. Let the cooked cherry turnovers sit for at least 10 minutes. Then drizzle the glaze over each turnover in a zigzag motion. Serve warm or at room temperature.

Peanut Butter S'mores

Servings:10
Cooking Time: 1 Minute
Ingredients:

- 10 Graham crackers (full, double-square cookies as they come out of the package)
- 5 tablespoons Natural-style creamy or crunchy peanut butter
- ½ cup Milk chocolate chips
- 10 Standard-size marshmallows (not minis and not jumbo campfire ones)

Directions:

1. Preheat the air fryer to 350°F .

2. Break the graham crackers in half widthwise at the marked place, so the rectangle is now in two squares. Set half of the squares flat side up on your work surface. Spread each with about 1½ teaspoons peanut butter, then set 10 to 12 chocolate chips point side up into the peanut butter on each, pressing gently so the chips stick.

3. Flatten a marshmallow between your clean, dry hands and set it atop the chips. Do the same with the remaining marshmallows on the other coated graham crackers. Do not set the other half of the graham crackers on top of these coated graham crackers.

4. When the machine is at temperature, set the treats graham cracker side down in a single layer in the basket. They may touch, but even a fraction of an inch between them will provide better air flow. Air-fry undisturbed for 45 seconds.

5. Use a nonstick-safe spatula to transfer the topped graham crackers to a wire rack. Set the other graham cracker squares flat side down over the marshmallows. Cool for a couple of minutes before serving.

Chocolate Lava Cake

Servings: 2
Cooking Time: 9 Minutes
Ingredients:

- 1 egg
- ½ teaspoon baking powder
- 1 tablespoon coconut oil, melted
- 1 tablespoon flax meal
- 2 tablespoons erythritol
- 2 tablespoons water
- 2 tablespoons unsweetened cocoa powder
- Pinch of salt

Directions:

1. Before cooking, heat your air fryer to 350 degrees F/ 175 degrees C.

2. In a bowl, whisk all the ingredients. Then divide the mixture into 2 ramekins.

3. Transfer the ramekins inside the air fryer basket and bake in the preheated air fryer for 8 to 9 minutes.

4. When cooked, remove from the air fryer and set aside to cool for 10 minutes. Serve and enjoy!

Spiced Fruit Skewers

Servings: 4
Cooking Time: 15 Minutes
Ingredients:

- 2 peeled peaches, thickly sliced
- 3 plums, halved and pitted
- 3 peeled kiwi, quartered
- 1 tbsp honey
- ½ tsp ground cinnamon
- ¼ tsp ground allspice
- ¼ tsp cayenne pepper

Directions:

1. Preheat air fryer to 400°F. Combine the honey, cinnamon, allspice, and cayenne and set aside. Alternate fruits on 8 bamboo skewers, then brush the fruit with the honey mix. Lay the skewers in the air fryer and Air Fry for 3-5 minutes. Allow to chill for 5 minutes before serving.

Mixed Berry Pie

Servings: 4
Cooking Time: 25 Minutes
Ingredients:

- 2/3 cup blackberries, cut into thirds
- ¼ cup sugar
- 2 tbsp cornstarch

- ¼ tsp vanilla extract
- ¼ tsp peppermint extract
- ½ tsp lemon zest
- 1 cup sliced strawberries
- 1 cup raspberries
- 1 refrigerated piecrust
- 1 large egg

Directions:

1. Mix the sugar, cornstarch, vanilla, peppermint extract, and lemon zest in a bowl. Toss in all berries gently until combined. Pour into a greased dish. On a clean workspace, lay out the dough and cut into a 7-inch diameter round. Cover the baking dish with the round and crimp the edges. With a knife, cut 4 slits in the top to vent.

2. Beat 1 egg and 1 tbsp of water to make an egg wash. Brush the egg wash over the crust. Preheat air fryer to 350°F. Put the baking dish into the frying basket. Bake for 15 minutes or until the crust is golden and the berries are bubbling through the vents. Remove from the air fryer and let cool for 15 minutes. Serve warm.

Tasty Berry Cobbler

Servings: 6
Cooking Time: 10 Minutes
Ingredients:
- 1 egg, lightly beaten
- 1 tablespoon butter, melted
- 2 teaspoons swerve
- ½ teaspoon vanilla
- 1 cup almond flour
- ½ cup raspberries, sliced
- ½ cup strawberries, sliced

Directions:

1. At 360 degrees F/ 180 degrees C, preheat your air fryer.
2. Add sliced strawberries and raspberries into the air fryer basket.
3. Sprinkle sweetener over berries.
4. Mix together almond flour, vanilla, and butter in the bowl.
5. Add egg in almond flour mixture and stir well to combine.
6. Spread almond flour mixture over sliced berries.
7. Cover dish with foil and place into the air fryer and cook for almost 10 minutes.
8. Serve and enjoy.

Walnut Banana Split

Servings: 8
Cooking Time: 15 Minutes
Ingredients:
- 3 tablespoons coconut oil
- 1 cup panko breadcrumbs
- ½ cup of corn flour
- 2 eggs
- 4 bananas, peeled and halved lengthwise
- 3 tablespoons sugar

- ¼ teaspoon ground cinnamon
- 2 tablespoons walnuts, chopped

Directions:

1. In a suitable skillet, melt the coconut oil over medium heat and cook the breadcrumbs until they are golden brown and crumbly, for about 4 minutes. Stir constantly.
2. Transfer the breadcrumbs to a shallow bowl and set aside to cool.
3. In a second bowl, place the cornmeal.
4. In a third bowl, beat the eggs.
5. Coat the banana slices with the flour, dip them in the eggs and finally coat them evenly with the breadcrumbs.
6. In a suitable bowl, mix the sugar and cinnamon.
7. Set the cook time to 10 minutes and set the temperature to 280 degrees F/ 140 degrees C on the air fryer.
8. Arrange banana slices in Air Fry Basket and sprinkle with cinnamon sugar.
9. Transfer banana slices to plates to cool slightly.
10. Sprinkle with chopped walnuts.

Easy Keto Danish

Servings: 6
Cooking Time: 12 Minutes
Ingredients:
- 1½ cups shredded mozzarella cheese
- ½ cup blanched finely ground almond flour
- 3 ounces cream cheese, divided
- ¼ cup confectioners' erythritol
- 1 tablespoon lemon juice

Directions:

1. Place mozzarella, flour, and 1 ounce cream cheese in a large microwave-safe bowl. Microwave on high 45 seconds, then stir with a fork until a soft dough forms.
2. Separate dough into six equal sections and press each in a single layer into an ungreased 4" × 4" square nonstick baking dish to form six even squares that touch.
3. In a small bowl, mix remaining cream cheese, erythritol, and lemon juice. Place 1 tablespoon mixture in center of each piece of dough in baking dish. Fold all four corners of each dough piece halfway to center to reach cream cheese mixture.
4. Place dish into air fryer. Adjust the temperature to 320°F and set the timer for 12 minutes. The center and edges will be browned when done. Let cool 10 minutes before serving.

Black Forest Hand Pies

Servings: 6
Cooking Time: 15 Minutes
Ingredients:
- 3 tablespoons milk or dark chocolate chips
- 2 tablespoons thick, hot fudge sauce
- 2 tablespoons chopped dried cherries
- 1 (10-by-15-inch) sheet puff pastry, thawed
- 1 egg white, beaten
- 2 tablespoons sugar

- ½ teaspoon cinnamon

Directions:

1. In a small bowl, combine the chocolate chips, fudge sauce, and dried cherries.
2. Roll out the puff pastry on a floured surface. Cut into 6 squares with a sharp knife.
3. Divide the chocolate chip mixture onto the center of each puff pastry square. Fold the squares in half to make triangles. Firmly press the edges with the tines of a fork to seal.
4. Brush the triangles on all sides sparingly with the beaten egg white. Sprinkle the tops with sugar and cinnamon.
5. Place in the air fryer basket and bake for 15 minutes or until the triangles are golden brown. The filling will be hot, so cool for at least 20 minutes before serving.

Giant Oatmeal-peanut Butter Cookie

Servings: 4
Cooking Time: 18 Minutes
Ingredients:

- 1 cup Rolled oats (not quick-cooking or steel-cut oats)
- ½ cup All-purpose flour
- ½ teaspoon Ground cinnamon
- ½ teaspoon Baking soda
- ⅓ cup Packed light brown sugar
- ¼ cup Solid vegetable shortening
- 2 tablespoons Natural-style creamy peanut butter
- 3 tablespoons Granulated white sugar
- 2 tablespoons (or 1 small egg, well beaten) Pasteurized egg substitute, such as Egg Beaters
- ⅓ cup Roasted, salted peanuts, chopped
- Baking spray

Directions:

1. Preheat the air fryer to 350°F .
2. Stir the oats, flour, cinnamon, and baking soda in a bowl until well combined.
3. Using an electric hand mixer at medium speed, beat the brown sugar, shortening, peanut butter, granulated white sugar, and egg substitute or egg (as applicable) until smooth and creamy, about 3 minutes, scraping down the inside of the bowl occasionally.
4. Scrape down and remove the beaters. Fold in the flour mixture and peanuts with a rubber spatula just until all the flour is moistened and the peanut bits are evenly distributed in the dough.
5. For a small air fryer, coat the inside of a 6-inch round cake pan with baking spray. For a medium air fryer, coat the inside of a 7-inch round cake pan with baking spray. And for a large air fryer, coat the inside of an 8-inch round cake pan with baking spray. Scrape and gently press the dough into the prepared pan, spreading it into an even layer to the perimeter.
6. Set the pan in the basket and air-fry undisturbed for 18 minutes, or until well browned.
7. Transfer the pan to a wire rack and cool for 15 minutes. Loosen the cookie from the perimeter with a spatula, then invert the pan onto a cutting board and let the cookie come free. Remove the pan and reinvert the cookie onto the wire rack. Cool for 5 minutes more before slicing into wedges to serve.

Cocoa Bombs

Servings: 12
Cooking Time: 8 Minutes
Ingredients:

- 2 cups macadamia nuts, chopped
- 4 tablespoons coconut oil, melted
- 1 teaspoon vanilla extract
- ¼ cup cocoa powder
- 1/3 cup swerve

Directions:

1. In a bowl, mix all the ingredients and whisk well. Shape medium balls out of this mix, place them in your air fryer and cook at 300°F for 8 minutes. Serve cold.

Almond-roasted Pears

Servings: 4
Cooking Time: 15 Minutes
Ingredients:

- Yogurt Topping
- 1 container vanilla Greek yogurt (5–6 ounces)
- ¼ teaspoon almond flavoring
- 2 whole pears
- ¼ cup crushed Biscoff cookies (approx. 4 cookies)
- 1 tablespoon sliced almonds
- 1 tablespoon butter

Directions:

1. Stir almond flavoring into yogurt and set aside while preparing pears.
2. Halve each pear and spoon out the core.
3. Place pear halves in air fryer basket.
4. Stir together the cookie crumbs and almonds. Place a quarter of this mixture into the hollow of each pear half.
5. Cut butter into 4 pieces and place one piece on top of crumb mixture in each pear.
6. Cook at 360°F for 15 minutes or until pears have cooked through but are still slightly firm.
7. Serve pears warm with a dollop of yogurt topping.

Home-style Pumpkin Pie Pudding

Servings: 4
Cooking Time: 30 Minutes
Ingredients:

- 1 cup canned pumpkin purée
- ¼ cup sugar
- 3 tbsp all-purpose flour
- 1 tbsp butter, melted
- 1 egg
- 1 orange, zested
- 2 tbsp milk
- 1 tsp vanilla extract
- 4 vanilla wafers, crumbled

Directions:

1.   Preheat air fryer to 350°F. Beat the pumpkin puree, sugar, flour, butter, egg, orange zest, milk, and vanilla until well-mixed. Spritz a baking pan with the cooking spray, then pour the pumpkin mix in. Place it in the air fryer and Bake for 11-17 minutes or until golden brown. Take the pudding out of the fryer and let it chill. Serve with vanilla wager crumbs.

Honey-roasted Pears With Ricotta

Servings: 4
Cooking Time:18 To 23 Minutes
Ingredients:
- 2 large Bosc pears, halved and seeded (see Tip)
- 3 tablespoons honey
- 1 tablespoon unsalted butter
- ½ teaspoon ground cinnamon
- ¼ cup walnuts, chopped
- ¼ cup part skim low-fat ricotta cheese, divided

Directions:
1.   In a 6-by-2-inch pan, place the pears cut-side up.
2.   In a small microwave-safe bowl, melt the honey, butter, and cinnamon. Brush this mixture over the cut sides of the pears.
3.   Pour 3 tablespoons of water around the pears in the pan. Roast the pears for 18 to 23 minutes, or until tender when pierced with a fork and slightly crisp on the edges, basting once with the liquid in the pan.
4.   Carefully remove the pears from the pan and place on a serving plate. Drizzle each with some liquid from the pan, sprinkle the walnuts on top, and serve with a spoonful of ricotta cheese.

Brownies

Servings: 8
Cooking Time: 20 Minutes
Ingredients:
- ½ cup all-purpose flour
- 1 cup granulated sugar
- ¼ cup cocoa powder
- ½ teaspoon baking powder
- 6 tablespoons salted butter, melted
- 1 large egg
- ½ cup semisweet chocolate chips

Directions:
1.   Preheat the air fryer to 350°F. Generously grease two 6" round cake pans.
2.   In a large bowl, combine flour, sugar, cocoa powder, and baking powder.
3.   Add butter, egg, and chocolate chips to dry ingredients. Stir until well combined.
4.   Divide batter between prepared pans. Place in the air fryer basket and cook 20 minutes until a toothpick inserted into the center comes out clean. Cool 5 minutes before serving.

Strawberry Donut Bites

Servings: 6
Cooking Time: 25 Minutes
Ingredients:
- 2/3 cup flour
- A pinch of salt
- ½ tsp baking powder
- 1 tsp vanilla extract
- 2 tbsp light brown sugar
- 1 tbsp honey
- ½ cup diced strawberries
- 1 tbsp butter, melted
- 2 tbsp powdered sugar
- 2 tsp sour cream
- ¼ cup crushed pretzels

Directions:
1.   Preheat air fryer at 325°F. In a bowl, sift flour, baking powder, and salt. Add in vanilla, brown sugar, honey, 2 tbsp of water, butter, and strawberries and whisk until combined. Form dough into balls. Place the balls on a lightly greased pizza pan, place them in the frying basket, and Air Fry for 10-12 minutes. Let cool onto a cooling rack for 5 minutes. Mix the powdered sugar and sour cream in a small bowl, 1 tsp of sour cream at a time until you reach your desired consistency. Gently pour over the donut bites. Scatter with crushed pretzels and serve.

Chocolate Chip Cookie Cake

Servings:8
Cooking Time: 15 Minutes
Ingredients:
- 4 tablespoons salted butter, melted
- ⅓ cup granular brown erythritol
- 1 large egg
- ½ teaspoon vanilla extract
- 1 cup blanched finely ground almond flour
- ½ teaspoon baking powder
- ¼ cup low-carb chocolate chips

Directions:
1.   In a large bowl, whisk together butter, erythritol, egg, and vanilla. Add flour and baking powder, and stir until combined.
2.   Fold in chocolate chips, then spoon batter into an ungreased 6" round nonstick baking dish.
3.   Place dish into air fryer basket. Adjust the temperature to 300°F and set the timer for 15 minutes. When edges are browned, cookie cake will be done.
4.   Slice and serve warm.

Banana-almond Delights

Servings: 4
Cooking Time: 30 Minutes
Ingredients:
- 1 ripe banana, mashed
- 1 tbsp almond liqueur
- ½ tsp ground cinnamon
- 2 tbsp coconut sugar
- 1 cup almond flour
- ¼ tsp baking soda
- 8 raw almonds

Directions:

1. Preheat air fryer to 300°F. Add the banana to a bowl and stir in almond liqueur, cinnamon, and coconut sugar until well combined. Toss in almond flour and baking soda until smooth. Make 8 balls out of the mixture. Place the balls onto the parchment-lined frying basket, flatten each into ½-inch thick, and press 1 almond into the center. Bake for 12 minutes, turn and Bake for 6 more minutes. Let cool slightly before serving.

Boston Cream Donut Holes

Servings: 24
Cooking Time: 12 Minutes
Ingredients:
- 1½ cups bread flour
- 1 teaspoon active dry yeast
- 1 tablespoon sugar
- ¼ teaspoon salt
- ½ cup warm milk
- ½ teaspoon pure vanilla extract
- 2 egg yolks
- 2 tablespoons butter, melted
- vegetable oil
- Custard Filling:
- 1 (3.4-ounce) box French vanilla instant pudding mix
- ¾ cup whole milk
- ¼ cup heavy cream
- Chocolate Glaze:
- 1 cup chocolate chips
- ⅓ cup heavy cream

Directions:
1. Combine the flour, yeast, sugar and salt in the bowl of a stand mixer. Add the milk, vanilla, egg yolks and butter. Mix until the dough starts to come together in a ball. Transfer the dough to a floured surface and knead the dough by hand for 2 minutes. Shape the dough into a ball, place it in a large oiled bowl, cover the bowl with a clean kitchen towel and let the dough rise for 1 to 1½ hours or until the dough has doubled in size.
2. When the dough has risen, punch it down and roll it into a 24-inch log. Cut the dough into 24 pieces and roll each piece into a ball. Place the dough balls on a baking sheet and let them rise for another 30 minutes.
3. Preheat the air fryer to 400°F.
4. Spray or brush the dough balls lightly with vegetable oil and air-fry eight at a time for 4 minutes, turning them over halfway through the cooking time.
5. While donut holes are cooking, make the filling and chocolate glaze. To make the filling, use an electric hand mixer to beat the French vanilla pudding, milk and ¼ cup of heavy cream together for 2 minutes.
6. To make the chocolate glaze, place the chocolate chips in a medium-sized bowl. Bring the heavy cream to a boil on the stovetop and pour it over the chocolate chips. Stir until the chips are melted and the glaze is smooth.
7. To fill the donut holes, place the custard filling in a pastry bag with a long tip. Poke a hole into the side of

the donut hole with a small knife. Wiggle the knife around to make room for the filling. Place the pastry bag tip into the hole and slowly squeeze the custard into the center of the donut. Dip the top half of the donut into the chocolate glaze, letting any excess glaze drip back into the bowl. Let the glazed donut holes sit for a few minutes before serving.

Apple Crisp

Servings: 4
Cooking Time: 16 Minutes
Ingredients:
- Filling
- 3 Granny Smith apples, thinly sliced (about 4 cups)
- ¼ teaspoon ground cinnamon
- ⅛ teaspoon salt
- 1½ teaspoons lemon juice
- 2 tablespoons honey
- 1 tablespoon brown sugar
- cooking spray
- Crumb Topping
- 2 tablespoons oats
- 2 tablespoons oat bran
- 2 tablespoons cooked quinoa
- 2 tablespoons chopped walnuts
- 2 tablespoons brown sugar
- 2 teaspoons coconut oil

Directions:
1. Combine all filling ingredients and stir well so that apples are evenly coated.
2. Spray air fryer baking pan with nonstick cooking spray and spoon in the apple mixture.
3. Cook at 360°F for 5minutes. Stir well, scooping up from the bottom to mix apples and sauce.
4. At this point, the apples should be crisp-tender. Continue cooking in 3-minute intervals until apples are as soft as you like.
5. While apples are cooking, combine all topping ingredients in a small bowl. Stir until coconut oil mixes in well and distributes evenly. If your coconut oil is cold, it may be easier to mix in by hand.
6. When apples are cooked to your liking, sprinkle crumb mixture on top. Cook at 360°F for 8 minutes or until crumb topping is golden brown and crispy.

Vanilla Custard

Servings: 2
Cooking Time: 25 Minutes
Ingredients:
- 5 eggs
- 2 tablespoons swerve
- 1 teaspoon vanilla
- ½ cup unsweetened almond milk
- ½ cup cream cheese

Directions:
1. Add eggs in a suitable bowl and beat using a hand mixer.

2. Add cream cheese, sweetener, vanilla, and almond milk and beat for 2 minutes more.
3. Spray 2 ramekins with cooking spray.
4. Pour batter into the prepared ramekins.
5. At 350 degrees F/ 175 degrees C, preheat your Air fryer.
6. Place ramekins into the air fryer and cook for 20 minutes.
7. Serve and enjoy.

Choco-granola Bars With Cranberries

Servings: 6
Cooking Time: 20 Minutes
Ingredients:
- 2 tbsp dark chocolate chunks
- 2 cups quick oats
- 2 tbsp dried cranberries
- 3 tbsp shredded coconut
- ½ cup maple syrup
- 1 tsp ground cinnamon
- ⅛ tsp salt
- 2 tbsp smooth peanut butter

Directions:
1. Preheat air fryer to 360°F. Stir together all the ingredients in a bowl until well combined. Press the oat mixture into a parchment-lined baking pan in a single layer. Put the pan into the frying basket and Bake for 15 minutes. Remove the pan from the fryer, and lift the granola cake out of the pan using the edges of the parchment paper. Leave to cool for 5 minutes. Serve sliced and enjoy!.

Fruity Oatmeal Crisp

Servings: 6
Cooking Time: 25 Minutes
Ingredients:
- 2 peeled nectarines, chopped
- 1 peeled apple, chopped
- 1/3 cup raisins
- 2 tbsp honey
- 1/3 cup brown sugar
- ¼ cup flour
- ½ cup oatmeal
- 3 tbsp softened butter

Directions:
1. Preheat air fryer to 380°F. Mix together nectarines, apple, raisins, and honey in a baking pan. Set aside. Mix brown sugar, flour, oatmeal and butter in a medium bowl until crumbly. Top the fruit in a greased pan with the crumble.Bake until bubbly and the topping is golden, 10-12 minutes. Serve warm and top with vanilla ice cream if desired.

Recipes Index

Printed in Great Britain
by Amazon